The Church,
Community of Salvation

An Ecumenical Ecclesiology

George H. Tavard

A Michael Glazier Book
THE LITURGICAL PRESS
Collegeville, Minnesota

NEW THEOLOGY STUDIES
General Editor: Peter C. Phan
*

Editorial Consultants:
Monika Hellwig
Robert Imbelli
Robert Schreiter
*

Volume 1: The Church, Community of Salvation

A Michael Glazier Book published by The Liturgical Press

Cover design by David Manahan, O.S.B.

	2	3	4	5	6	7	8	9

Library of Congress Cataloging-in-Publication Data

Tavard, George H. (George Henry), 1922–
    The church, community of salvation : an ecumenical ecclesiology / George H. Tavard.
        p.   cm. — (New theology studies ; v 1)
    "A Michael Glazier book."
    Includes bibliographical references.
    ISBN 0-8146-5789-3
    1. Church.   2. Catholic Church—Doctrines.   3. Catholic Church--Relations.   4. Ecumenical movement.   5. Christian union.
    I. Title. II. Series.
    BX1746.T37   1992
    262—dc20   92-9598
                                             CIP

Contents

Abbreviations

AG	*Ad Gentes*, Vatican II's Decree on Missions
ARCIC-I	Anglican-Roman Catholic International Conversations, First Joint Commission
ARCIC-II	Anglican-Roman Catholic International Conversations, Second Commission
BCEIA	(American) Bishops' Commission for Ecumenical and Interreligious Affairs
CA	*Confession of Augsburg*
CD	*Christus Dominus*, Vatican II's Decree on Bishops
DH	*Dignitatis Humanae*, Vatican II's Declaration on Religious Freedom
DS	Denzinger-Schönmetzer, *Enchiridion Symbolorum*, 32nd edition
DV	*Dei Verbum*, Vatican II's Constitution on Divine Revelation
DVif	*Dominum et vivificantem*, John Paul II's Encyclical on the Holy Spirit
ES	*Ecclesiam suam*, Paul VI's Encyclical on the Church
GS	*Gaudium et spes*, Vatican II's Pastoral Constitution on the Church in the Modern World
HV	*Humanae vitae*, Paul VI's Encyclical on Birth Control
LG	*Lumen Gentium*, Vatican II's Constitution on the Church
NA	*Nostra Aetate*, Vatican II's Declaration on Judaism and Other Religions
PG	Migne, *Patrologia graeca*
PL	Migne, *Patrologia latina*
RM	*Redemptoris Mater*, John Paul II's Encyclical on the Virgin Mary
SC	*Sources chrétiennes*, Paris: Le Cerf
UR	*Unitatis redintegratio*, Vatican II's Decree on Ecumenism
WCC	World Council of Churches

Editor's Preface

This series entitled *New Theology Studies,* composed of eight volumes, is an attempt to answer the need felt by professors and students alike for scholarly yet readable books dealing with certain Catholic beliefs traditionally associated with dogmatic theology. The volumes treat of fundamental theology (revelation, the nature and method of theology, the credibility of the Christian faith), trinitarian theology, christology, ecclesiology, anthropology, and eschatology.

There has been, of course, no lack of books, published singly or in series, both in this continent and elsewhere, which are concerned with these central truths of Christianity. Nevertheless, there is room, we believe, for yet another series of texts on systematic theology, not because these offer entirely novel insights into the aforementioned teachings, but because it is incumbent upon Christians of every age to reflect upon their faith in light of their cultural and religious experiences and to articulate their understanding in terms accessible to their contemporaries.

Theology is traditionally described as faith in search of understanding, *fides quaerens intellectum*. The faith to which the contributors to this series are committed is the Christian faith as lived and taught by the (Roman) Catholic Church. It is, however, a faith that is ecumenically sensitive, open to ways of living and thinking practiced by other Christian communities and other religions. The understanding which the series seeks to foster goes beyond an accumulation of information, however interesting, on the Christian past to retrieve and renew, by means of the analogical imagination, the Christian Tradition embodied in its various classics. In this way, it is hoped, one can understand afresh both the meaning and the truth of the Christian beliefs and their multiple interconnections. Lastly, the contributors are convinced that theology is a never-ending quest for insights into faith, a *cogitatio fidei.* Its ultimate purpose is not to provide definite and definitive answers to every conceivable problem posed by faith, but to gain an understanding, which will always be imperfect and fragmentary, of its subject, God the incomprehensible Mystery. Thus, theology remains an essentially unfinished business, to be taken up over and again in light of and in confrontation with the challenges found in every age. And our age is no exception, when, to cite only two examples, massive poverty and injustice structured into the present economic order, and the unprecedented meeting of religious faiths in new contexts of dialogue, have impelled theologians to reconceptualize the Christian faith in radical terms.

Contrary to some recent series of textbooks, *New Theology Studies* does not intend to advocate and advance a uniform or even unified viewpoint. Contributors are left free to present their own understanding and approach to the subject matter assigned to them. They are only requested to treat their themes in an integrating manner by situating them in the context of Tradition (highlighting their biblical, patristic, medieval, and modern developments), by expounding their theological meaning and function in light of current pronouncements of the Magisterium, by exploring their implications for Christian living, and by indicating possible different contemporary conceptualizations of these doctrines. The goal is to achieve some measure of comprehensiveness and balance by taking into account all the important issues of the subject matter under discussion and at the same time exhibit some thematic unity by means of a consistent method and a unifying perspective.

The eight volumes are intended primarily as resource books, "launching and landing bases," for upper-division theology courses in Catholic colleges and seminaries, but it is hoped that they will be useful also to people—priests, permanent deacons, religious, and educated laity, inside and outside of the Roman Catholic communion—interested in understanding the Christian faith in contemporary cultural and ecclesial contexts. We hope that these volumes will make a contribution, however modest, to the intellectual and spiritual life of the Christian Church as it prepares to enter its third millenium.

Peter C. Phan
The Catholic University of America

Introduction

Ecclesiology is now taken for granted as an area of theological research. Before the modern age, however, the Church felt no need to define itself. Even during the period of the great ecumenical councils, from the fourth to the eighth century, no council made an explicit statement on the nature of the Church although by their very nature all conciliar decisions are bound to affect the community that considers itself to be the Church. Only with the dogmatic constitution of Vatican I, *Pastor aeternus*, in 1870, did a council attempt to explain the nature and structure of the Church. Of nature and structure, structure dominated. This was followed in due time, at Vatican II (1962–1965), by the constitution *Lumen gentium* and the pastoral constitution on the Church in the modern world, *Gaudium et spes*. These documents looked closely at the nature of the Church.

Not surprisingly, this movement has a parallel in theological reflection. No systematic treatment of ecclesiology developed before the pre-scholastic period, when Hugh of Rouen (c.1080–1164) wrote an opusculum, *Contra haereticos sui temporis, sive De ecclesia et ejus ministris libri tres*. This was prompted by the emergence in Brittany of a sect that denied all authority to the Church. About the same time, Hugh of St.-Victor (c. 1096–1141) opened his treatise *De sacramentis* with an explanation of what he regarded as the first sacrament, the consecration of a church. Underlying this approach was the idea that what a church building is to the administration of the sacraments, the Church as such is to the sacramental life of the people of God. Such medieval initiatives, however, had no immediate sequel.

The great Western schism exploded in 1378. For reasons that are far from simple, opposite factions of cardinals supported two different popes, the one at Avignon, the other in Rome, then three, the third being in Spain. This clearly raised constitutional questions regarding the nature and structure of the Church's unity. Tractates *De unitate ecclesiae* began to appear that proposed various means to end the internal schism of the Church of Rome. The schism ended in 1418, thanks to the council of Constance and its decrees, *Haec frequens* (30 March 1415), *Frequens*, and *Si vero* (9 October 1417). Yet the popes who were legitimized by these decrees later refused to apply the provisions that were made in them.

Finally, in 1530, the *Confession of Augsburg*, written by Philip Melanchthon (1497-1560) and presented to Emperor Charles V at the diet of Augsburg by the political supporters of Luther, formally identified the question, "Where is the Church?" The Reformers' answer was given in Article IV of the Confession: "where the Word of God is preached and the sacraments are administered according to the gospel."

Between the Reformation and Vatican Council II, the problem of the identity of the Church and of its visible signs or marks dominated ecclesiological reflection. Protestants generally followed Melanchthon's determination of the locus of the Church. Most Calvinist confessions included similar formulations. The Thirty-nine Articles of the Church of England endorsed Melanchthon's doctrine: "The visible Church of Christ is a congregation of faithful men, in the which the pure Word of God is preached, and the Sacraments be duly administered according to God's ordinance, in all those things that of necessity are requisite to the same" (Art. XIX). This became Article XIII in the Twenty-eight Articles of Methodism.

Meanwhile, Cardinal Robert Bellarmine (1542-1621), in the treatise on the Church Militant that is included in his *De controversiis*, formulated the standard Roman Catholic answer in the spirit of the Counter Reformation: "The one and true Church is the community of people brought together by the same Christian faith and united in the communion of the same sacraments under the government of the legitimate pastors, and especially the one vicar of Christ on earth, the Roman pontiff."[1] This remained the common teaching of Roman Catholic catechisms until the time of Vatican II.

Modern Catholic ecclesiology, however, began to mushroom in the second half of the nineteenth century. The movement started in Germany where the school of Tübingen, notably with Johann Adam Möhler (1796-1838), saw the Church primarily as a living organism led by the Spirit.[2] This line of thought was pursued by Matthias Scheeben (1835-1888) whose ecclesiology is focused on a theology of the Christian "mystery." Meanwhile, the reflection of French ecclesiologists took a more institutional turn. After the mildly Gallican book by Abbé Henry Maret (1805-1884), *Du Concile général et de*

---

[1]Quoted in Avery Dulles, *Models of the Church* (New York: Doubleday, 1976), 20.

[2]On Möhler see Louis Bouyer, *The Church of God, Body of Christ and Temple of the Spirit* (Chicago: Franciscan Herald Press, 1982), 91-104; Matthias Scheeben, *The Mysteries of Christianity* (St. Louis: Herder Book Company, 1964, original German edition, 1864); Adrien Gréa, *L'Eglise et sa divine constitution* (Paris: Casterman, 1965).

la paix religieuse (1869), the major work is the frankly ultramontane *L'Eglise et sa divine constitution* (1884) by Dom Adrien Gréa (1828-1917), where the Church and its institutions are entirely ruled by their liturgical tasks. In England, George William Ward (1812-1882), one of the early converts of the Oxford movement, held ecclesiology to be a "general statement of principles," although he admitted an "admixture of temporary and accidental matters" in his book, *The Ideal of a Christian Church* (1845).

In plain contradiction of the belief that the Church's constitution, being divine, is permanent and unchanging, the more recent Catholic ecclesiology of Christian Duquoc has explored the unfinished and provisional aspect of the Church, taking its point of departure in "the historicity and institutionality of the Church" as manifested in "the necessary provisionality of the empirical Churches."[3] In this perspective, it is precisely the temporary and accidental that throws light on the nature of the Church.

Any number of intermediate positions could be cited in recent theology. According to Hans Küng, one can know what the Church should be now only if one already knows what it was originally. This means treating the New Testament as the norm of what the Church should be, whatever concrete forms it has taken and may still take in its ongoing history. Küng's inquiry is therefore led chiefly in the confines of the New Testament. Yet Hans Küng has also made a careful study of the "structures of the Church" that owes little to the Scriptures, being a research into the late medieval ecclesiology of conciliarism as endorsed at the council of Constance. Bishop Christopher Butler (1902-1986) had the modest ambition to explore whether "the word, Church, when restricted in its application [to the Church militant exclusively] . . . relates to any coherent object and can express a consistent idea."[4] But Avery Dulles, in an exercise in "comparative ecclesiology," later identified five different "models of the Church": institution, mystical communion, sacrament, herald, servant. Diverse combinations of these models determine "the various points of view on the relationships between the Church and the churches."[5]

By and large, the insight that Frederick Denison Maurice (1805-1872) formulated in 1833 is still largely valid: "The three words, *respice, circumspice, prospice,* contain the three dogmas of our day respecting the Church."[6] That is, one class of "thoughtful and intelligent divines" points to the Church by looking back (*respice*): they find the proper model in the past, whether of the Scriptures or of the first Christian centuries; it has the shape of a consensus in doctrine, organization, and life that lasted several centuries until the first schisms between East and West. But "the teachers of another school" say,

---

[3]Duquoc, *Des Eglises provisoires: Essai d'ecclésiologie oecuménique* (Paris: Le Cerf, 1985).

[4]Butler, *The Idea of the Church* (Baltimore: Helicon Press, 1962).

[5]Dulles, op. cit., 9.

[6]F. D. Maurice, *The Kingdom of Christ*, 2 vol. (London: SCM Press, 1958), vol. 1, 15.

"Look around you" (*circumspice*) as they see an amazing diversity of thought and worship in the Christian world," that is yet fundamentally at one in the wish to preach and promote the Gospel. Finally, "Look forward, say a third party" (*prospice*): the turmoils of the past and the present have prepared us for a "new dispensation," and the New Jerusalem is just around the corner. When he wrote this, Maurice was chiefly concerned with the contention of the Quakers that the Church needs no shape or structure. His three models corresponded to three styles of churchmanship in the Church of England— the High-Church, Low-Church, and Broad-Church parties. Yet they fit remarkably well the moods that characterize present divisions in ecclesiology between the Orthodox and Catholic, the classical Protestant, and the Pentecostal points of view. In order to be complete today, one would have to add two more categories: the liberal Protestant and the fundamentalist, which place different emphases on certain elements of the classical Protestant ecclesiology—the indetermination of the Church's form (liberal) and the ties of the Church to a prescientific reading of Scripture (fundamentalist).

At least in the Catholic realm it is universally agreed that something entirely new in relation to ecclesiology happened at Vatican II. When Cardinal Léon Suenens asked his seminal question, *Ecclesia Dei, quid dicis de te ipso?* ("Church of God, what do you say of yourself?"), he invited the Church's bishops and theologians to undertake self-criticism. In 1964 Pope Paul VI gave his profound yet mostly overlooked personal answer in his first encyclical, *Ecclesiam suam*. His thought was not couched in the dogmatic categories that were familiar to the deductive ecclesiology of the Counter Reformation when the nature of the true Church was logically deduced from certain principles that were assumed to rank with the articles of faith. Unlike Pius XII in *Mystici corporis* (1943), Pope Paul took his starting point in experience, and specifically in the experience of being Church. This could have been a futile exercise in tautology. For Paul VI, not unnaturally, assumed that the experience of being Church is located precisely in the Roman Catholic Communion. However, the chief characteristics of the experience of being Church that Paul VI identified can also be found in groups of Christians that are not in communion with the bishop of Rome. In *Ecclesiam suam* there are two such characteristics: the awareness of being Church, for the Church knows itself whenever it knows its Lord; and the awareness of participating in both an internal and external dialogue. Following Pope Paul's lead, the constitutions and decrees of Vatican II attempted to express what it means to be, in the middle decades of the twentieth century, a Church in dialogue.[7]

The reflection that will unfold in the following chapters takes its departure at this point: being Church means sharing a distinctive self-awareness and, on the basis of this self-awareness, engaging in a multisided dialogue.

---

[7] *"Ecclesiam suam": Première lettre encyclique de Paul VI. Colloque International, Rome, 24–26 octobre 1980* (Brescia: Istituto Paolo VI, 1982); see my remarks, 170–171.

The distinctive self-awareness in question derives from a principle that is at work in the birthing and shaping of the Church. This may be labeled a principle of correlation, though not in Paul Tillich's sense of the expression. Tillich (1886–1965) grounded his *Systematic Theology* in a correlation between human or philosophical question and divine or theological answer.[8] The ecclesial correlation that I have in mind lies between offer and reception, divine gift and human response, the gift having primacy and the response being itself implied in the gift. There can be no Church without God's prevenient initiative. By the same token, the Church comes to be wherever women and men respond with trust to God's numerous gifts, even though this be only in the interior forum of conscience. The exchange of offer and response between Creator and creature provides the basic ground for acknowledging the invisible Church, or the Church that is present in the hearts. Yet it provides no clue to what or where the Church of God is in the texture of human society.

The interior dialectic of offer and response has its counterpart at the social level when those who have received God's gift in their hearts testify to it in words and deeds. When they recognize one another and give thanks together for the gift of God in Jesus Christ and for the response that they have given to it in the Spirit, they form the visible Church, the community of God with the human creatures who are united by their faith in Jesus Christ the Savior. Here, also, the dialectic of offer and response is at work, for it is by God's guidance that the disciples discover one another in Christ and, in this discovery, become a community that anticipates the kingdom of God. The Christian Church is precisely the community of those who acknowledge Jesus the Christ as the one Mediator of both the gift they receive and the response they make. The dialogical structure that Paul VI discerned in the making of the Church is implicit in this social dimension of divine gift and human response.

Such a response to God's gift and the ensuing formation of the Christian community need no other apologetics than themselves. For experience is known only to those who share it. Demonstrations of the credibility and the credentity of the divine gift, and of the correlative intelligibility and rationality of the human response to God, used to constitute the heart of Christian apologetics. Yet they can never lead unbelievers beyond the fact that they have met with a surd that may not be properly explainable in their terms. The ecclesiology that I propose will therefore not attempt to justify the existence of the Christian Church, whether at the tribunal of secular rationalism or in the courts of other religions and religious institutions. Nor shall I endeavor to prove beyond doubt that Jesus Christ instituted a Church or that the institution created by his disciples correctly expressed the divine revelation given in him.

---

[8] Tillich, *Systematic Theology*, 3 vol. (Chicago: Chicago University Press, 1951, 1957, 1963); the method is explained in vol. I, 59–66.

I expect to do justice to the Scriptures and to history. Yet this is not a book of biblical or historical research. It is a systematic organization of the essential Christian beliefs about what the Church has been, is, and ought to be. It is focused on the awareness of being the Church that is inseparable from the profession of the Christian faith and on the dialectical or dialogical dimension of this awareness. In traditional Catholic terms, I intend to investigate the dogmatic or doctrinal nature and structure of the Church. But at the present historical moment, this must be done in an ecumenical spirit. Catholics cannot rest content with repeating what their forerunners said about the Church and its visible center in the bishop of Rome whom they consider to be in some sense the successor of the chief apostle Peter. One should also draw on the profound insights that have been preserved in the Orthodox Church and on those that were nurtured by the Reformers and pursued by their followers in the Churches of the Reformation. I will therefore appeal to what should be identified as the central Catholic tradition: along with the witness of the Scriptures, of the Greek and Latin Fathers, and of the Latin Middle Ages to which Catholics are wont to appeal, this includes the echoes of the Fathers that still reverberate in the Byzantine tradition of Orthodoxy, in the testimony of the great divines of the Anglican Communion, and in the voices of Martin Luther and John Calvin.

A preliminary chapter (ch. 1) will ask if there is a sense in which one may find the Church before and outside of the Christian faith. Following this, the book will be divided in three parts. The awareness of being the Church implies a certain *Vision* of oneself as the Church (part I). This vision is Trinitarian. It is grounded in a Christological foundation (ch. 2). It is nurtured by a life of grace inspired by the Spirit (ch. 3). And by it, one is aware of living in the presence of the glory of God (ch. 4).

This vision lies at the heart of a historical *Tradition* (part II). The first recorded form of this tradition is conveyed in the manifold images which the Scriptures of the New Testament use to designate the communities of the early Christian believers (ch. 5). The patristic unfolding of this tradition sought for and gave shape to a conciliar mold for ecclesial life (ch. 6) which the Middle Ages further developed into a monastic model (ch. 7).

Out of this tradition, there have emerged certain specific *Structures* (part III) that are connected with the ministerial service of the people (ch. 8) and with teaching responsibility or magisterium (ch. 9), both of which operate in the broad horizon of the world to which the Church necessarily relates (ch. 10).

Both history and structures bring to light the *Dialogue* (part IV) that is essential to the being of the Church. This dialogue is ecumenical as it embraces all the communities where the gospel is preached (ch. 11). It is interreligious as it extends to the great religions of the world (ch. 12). And it entails a radical orientation of Christian self-awareness toward future gifts of the Spirit and the eschatological kingdom of God (ch. 13).

The ecclesiology that I propose varies considerably from that of Emmanuel d'Alzon (1810-1880), the founder of the Augustinians of the Assumption, my religious community. Profoundly marked by his time and place, d'Alzon was a determined ultramontane, devoted to Pius IX, the pope of the Syllabus (1864) and of the proclamation of papal infallibility (1870). The Church to which he gave his loyalty was very different from the Church of today. Yet it is one and the same Church. The cult of the papacy was tempered by d'Alzon's view of a general council as "a new alliance in the truth between the human spirit and the Spirit of God."[9] It was also tempered by the eschatological overtones of his total ecclesial perspective: "God," d'Alzon wrote, "Jesus Christ, the elect: such is the last word on the Church, on its history, on the history of humankind and of all the historical and social sciences. Society and history have their source in the society of the elect, the heavenly Church, which has its grounding in Jesus Christ . . . who himself goes back to God. . . ." It is on this horizon that I wish to set the present study.

There naturally are similarities and dissimilarities between the present essay and the many ecclesiological productions of recent theology. I need not list the numerous theologians, past and present, who have taught me most of what I know. But I wish to emphasize my fundamental debt to Vatican Council II which I attended as a *peritus* and in which I shared the work of the Secretariat for Christian Unity. Above all I have tried to bring out the insights into the nature and task of the Church that emerged at Vatican II. Even though these insights have not yet found adequate institutional expression, they remain central to what the Church is to be in the twenty-first century.[10]

Assumption Center   George H. Tavard
Brighton, Massachusetts

---

[9] *Ecrits spirituels*, Rome: Maison généralice, 1956, p. 177 and 111; George H. Tavard, *The Weight of God: The Spiritual Doctrine of Emmanuel d'Alzon* (Rome: Centennial Series, 1980).

[10] Footnotes will be reduced to a minimum. References to most conciliar decrees and papal documents will be given in the text. Each chapter will be followed by a short bibliography. Books cited in footnotes will not be mentioned again in the bibliographies. I list here once for all some of my previous writings that relate directly to ecclesiology: *The Church, the Layman, and the Modern World* (New York: Macmillan, 1959); *Holy Writ or Holy Church: The Crisis of the Protestant Reformation* (New York: Harper, 1959); *The Quest for Catholicity: The Development of High Church Anglicanism* (New York: Herder and Herder, 1963); *The Church Tomorrow* (New York: Herder and Herder, 1965); *The Pilgrim Church* (New York: Herder and Herder, 1967); *The Seventeenth-Century Tradition: A Study in Recusant Thought* (Leiden: E. J. Brill, 1978); *A Theology for Ministry* (Wilmington: Michael Glazier, 1983). Two shorter essays should be added: "The Church as Eucharistic Communion in Medieval Theology," in F. Forrester Church and Timothy George, eds., *Continuity and Discontinuity in Church History: Essays Presented to George Hunston Williams on the Occasion of his 65th Birthday* (Leiden: E. J. Brill, 1979), 92-103; "Is There a Catholic Ecclesiology?" in *Proceedings of the Twenty-ninth Annual Convention, The Catholic Theological Society of America*, vol. 29, 1974, 367-380.

1

Antecedents

"Church," "Assembly," or "Gathering," have been used since New Testament times to designate the social organization of the disciples of Christ. In Greek it was *ekklesia*, often preceded by the adjective *kyriake*. Etymologically, the word of the Germanic languages (*church, kirk, Kirche, kerk, kyrka, kirkja*) derives from the adjective, whereas the corresponding word in Romance languages (*église, chiesa, iglesia, igreja*) comes from the noun by way of its Latin form, *ecclesia*. In either case, it is intended to be equivalent to *qahal* in Hebrew, the term which, in the Book of Exodus, designates the assembly that was guided by God in the wilderness toward Mount Sinai.

The frequency of this word in the Scriptures and in early Christian literature implies that the followers of Jesus have never lived their faith and testified to it individually, as it were on their own, but socially, as part of a group. This group came into being as soon as an undetermined number of Jews believed that the prophet Jesus of Nazareth had "risen from the dead," was alive in their midst in the power of God's Spirit, and must therefore be the Messiah announced by the prophets.

It is not historically unreasonable to think that such a grouping of his posthumous disciples fulfills the wishes of Jesus himself. This can be inferred from various sayings and episodes of the New Testament. As recorded in Matthew's gospel, Jesus had envisaged the return of the Assembly (*qahal*) among his followers: "On this 'rock' I will build my Assembly" (Matt 16:18). St. Paul, who presumably reflected a widespread opinion among the disciples, further identified this Assembly as "the Israel of God" (Gal 6:16) which has received the "new covenant" in the blood of Jesus (2 Cor 3:6). One short step further, and the disciples of Jesus are seen as a New Israel that complements, or perhaps replaces, the Old.

If this grouping of Jesus' disciples is called the Church, then the Church is anterior to the Christian Scriptures since, as St. Augustine noted, the

Church produced these Scriptures and recognized them as inspired by the Spirit, on the model of the Jewish Scriptures, which were slowly relegated to the rank of "Old" Testament (in the sense of Covenant), the writings of the disciples becoming the "New" Testament. As later generations of the disciples of Jesus looked back at the origins of the Christian Church, they commonly explained the Church on the basis of the Christian Scriptures. But as they did so, they appealed to the Church's product to justify the Church's being, thus reasoning in a circle and thereby throwing doubt on the value of their demonstration.

This logical difficulty led the theologians of the first Christian centuries to seek a point of reference that would somehow transcend the history of the empirical social reality that is called Church. If it was to succeed, such a search was bound to lead, ultimately, to God's purpose for the world and sovereign initiative. But God's purpose can be known only by faith. One could thus end up with what would seem to an outsider to rest on another vicious circle: faith in the God of Jesus justifies faith regarding the Church that is itself the context where faith in the God of Jesus is born and nurtured.

At any rate, the Christian belief that the Church originates in God's initiative entails the notion that it may be, in some sense, anterior to humanity and even independent of creation: the Church resides first of all in God's eternal purpose. The traditional assumption, coming from Judaism, that the Creator called into existence spiritual creatures, the angels, before creating the physical universe, implies the notion that, at least when they were confirmed in grace, the angels constituted a Church in heaven, the heavenly Jerusalem, the Church of the celestial hierarchies, or the Church triumphant. Such a speculation about angels was common in the early centuries of Christianity. It identifies the Church as a community founded in grace which God has established with the creatures that are called to know and love him. Here, the core element that is constitutive of the Church is the gift and reception of divine grace.

The Church "from Abel the Just . . ."

The alternative to this approach is to look for a point of reference in history. Whatever may be thought about an angelic Church in heaven before the creation of humankind, the Church in history, or the Church militant, is the community that God has established with the human creatures, themselves called to know and love him. In this case, the Church of God received its shape from the Jewish people, organized religiously around the Temple of Jerusalem and its traditional priesthood, its liturgical worship, its official calendar of feasts, a weekly and a daily life of prayer structured around the synagogue and the family circle. This itself was the fruit of a long evolution that went back to the building of the first Temple by Solomon (c. 975-935

B.C.E.) and even beyond, when the Hebrews worshipped God in their wandering years in the desert under the leadership of Moses and his brother Aaron. Further, the work of Moses and Aaron had antecedents in the worship of God by the pre-Hebraic holy men and their clans who came to be honored as ancestors. Abraham (c. 1900 B.C.E.) and the more mythical Noah (undatable) were the most prominent (Gen 12-25 and 5-9). Through this long line of witnesses, the Jewish Scriptures go back to the acceptable worship that is ascribed in Genesis 4 to Abel, son of the first human couple, Adam and Eve. On this basis, Vatican Council II, following St. Augustine, spoke of the Church that stretches "from Abel the just to the last of the elect" (LG n. 2).

Seen from this perspective, the Church is indeed a social entity of this earth, made of men and women who believe in Jesus the Christ. It rests on two fundamental elements that are entirely due to God's initiative. First, the Church originates in God's creative intent and power: the first humans were placed on this earth (in whatever way we may imagine or reconstruct their emergence in the long process of evolution) in order to form a society that would be related to the Creator in knowledge and love. This society is called the Church. It has existed in different social forms since the beginning of humanity. And it is expected to last "to the last of the elect," that is, until humanity vanishes from the earth.

Second, this religious society actually came into being with God's gift of grace or divine friendship. Its most developed form before the birth of Jesus resulted from the divine initiative that the Hebrews conceptualized as an everlasting Covenant with their ancestors. In the course of time and the historical evolution of society, this Covenant was believed to have taken several forms: the Covenant with Abel, with Noah, with Abraham and the patriarchs, and with Moses. And to this list the Christians added Jesus. To each of these forms of the Covenant there corresponded a special status and organization of the Church of God. As the people who had received the Covenant and intended to live by it were constantly inclined to stray, God from time to time inspired prophets to call them back to their original fidelity. For its longest recorded period, the Covenant and its people were associated with a Promised Land. It was believed that the Covenant included, along with God's salvific graciousness and Law (Torah), the promise of life in a specific land, the land of Israel, located in Palestine.

We need not examine how the people of the Land functioned as the Church of God. The Epistle to the Hebrews sums it up in an image: the believers who lived before the coming of Jesus form "a great cloud of witnesses" around the Christian faithful, leading them, like the miraculous cloud that preceded the Hebrews in the desert, toward the Promised Land of heaven, their "eyes fixed on Jesus" (Heb 12:2). In their life, worship, and testimony, the people of the Land were the people of God. They witnessed to the living Lord who created the universe, established the Covenant, spoke through the prophets, and, according to the Christian faith, sent his Word in the humanity of Jesus of Nazareth. In their core, the Scriptures of both the Old and the New Testaments are the record of this witness, of which they also provide a series of successive interpretations.

The People Chosen by God

If indeed the Judeo-Christian tradition is correct, God the Creator selected one people to become the cradle of the Messiah so that at least a section of humanity would be ready to receive the salvific message of the Word made flesh. The choice fell on Abraham who is called, on this account, "father of the faithful," "our patriarch." God promised Abraham a great posterity, the sign of which was the birth of Isaac, the son of his old age. The divine choice was reaffirmed in his son Isaac and his grandson Jacob. Then, through the long years of obscurity that lasted from the "Hyksos" period of Middle Eastern history (c. 1780-1580 B.C.E.) to shortly after the reign of Pharaoh Akhenaton (Amenophis IV, 1375-1360 B.C.E.), nobody knows for certain what happened to Abraham's posterity. At any rate, Moses emerged as the leader of a people, the Hebrews, who are identified in the Book of Exodus as the legitimate posterity of Abraham. Under Moses' guidance, the Hebrews were forged into a nation with an ethical code based on the Ten Commandments, an organization, a ritual, and a purpose, namely the conquest of Palestine which they claimed as the land promised by God to their ancestors. The Covenant was renewed with Moses at Mount Horeb, or Sinai.

The Hebrews' subsequent history records their infidelities to the Covenant and periodic returns to God thanks to "judges" like Deborah or Gideon, kings like David, priests like the artisans of the Deuteronomic reform under King Josiah, prophets like Elijah, Samuel, and the great "writing prophets" whose preaching is recorded in the Bible. As Christians understand God's purpose, this long history reached its fulfillment in a final and eternal Covenant given through Jesus Christ, when the message and knowledge of God of which the Hebrews and Jews had been the bearers was extended to all humanity. Thus, what Christian theology has regarded as the Church of the Old Testament was structured around two poles: the worship of the God who spoke to Abraham and Moses and, no less important, the expectation and the preparation of the coming of a Savior sent by God whom Christians identify as Jesus of Nazareth, the Messiah (in Hebrew) or Christ (in Greek).

Further investigation of this point would bring into focus the nature of the anticipatory Church of the Old Testament. Briefly, the Covenant-consciousness of the people of God took new forms in the last century or so of the pre-Christian era. Some of them call for special comment.

Biblical Images of the Christ

This is not the place to outline a Christology. Yet if indeed the people of the Old Testament may be seen as the Church created and guided by God, then the two foci of its life are relevant to the nature of the Christian Church that will follow the acknowledgment of Jesus as the Messiah.[1]

The worship of the Hebrews and Jews was directed toward God as revealed to Moses. This revelation had two major moments: at the Burning Bush, Moses learned the holiness of God that is signified by his Name, *èhiè asher èhiè* ("I Shall Have Been Who I Shall Have Been": Exod 3:14), often summed up as "He Who Is"; and at Mount Horeb, Moses was given the "Ten Words" (Commandments) that are at the heart of Torah, the Law (Exod 20:1-17). It follows that the worship of God in the Old Testament resides as much in obedience to Torah as in adoration and prayer. In the course of time, more regulations were added by religious authorities precisely in order to protect the heart of the Law. But as the very weight and number of these regulations tended little by little to veil what they were intended to protect, there eventually arose a question that became of major importance for the Christian movement: what is, in this forest of rules, the heart of the Law that is truly essential to the worship of God? According to the Christian Scriptures, St. Paul had a major influence in declaring obsolete most of what was considered Law in Judaism.

In any case, the expectation of the Messiah was far from uniform. At the time of Jesus, many, especially those who were called the Zealots, expected God's messenger to be modeled on King David, the founder, after the death of King Saul, of the dynasty of the kings of Juda. After the rebellion of the ten northern tribes that followed the death of Solomon, this dynasty continued to rule the southern kingdom. After the conquest of the northern kingdom by Sargon II, king of the Assyrians, in 721 B.C.E., the Davidic dynasty remained the sole royal line of the Chosen People until the southern kingdom was itself conquered by Nebuchadnezzar II in 586 B.C.E.. The dynasty having vanished during the Babylonian exile, the hope remained that it would come back. There would be at some future time a new king especially anointed by God, a new David. This hope thrived after the exiles were liberated and sent back to Palestine by Cyrus, king of the Persians, in 538 B.C.E. The revolt of the Maccabees in 164 B.C.E. against the Greek-Egyptian dynasty of the Seleucids (King Antiochus Epiphanes, 165-161) gave a more political twist to this expectation of a Messiah (Anointed One).

Others expected the Messiah to be more like a prophet than like a king; he would be the New Prophet. There had been no prophet since Esdras the scribe had been instrumental in the reorganization that followed the return

---

[1]See Tavard, *Images of the Christ: An Enquiry into Christology* (Washington: University Press of America, 1982).

from exile. But God would not abandon the people. God would provide. Perhaps Elijah, the great northern prophet of the ninth century, who was believed to have been "taken up" by God, would be sent back to earth. Perhaps this New Prophet was the person described as the *'ebed Adonai*, the Servant of God, in the Book of Isaiah: an eschatological prophet who would be persecuted and would give his life for the many. In fact, at the time of Jesus, a new prophet was expected by the monks of Qumran, along with "the Messiahs of Aaron and Israel."[2] When John the Baptist came, living and speaking like a prophet, and when Jesus was baptized by him, questions concerning their identity could not but arise whether perchance one of them was "Elijah, . . . Jeremiah or one of the prophets" (Matt 16:13). When Jesus was persecuted and crucified, his disciples could well see him as Isaiah's prophetic Servant of God.

In the apocalyptic literature that developed in Judea in the last century or so before Christ, the messianic expectation took a new, more eschatological, turn. As was hinted at in the initiatory vision of the prophet Ezekiel, the glory of God could be visually perceived. Ezekiel saw "the likeness of a throne, in appearance like sapphire; and, seated above the likeness of a throne, was the likeness as it were of a human form" (Ezek 1:26). Daniel also described his vision of "one like a Son of Man" coming on the clouds of heaven to receive the Kingdom and give it to "the Saints of the Most High" (Dan 7:13-14, 27). This "Son of Man," or simply this "Man," was identified with the Messiah in such late Jewish extrabiblical literature as the fourth Book of Esdras, chapter 13, and the Ethiopian Book of Enoch, chapters 37–71. The kingdom thus restored by the Messiah-Son of Man will be eschatological. It will mark a total restoration of God's purpose for creation and humanity in what will be "the day of the Lord." Again, when Jesus came, it was possible for his disciples to identify him with this apocalyptic figure and to reinterpret the old expectation in the light of his remembered words and deeds.

Understood as the Church, as they have been in the Christian tradition, the people of the Old Testament were united in worship and in the expectation that God would again intervene in the future as he had done in the past. God would send his anointed messenger, the Messiah. Under whatever form he was imagined, the "One who is to come" (Luke 7:19) was expected to bring salvation to the people of God, to restore its liberties, to purify its worship and its keeping of Torah, to protect it from the heathen world around. Eventually, according to some of the prophets (Isaiah II, Zechariah II), God's messenger will bring all Gentiles to worship at Jerusalem, and there will be a pure offering, not only at the Temple, but even all over the earth (Malachi).

---

[2]The "Community Rule" expects the coming of "the Prophet and the Messiahs of Aaron and Israel" (CR. n.IX, in G. Vermes, *The Dead Sea Scrolls in English* [New York: Penguin Books, 1962], p. 87); the "Damascus Rule" alludes to a Lay Leader of the community and to an Anointed Messiah who will be the interpreter of the Law (DR n.VII, p. 104).

Christian theology should infer from this all-too-brief survey that ecclesiology cannot be the primary category. The heart of the messianic expectation in all its forms is hope in a God-given Savior. God creates the Church in view of the divine purpose. Ultimately, this purpose is no other than "the divine glory." But being the overflow of the goodness of the Creator that is manifested in the historical forms of the Covenant, this glory will be experienced by the members of God's people as their own salvation. The prime category for understanding the nature of the Church must therefore be soteriology. From the time of Abel the Just to the rising of Jesus from the dead, the Church of God underwent a succession of forms that were determined by the actual state of the expectation of salvation in its historical context. This expectation was itself the outcome of God's offering of love through the Law and the Prophets and of the human response to it. Furthermore, offering and response should both be understood as God's gift. In the language of the Bible, it is God who enlightens the mind and blinds it, who opens the heart and closes it.

But the Church, being the organization of the disciples of Jesus, has also a social structure. The evident continuity which, in the formative period of the Christian community, linked the Christian teachings and ethics to their biblical source, suggests that the main model for the Christian organization must have itself been Jewish. The Jews were one people, even though Pharisees, Sadducees, Zealots, the Qumran monks, and those who were simply called the "people of the land" (*'am 'aaretz*), understood their religion in differing ways. But within the broad communion of the people of God, the religious community of Judaism was active at three levels. First, it was focused on the Temple, its liturgy, and the levitical priesthood. But second, a monthly and weekly cycle of biblical reading, meditation, and prayer was organized around numerous synagogues. And third, the family circle played a major role in the celebration of feasts and in the communication of the tradition to women and children. In addition, other patterns of community could be found in the more or less informal circles of pious friends who gathered for holy meals on the model of the *'anawim*, the "Poor of Adonai" of the Psalms. And lastly, the monastic order of Qumran could also influence the early shape of the Christian community.

The Church among the Gentiles

The Bible is entirely focused on God's relation to one people, the Hebrews, and what was regarded as their ancestry. After the reconstruction in Judea that followed their return from exile, the descendants of the Hebrews were known as the Judeans or Jews. Even in its broad outline, however, this history cannot avoid raising the question: what about the numberless other tribes of humanity? These were not without some relation to the Creator.

As far back as archeologists have identified traces of human civilization, they have found signs of worship such as clay figurines or cave paintings that are presumed to carry religious significance. Women mold and carry amulets that, given certain conditions, will provide divine protection to themselves and their child during pregnancy; hunters invoke God, or gods, or a numinous power that is latent in wild animals so that their hunt may be successful. One may posit a continuity between these "primitive" forms of the human relation to God and the more elaborate and theoretical theogonies and theologies of the great religions of the world, all of which have their origin in prehistoric times. Thus the Rig Veda, which contains the oldest known religious writings of humankind, shows traces of long-established religious beliefs and practices.

In fact, the Bible presents the Covenants with Abel and with Noah as universal Covenants so that the first phases of the Church on earth must have been universal rather than specific to one particular people. And if the Church includes in some way all the just and pious of whatever tribe and tongue, then each tribal religion or religious organization, insofar as it presupposes God's initiative to which a human response is given, is itself already a tentative form of the Church of God. This is not the standard teaching of the Bible. Yet it is echoed in significant passages. Job, presented as a holy man who dialogues with God, lives "in the land of Uz" (Job 1:1: presumably in Edom) and is not a Jew. Jonah, son of Amittai, is said to have been sent as God's prophet to the inhabitants of "the great city of Nineveh," God having pity on its "hundred and twenty thousand who cannot tell their right hand from their left" (Jonah 4:11); Nineveh and its people were not in the land of Israel. To Naaman, "commander of the king of Aram's army," who has been healed of leprosy by the prophet Elisha (2 Kgs 5:1-14), is attributed a formulation of the dilemma that flows from the existence of sundry religions: "I will no longer offer whole-offering or sacrifice to any god but the Lord. In this one matter only may the Lord pardon me: when my master [the king] goes to the temple of Rimmon to worship, leaning on my arm, and I worship in the temple of Rimmon when he worships there, for this let the Lord pardon me" (2 Kgs 5:17-18). Vatican II itself noted: "religions, which are found throughout the world, attempt in various ways to calm the human hearts, proposing ways that include doctrines and precepts for living as well as sacred rites" (NA. n. 2).

All the non-biblical religions are themselves organized around communitarian structures. The Roman empire was filled with temples and religious societies. The Vestals were a monastic community at the heart of the empire and its official religion. As people everywhere were grouped in villages, tribes, and clans before entering the more confused mix of larger cities, so they formed communities around religious beliefs and practices. Outside of the Mediterranean world, Hindus have temples and *ashrams*; Buddhist monks "take refuge" in the Buddha, the *dharma* and the *sangha* (the Enlightened guide, the Law, and the Community), and *stupas* erected along roads and lanes remind the believers that they all belong to the *sangha*, where they discover the *dharma* as they walk in the steps of the Buddha.

"One must not doubt that the Gentiles also have their prophets."[3] This sentence was quoted by Pope Paul VI on December 9, 1964 as he returned from India. And the Pope added: "We must know far better the peoples with whom the Gospel brings us into contact, and recognize all the values they possess, not only through their histories but in the moral and religious traditions that they have preserved."

The question of ecclesial status may then be raised regarding the pagan religions: are they not themselves aspects of the Church? Is it not possible to establish a parallel between the preparation of the Christian Church in the Temple and the Synagogue and its preparation in non-biblical temples and cults? As well as the communities within Israel, the communal organisms of non-biblical religions have acted, and still act, as cocoons in which the Church of God already subsists in a more or less latent state. If the Church of God exists on earth in anticipatory ways before being embodied in the community that proclaims Christ as the Savior, then the Church must already subsist in a parallel way in the religions that have pursued other, non-biblical approaches to the Divine Mystery.

Further, would it be legitimate to say that in some sense the religious writings of India and other lands may, in the providence of God, act as "Old Testaments" in the context of their culture? In this case, there would be many Old Testaments converging upon one New Testament. We are not, at this point, in a position to formulate a final answer to such queries. But these questions and the perspectives that they open on the universality of the Church ought to be kept in mind as we proceed to study the Christian Church.

The problem of the identity of the Savior in relation to all religious expectations is thus not exhausted by the varieties of Jewish messianism. Likewise, one may suggest that the Christian Church is already preexisting as the Church of God, not only in the worshiping communities of the Old Testament, but also in all human communities that are unified by religious hope. Yet one may go beyond this suggestion and affirm two points. First, the fact that the disciples of Jesus soon broke out of the Jewish matrix in order to preach salvation to the whole world cannot be irrelevant to the issue of the nature of the Christian Church. The coming of Jesus responded not only to the quest of the Old Testament for the fulfillment of God's promises but also to the many religious movements that were thriving in the pagan world, seeking for divine light and guidance. Secondly, as a consequence, the Church

---

[3]"*Ac per hoc dubitandum non est, et gentes suos habere prophetas*" (*Contra Faustum Manichaeum*, bk XIX, ch. 2, composed in 397/98; PL 42, 348), cited at the general audience of December 9, 1964. Pope Paul, however, erroneously attributes the sentence to St. Augustine: it is in fact the opinion, not of Augustine, but of his adversary, Faustus the Manichean (*Documentation Catholique*, 3 Jan. 1965, vol. LVII, n. 1439, col. 23).

must have already led, so to speak, a subterranean existence in the diverse religions of the pagan world.

Religious Movements of Humankind

A brief overview of the religious movements of humankind outside of Judaism will delineate the horizon of these questions. Knowledge of God, for most people, has been built on two bases. From the perception of a numinous background to nature, an argument has been made for the existence of God and for some of the attributes of God the Creator who is hidden by, yet also expresses himself through, the veil of creation. Thus St. Paul could affirm: "His invisible attributes . . . have been visible, ever since the world began, to the eye of reason in the things he has made" (Rom 1:20). In the final analysis, the cosmological proofs of God's existence that were eventually systematized by St. Thomas Aquinas derive from this affirmation. They unfold systematically the conviction, universally held in pre-modern society, that nature has a holy origin and that this origin is to be found in a holy Being in whom it also has its meaning and goal. In addition, most religions hold that God has been revealed through prophets, sacred objects, or sacred writings. Thus the religions of the world should be seen by Christians neither as false worship nor as doctrines to be refuted. They go deeper in the direction of God than the mere perception of the marks of the Holy in nature that is also universal in humankind. Through their myths, their images, their rites of initiation, and their forms of worship, the religions act as tentative and partial unveilings of the mystery of God. If they undoubtedly differ from the Covenants of the Biblical tradition, this is not to say that they are worthless and that one cannot learn anything from them as to the nature of the Church of God and of Christ.

It is not necessary here to enter into anthropological theories about the origin of religion or even into Karl Jaspers' analysis of what he called the religious "axes" or "axial periods" of humankind.[4] Yet one cannot deny that there have been waves of religiosity at different periods of history. These waves of religiosity were occasioned by seemingly inspired personalities. Some were kings, like Amenophis IV in Egypt who took the name Akhenaton after his conversion to the religion of Aton; or sons of kings, like Sakyamuni the Buddha (the Enlightened One). Some were poets, like the authors of the Rig Veda in northern India. Others were philosophers, like Lao-tzu in China or the authors of the Upanishads. Others, finally, were more obviously prophets, like Zoroaster in Persia and possibly, though the evidence is more obscure, Quetzalcoatl among the Aztecs. Further, these movements were

---

[4]Karl Jaspers, *The Origin and Goal of History* (London: Routledge and Kegan Paul, 1953), p. 1-77.

not without widespread social influence: they sparked the emergence of new communities, monastic as in Buddhism or secret gatherings like those of the Mithraic cult and other mystery religions.

The Search for a Savior

Above all, an expectation of salvation underlies all the great world religions. One of their common characteristics lies in the conviction that something is fundamentally wrong with the world as it is. The diversity comes when they identify the proper remedy for what is wrong with the world. As the Buddha taught his disciples, humankind is caught in a wheel of suffering, and one should seek for a way to stop the wheel. Or as was perceived by the great tragedians of Greece, humans suffer under an untolerable yoke, a destiny that is perhaps due to "some manslaying of old, some ancient tale of murder among my kin."[5] Yet as the goddess Artemis asserts when she tries to bring consolation to Hippolytus, "You die beloved by me." In other words, the way of fate and suffering may turn out to be a way of salvation. In the mysteries that spread in the Roman empire at the same time as Christianity, the initiate enters a special relationship with God and is assured of rebirth in a land of happiness after the tragedy of this life.

Thus, the great world religions have nurtured personal and collective hope in and beyond this world. Structured in view of a soteriological focus, they have acted as ways of salvation. This appears more clearly in those forms that have expected not only salvation in general, but a particular Savior. The Savior may be a human person or at least appear under human features, as the Shaoshyant of late Zoroastrianism or Maitreya Buddha in Mahayana Buddhism. Often, the expected one is a Mediator in the strict sense, like the many *boddhisattvas* of Mahayana or Amida in Pure Land Buddhism, who lead their followers to final liberation. In Hindu *bakhti*, it is God himself, the Absolute and Ineffable, who becomes Mediator under a visible form and is so designated by some of the divine Names—thus Krishna in the *Bhagavad gîta*. At times, there is a mediatory or salvific event. It may be initiation, as in the Mysteries, when the initiate dies and rises with Isis, Osiris, Mithra, or any of the other mysteric god-figures. It may be liberation or Nirvâna as in Hinduism and in classical Buddhism or an ineffable moment of enlightenment as in Zen.

Insofar as such expectations of salvation were taught by a college of priests or by a school of prophets or inspired the monastic life or acted as catalysts of hope and peace for the worshippers and provided inspiration for their social life, then Christians may speak of an invisible Church being at work,

---

[5]David Greene and Richmond Lattimore, eds., *Euripides*, vol. I (*The Complete Greek Tragedies*, vol. V) (New York: Modern Library, no date), p. 235, verses 1380-81, and p. 236, verse 1398.

outside of the biblical realm, in the religious institutions of the world at large from the time of "Abel the just."

Students of Christology and Christian soteriology cannot prescind from the diverse forms of the expectation of salvation among the Gentiles. Likewise, the ecclesiological question should obtain some light from investigation of latent forms of the Church in the past and present religions in which people have found spiritual help and consolation. Indeed, Karl Marx was not entirely mistaken when he affirmed that religion acts as "the opium of the people."[6] For people were forced by their sufferings to seek for an opium. Whatever organization provided them with the opium they sought anticipated the soteriological dimension and task of the Christian Church. Christians of course may, indeed should, be dissatisfied with the opiate solution that has often bred delusions and has led to partial or false securities. But this is not to deny the prophetic dimension of the search.

The Focus for Ecclesiology

Both the Hebrew-Jewish and the Gentile antecedents of the Christian Church point to what should be the focus of Christian ecclesiology. This focus will be twofold in keeping with the double reference that has been discovered both in biblical religion and in the religious movements of the pagan world: worship of God and quest for salvation. Worship of God has informed many different attitudes: the offering of sacrifice, the recitation of prayer, participation in liturgies of adoration, mental recollection and meditation, prayer of petition, invocation of mediators and saints, the consecration of one's life in a monastic community or in eremitical solitude, total reliance on Divine Providence in spiritual and material poverty, devotion to the spiritual and material service of neighbor.

The quest for salvation also has taken many forms: endeavors to stop or reverse the wheel of suffering, renunciation of desire and of acquisitiveness, flight from illusion and from reliance on the contingent and temporary, regret for the sins of one's past or present, acceptance of responsibility for collective sins, begging for forgiveness, searching for holiness and the means of perfection, waiting for divine grace, visiting holy places and shrines in pilgrimage, doing good works, accumulating what was believed to be meritorious in God's eyes.

The quest for salvation and the urge to adoration that are at the heart of all religions may be traced back to a natural desire for God that is, by God's design, constitutive of spiritual creatures. In this case, the Holy Spirit is al-

---

[6]This famous expression is in the introduction to *Contribution to the Critique of Hegel's Philosophy of Right* (1844), in K. Marx and F. Engels, *On Religion* (Moscow: Foreign Languages Publishing House, 1957), p. 42.

ready at work in the religions of the world, giving them a salvific dimension and an orientation, however obscure and misunderstood it may remain, toward the only Savior.

Christian ecclesiology should be both continuous and discontinuous with this general tally of the religious quest. Christianity is based on the belief that in Jesus the Christ, who is the divine Word incarnate, God has sent to humanity the only Mediator of adoration and salvation. This is continuous with the religious quest of humanity, both in its biblical and in its extrabiblical forms. But it is discontinuous with the precise forms of adoration and means of salvation that biblical and extrabiblical religions have proposed and practised. The coming of the Christ, made evident to faith by the rising of Jesus from the dead, marks the point of discontinuity.

Ecclesiology, or the doctrine about the Church, stands therefore in continuity with the doctrine of creation: the God who is worshipped is the Creator. It is also continuous with the doctrines of the incarnation and of redemption: the God who saves from sin and ultimately from death, which is, for St. Paul, "the last enemy" (I Cor 15:26), is also the one who creates the universe and who is worshipped in adoration and love. This is the fundamental reason why, in the dogmatic constitution *Dei Filius*, Vatican I asserted: "Faith and reason can never disagree with each other. . . ." (DS n. 3019).

Yet there is discontinuity between God's revelation and salvific action in Christ on the one hand, and what the human mind has by itself discovered or invented about God and salvation as well as what the human will can by itself decide and do in relation to God and salvation on the other. For this reason Vatican I also declared: "The doctrine of faith, which God has revealed, has not been proposed as a philosophical theory to be perfected by human minds, but as a divine deposit handed on to the Bride of Christ, to be faithfully preserved and infallibly declared" (DS n. 3020). The Church that is called here the Bride of Christ does not emerge from its latent state in biblical and extrabiblical religions by evolutionary unfolding. It passes through the discontinuity of the death and rising of the Christ.

Just like the Church itself, ecclesiology is therefore entirely centered on faith in the Christ who died and rose again. And faith is God's pure and total gift. It owes nothing to previous human quests or prayers or spiritual achievements or philosophical theories about God, the world, and salvation. On the one hand, Vatican Council I affirmed that human beings have the capacity, "from creaturely realities," to "know God with certainty as the beginning and end of all things by the natural light of human reason" (DS n. 3004). On the other hand, such knowledge is not to be equated with the faith that is "the beginning of human salvation." Rather, faith is such that by it one "gives the revealing God full obedience of intellect and will" (DS n. 3009). Obedience of intellect implies the belief that God's revelation is true. Obedience of will implies total trust in God's love and guidance. This divine revelation has followed the order that is outlined in the Epistle to the Hebrews: "When in former times God spoke to our forefathers, he spoke in fragmentary and varied fashion through the prophets. But in this the final age he has spoken to us in the Son. . . ." (Heb 1:1-2; DS n. 3004). In itself, faith is "a supernatural power by which, [moved] by God's grace that draws and assists [us], we believe. . . ." (DS n. 3008).

Perspective

In its stance toward other religions, Christian ecclesiology is in principle, whatever historical deviations there may have been here and there, neither polemical nor apologetic. It has often degenerated into the one or the other. Yet it is radically turned to understanding. And one cannot understand without sympathy and empathy.

Yet the investigation of the religious quest is only the beginning of ecclesiology. The Christian Church conceives itself to be not the product of human longings and efforts, but the gift of God. The theologians of the Middle Ages commonly spoke of it as *ecclesia ex Trinitate*, the gathering that has its origin in the Three Persons. The Church is necessarily tied to the belief that God is not just a divine nature or substance or essence but is Three divine Persons. Martin Luther, still in the context of Trinitarian theology but with a special concern for the transmission of the divine revelation by word of mouth, insisted that the Church is the creature of the Word, *creatura verbi*.

No less than the incarnational perspective, the Trinitarian context is essential to understand the Church.

For Further Reading

Titles will be listed only once, at the place where they seem to be the most relevant.

Yves Congar. *The Mystery of the Temple*. Westminster, Md: Newman Press, 1958.
The Church: Readings in Theology. New York: Kenedy, 1963.
Louis Bouyer. *Rite and Man: Natural Sacredness and Christian Liturgy*, Notre Dame: University of Notre Dame Press, 1963.
Otto Karrer. *The Kingdom of God Today*. New York: Herder and Herder, 1964.
Christopher Derrick (ed.). *Light of Revelation and Non-Christians*. New York: Alba House, 1965.
Raymond Panikkar. *The Unknown Christ of Hinduism*. London: Longman, Darton, and Todd, 1968.

PART ONE

VISION

The Trinitarian framework of the ecclesiology of Vatican Council II is of great importance even though it has not had much of an impact on subsequent developments in the Church's life. The council opened its decree on the Church's missionary activity with an evocation of the Holy Trinity: "By its very nature, the Church in its pilgrimage on earth is missionary, since it originates in the mission of the Son and the mission of the Holy Spirit according to the design of God the Father" (NA, n. 2). The pastoral constitution on the Church in the modern world starts on a similar note: the community of the disciples "is made of humans who, united in Christ, are led by the Holy Spirit in their pilgrimage toward the Father's kingdom. . . ." (GS, n. 1). The constitution on the Church also begins its description of the "mystery of the Church" with a threefold explanation of the creative and salvific project formed by "the Eternal Father," the mission of the Son sent by the Father, and the mission of the Holy Spirit on the day of Pentecost. "Thus," it concludes, with the words of St. Cyprian, "the universal Church is manifested as 'the people that is made one with the unity of the Father, the Son, and the Holy Spirit'" (LG, 2-4).

The Trinitarian approach may surprise some readers. Yet in taking this road, Vatican II was faithful to a long tradition. Already in the twelfth century, Hugh of Rouen introduced his ecclesiological reflections with a confession of the Trinitarian faith: "The sane doctrine professes and preaches that the Creator of all, the almighty and only God, is Father, Son, and Holy Spirit, unconfused Trinity, undivided Deity."[1] From this vantage point, Hugh saw the Church primarily as the bride (*sponsa*) of the Incarnate Son.

---

[1] Also called Hugh of Amiens, *Contra haereticos sui temporis, sive De Ecclesia et ejus ministris*, PL 192, 1255–1289.

Part One proceeds along similar lines. But since knowledge of the Divine Persons comes only from the revelation given in Christ, it starts with the Christological foundation of the Church (ch. 2). This leads to the Church's pneumatological life, or life of grace in the Spirit (ch. 3), and lastly, to the Church's approach to the First Person whose doxological epiphany is perceived in the Glory of God that accompanies liturgical celebrations (ch. 4). Thus one should be able to grasp three basic dimensions of the Church, namely *diakonia* or service, *koinonia* or communion, *liturgeia* or worship.

2

Christological Basis

In no way can the institution of the Church as a social and spiritual entity be traced directly to the recorded words of Jesus, even if these words are believed to have been truly spoken by the Jewish prophet from Nazareth. What can be asserted with certainty is that Jesus did have Jewish men and women as his followers and disciples, that a small band of men called the Twelve, or the apostles, were particularly close to him. When Paul wrote his Letters and the four Gospels were composed, the apostles were regarded as pillars of the Christian community. They were living links with Jesus and witnesses of his rising from the dead. They exemplified in their person and mission the divine promise that Jesus would return as the Messiah to inaugurate the kingdom of God in the last days. Among the Twelve, three—Peter, James, and John—had been Jesus's special confidants. And one of these, Peter, was generally considered to hold the first place. It is also clear from the Gospel of John that someone who was a disciple but not an apostle was so close to Jesus that he was later designated, at least in the Johannine communities, as "the disciple whom Jesus loved" (John 21:20).

In view of this, it is most likely that the formation of a distinct community by his followers did correspond to Jesus' intent. But that such an intent was explicitly formulated in his teaching is a much more hazardous proposition.

From time to time, theologians have attempted to determine a priori what structures a community of Christ's disciples must necessarily have. Some of these essays will be evoked when we examine the Church's structure. One point is sufficient at this time: since the disciples were to "baptize all nations in the Name of the Father, and of the Son, and of the Holy Spirit," (Matt 28:19) and were to be witnesses to what they had "seen and heard and perceived and touched of the Word of life" (1 John 1:1), their common experience as a community must have been related from the beginning to baptism in the Threefold Name and to preaching and hearing the Word of Salvation. These basic missionary acts were later expanded into the credal formulations of faith and the sacramental system. Yet already in the New Testament, the Christian Church appears as that community from which the Word of Salvation is proclaimed and into which believers are baptized. In other words, it takes its point of departure in Jesus' salvific mission. Its nature is determined by its relation to that mission. It is the soteriological community par excellence, soteriology being the study of the ways in which Jesus brings salvation to those who believe in him. This fits the conclusion of our first chapter: the Assembly of God that is foreseen in the Old Testament and is adumbrated in pagan religions is focused on the worship of God and the experience of Divine Grace.

The Old Testament sees the people of God as a unit. There is one people of God as there is one Temple, located in Jerusalem. By and large, the former high places, set on tops of mountains, were not reconstructed after the return from exile in Babylon in 538 B.C.E. The chief exception, the sanctuary on Mount Garizim, confirms the rule since it is identified with the heterodox worship of the Samaritans. The New Testament, however, opens another perspective. In the plural, Churches are established in different cities: the Churches of God in Corinth, in Ephesus, in Rome. But the Church is also spoken of in the singular, as in "On this rock I will build my Church" (Matt 16:18). It is not immediately evident whether this is a singular of abstraction designating what some theologians have called "the idea of the Church"[2] or a singular of universality corresponding to a Church spread over the whole world.

Neither the New Testament nor the Trinitarian principle as such or even the conciliar passages that I have quoted determine the locus of the Church. Is it the local community of those who, to use the expression of the New Delhi Assembly of the World Council of Churches, "gather in one place" as Christian believers or a universal association of local gatherings of believers? For the time being we will prescind from this question. Whether the Church, seen theologically, is local before being universal or vice versa is a matter of structure. It will be examined later. The eventual concentration of the universal Church around five patriarchates, among which the patriarchate of Rome has primacy, should not be read back into the New Testament. The further concentration of authority in the see of Rome, whose bishop is perceived by Roman Catholics to be Peter's vicar and successor through whom the first Apostle speaks, as it were, mystically, does make it difficult to recover the New Testament vision. Yet the effort must be made if one is to view the Church of Christ, insofar as is still possible, as it appeared in its early years. In empirical terms, it was a sisterly association of believing communities.

[2]Christopher Butler, *The Idea of the Church* (Baltimore: Helicon, 1962).

The New Testament adds an important precision: it is in the experience of Divine Grace as God's gift of salvation in and through Jesus Christ that the Christian faithful are enabled to worship God as they ought. In the double focus of the believers' community, the coming of Jesus underlines salvation in Christ as the source of the worship of God. As it is presented in the Scriptures, the salvific mission of Jesus should be all the more enlightening regarding the nature of the Christian Church as there is a growing ecumenical consensus on the picture of Jesus in the New Testament. We will briefly look at the letters of Paul, the Synoptic Gospels, and the Johannine writings.

The Pauline Epistles

In St. Paul's mind, a Church is the community of those who gather, not around the Law (Torah), the Temple, or the Synagogue, but around Christ who has risen from the dead and is now present in the Spirit among those who believe. In a realistic perspective, Paul affirms that the believers are "in Christ," that they are "co-heirs" with him, and that the bond of their association with Christ is neither the works of the Law nor the works of the flesh but faith. Through faith they are "justified" or declared just by God. And it is their justification in Christ that distinguishes them, individually and as a group, both from pagans who try to follow the law of their conscience and from the Jews of the Old Israel who profess to follow the Law of Moses.

In the cities where he proclaims the Gospel, Paul groups into one fellowship those who come to believe. These are chiefly Jews and proselytes. The *ecclesia* is their assembly as they gather to take part in the Supper of the Lord, to pray in common, and to hear the word of the Gospel. These communities are linked by Paul's own ministry as he visits them, by their fidelity to his presentation of the Gospel as liberating from the traditional shackles of the Law, by the messengers he sends to them from time to time, and by his letters that were presumably more numerous than what was collected in the New Testament.

Yet in spite of the freedom from Torah that he teaches and practices, Paul views the totality of the Churches on the basic model of Judaism: there are "the saints" in Jerusalem, and a diaspora among the Gentiles. Paul therefore carefully maintains ties between his Churches and those that he has not founded. He initiates and organizes a collection for the support of "the saints" even though his understanding of the Gospel has met with opposition from some of their leaders. Likewise, Paul addresses a doctrinal letter to the Christians in Rome whom he intends to visit on a projected journey to Spain. As this letter explains it, the salvific mission of Christ that Paul has experienced in his own life provides the core of his message. It is by the same token the basis for his conception of the Church. Paul's dedications of his letters are enlightening on this point. The Church is that group of believers who receive "the grace and peace of God our Father and of the Lord Jesus Christ, who in order to rescue us from the present world sacrificed himself for our sins. . . ." (Gal 1:3-4). It encompasses those "who are God's beloved in Rome, called to be saints. . . ." (Rom 1:7). The "Church of God in Corinth" is made of those "holy people of Jesus Christ, who are called to take their place among all saints everywhere who pray to the Lord Jesus Christ. . . ." (1 Cor 1:2). In Philippians 1:1, Paul addresses his letter to "all the saints in Christ Jesus. . . ." Likewise, he writes to "the Church in Thessalonika which is in God the Father and the Lord Jesus Christ" (1 Thess 1:1). And in his short word to Philemon, he salutes "the Church that meets in your house," wishing all its members "the grace and the peace of God our Father and of our Lord Jesus Christ" (Phlm 1:2-3).

Their relation to God the Father and to the Lord Jesus is, in this case, constitutive of the Churches to which Paul writes. This relation is "the Good News that God promised long ago through his prophets in the Scriptures" (Rom 1:1-2). It is God's gift, "eternal life in Christ Jesus our Lord" (Rom 6:23).

The Deutero-Pauline Letters

In these documents, the limits of the Church have been broadened. The angels and the "powers" are subject to Christ (Eph 1:21). They were even created for him (Col 1:16). Christ is the head not only of the community of believers but of "all" since the design of God is "to reconcile all through him and for him" (Col 1:20), "to reunite all in Christ, all in heaven and all on earth" (Eph 1:10). It is precisely as "head of the Church" (1:22) that Christ has power over the whole cosmos. This is in line with the affirmation of the preexistence of Christ: "Before anything was created, he existed, and he holds all things in unity" (Col 1:17). His historical task, when "he made peace by his death on the cross" (Col 1:20), reflects his eternal standing.

The Church is therefore more than a community on earth. It is "his body, the fulness [*pleroma*] of him who fills the whole creation" (Eph 1:23). In the believers' immediate experience, the fulness of the Church as Christ's body is chiefly evident in the abolition of human "walls." There is the wall between Jews and Gentiles, but now Christ "has made the two into one. . . ." (2:14), "one single new man out of the two of them" (2:15). One may debate whether this "new man" is Christ himself or the Christian or the Church. But the general sense is clear. The newness of Christ abolishes the older divisions of humanity. There have been walls between sexes, between children and parents, between slaves and masters. But now husband and wife should "give way to one another in obedience to Christ" (5:21), for their union has its model in Christ and the Church (5:32). As to children and parents, it is in and for the Lord that they should obey and should guide (6:1-4). As to slaves and free men, they now "have the same master in heaven" who "is not impressed by one person more than by another" (6:9). This is neatly summed up by the author of Ephesians: "You are part of a building that has the apostles and prophets for its foundations, and Christ Jesus himself for its main cornerstone. As every structure is aligned upon him, all grow into one holy temple in the Lord" (2:20-21).

The Synoptic Gospels

As the gospels were composed within particular communities, their authors illustrated what was remembered of Jesus in those communities with examples, applications, and images taken from their beliefs, their life, and their organization. The memory of Jesus was filtered through their usual preaching and catechesis, through their practice of the worship of God, and through their experience of the continuing presence of Jesus and of the impact of the Spirit.

The Gospel of Mark never mentions the Church. It is entirely focused on the expectation of the kingdom of God. That the kingdom is "close at hand" (Mark 1:15) is the chief point of Jesus' preaching. The kingdom requires repentance and belief. But it does not result from these or from any human virtue or power. It is brought about by the healing and the forgiveness of sins that are wrought by God's power in answer to faith. The coming of the kingdom finally takes the form of the rising of Jesus from the dead. At this point, however, there is not yet a community of those who have been saved, although there could be a community of those who perceive the coming of the kingdom. In itself, the group of the disciples suffers from the failings that the Gospel ascribes to Jesus' relatives who believe that he is "out of his mind" (3:21); to Peter (8:32-33); to the disciples, in general, who fail to understand the parables (4:13), who argue as to who is the greatest (9:33); to the women who have found the tomb empty and are frightened by the angelic message that Jesus has risen from the dead (16:8). Like the messianic teaching that should remain secret until the kingdom of God comes "with power" (9:1), the messianic community lies undisclosed.

All this suggests that the community of faith does not come into being by human effort or according to human expectations and lights. This seems to be the intent of the short ending of the gospel in Mark 16:8—the women at the tomb "were afraid." The community is not even made of Jesus' "mother and brothers." It is made rather of "anyone who does the will of God" and is thus "brother and sister and mother" to Jesus (3:35). Yet the "long ending" (16:9-20) functions as an ecclesiological codicil that has been added to the Gospel of Mark: the community finally came into being when the risen Jesus personally appeared to the Eleven and gave them their mission—"Proclaim the good news to all creation" (16:15). It is in their messianic proclamation of the kingdom of God and their discernment of its signs that the disciples become the Church. The first of these signs is healing by the "casting out of devils" (16:16). The last is healing by the laying on of hands. Other signs are ancillary to those: speaking "new tongues" during their missionary journeys and protection from harm even in extraordinary circumstances. If, then, one identifies as Church the audience for which Mark writes his Gospel, the Church is made of those who, after expecting the kingdom of God, hear now the good news of its coming, perceive its signs, and in turn proclaim the messianic kingdom.

The Gospel of Matthew contains the verse that has epitomized the Catholic idea of the Church since the days of Pope Siricius, bishop of Rome (384–399): "You are *Petros* [*Cephas, Petrus:* Rock, Peter] and on this *petra* [rock] I will build my *ecclesia*" (Matt 16:18). In fact, the word "Church" occurs in Matthew more often than in any other single book of the New Testament. The model for Matthew's use of the term is taken from the people of God under the Old Covenant and from the assembly of God at the time of the exodus from Egypt. But as the past is reflected in the present and is projected into the eschatological future, the Church is seen as the ideal covenantal community for all peoples and for all times.

Matthew reflects the tradition that the prophet Jesus initiated the messianic community among his disciples and that these were the true "remnant," the new people of Israel, coming to life when the old one falters. They were brought into being through the salvation that was finally won by Jesus. They are the fruit of the shedding of his blood in the supreme sacrifice of atonement. And now they are also the foundation and the heralds of God's final kingdom.

The diatribes against scribes and Pharisees that are interspersed in Matthew's Gospel show that his community, probably located in Palestine, was engaged in a sharp polemic with Jews. And this very polemic underlines the basic principle of the Matthaean understanding of the Church. Salvation is offered through Jesus to believing Gentiles as well as to Jews: "in no one in Israel" did Jesus find more faith than in the Roman centurion (8:10). No longer the Old Law, but its reinterpretation and even its replacement by Jesus, is the gate to salvation. As is indicated by the "great commission" given in the last verses of the Gospel, the Matthaean community, though not missionary, admits no ethnic or geographic boundary and is, in regard to time, open-ended. This directly reflects the new experience of salvation that the members of this community have made. They are the Church of God, as at the time of the Exodus when Moses led the people out of Egypt.

In his Gospel and in the Acts of the Apostles, Luke provides a clearer picture of the Church. The Book of Acts describes the origin of the churches in the Diaspora, outside of Palestine, according to a simple pattern. The impetus is given at the Ascension. At Pentecost, the apostles are equipped for their mission, and Peter immediately starts preaching in Judaea. Philip the deacon initiates the mission to the Samaritans with the subsequent approval of the apostles, especially Peter and John. At Caesarea, Peter further extends the mission to spiritually prepared pagans. The Church is established at Antioch, outside of traditionally Jewish lands, by hellenistic Jews of the Diaspora who preach to the Gentiles. Finally, Paul, converted some three years before, joins the Church in Antioch. His association with the Antiochean Christians marks the start of his extensive missionary journeys in Greek lands. Luke then explains what he knows of these journeys which finally led Paul to the capital of the Roman Empire.

Luke's major originality lies in the underlying theology that he uses to bolster up his historical reconstruction.[3] This is history of salvation (*Heilsgeschichte*) in the proper sense of the expression. In God's design, the process of salvation goes through three phases. The many centuries of Israel formed the first phase. The recent life, death, and rising of Jesus have been the second. And now the third phase is the time of the Church. In geographic terms, salvation is identified firstly with the people of Israel and its land. Secondly, it is concentrated in the person of Jesus and his career. Thirdly, because of who Jesus was and what he did, it is extended to all nations and the whole world. There will be a fourth phase when Jesus "who was taken up from you into heaven . . . will come back in the same way as you have seen him go there" (Acts 1:11). Then, as is already stated in Luke's Gospel, Jesus will be seen as "the Son of Man coming in a cloud with power and great glory" (Luke 21:27).

Part of Luke's originality has to do with Jesus himself. In his Gospel, the messianic announcement begins with the sending of the angel to the priest Zechariah and the conception of John the Baptist followed by Mary's visit to Elizabeth who blesses her younger kinswoman and by the annunciation to Mary and the birth of Jesus. Likewise, the preaching of the Baptist is followed by Jesus' visit when he is baptized by the prophet in the Jordan river. Thus continuity is ensured between the first two phases of the salvation process. In later terms, the Old Covenant pours into the New. From then on, Jesus is the only point of reference for those who wish to be saved. In Galilee, he heals the sick, selects the Twelve, reinterprets the Law; and he departs from contemporary prejudices by accepting women among his immediate followers. On the way to Judea and in Judea itself, Jesus brings his ministry to its high point: the Last Supper, his testimony before the Roman governor Pilate, followed by his crucifixion and his rising from the dead.

Luke's central point emerges clearly: the mission given to the Twelve, and more generally to all the disciples, is to be Jesus' "witnesses" (Acts 1:8). The Gospel consists in telling Jews and Gentiles about the deeds and the person of Jesus. But this is no mere story telling or myth making or composing poems

[3]Robert C. Tannehill, *The Narrative Unity of Luke-Acts: A Literary Interpretation*, 2 vol., (Minneapolis: Fortress Press, 1986 and 1990). Contrast vol. 1, p. 203-74 (Jesus and His Disciples), and vol. 2, p. 43-47 (The Communal Life of the Jerusalem Believers).

and epics as found in the oral traditions and the literature of all tribes and nations. Communicating the gospel requires a special "power" which the disciples were told to wait for and which they received at Pentecost. The very structure of Luke's work points to a close connection between the events of Jesus' last days, from the Last Supper to the ascension and the heart of the good news. These events took place, as Jesus said of the pouring of his blood, "for you" (22:19). It is salvation through the sacrifice of Jesus that sets the believers apart from their original Judaism or Gentility. By the same token, salvation through his body and blood constitutes them as the Church of Christ. Hence the centrality of "the breaking of the bread" in the early communities as reported in Acts 2:46. Hence also the "joy" that flows from breaking the bread, the sense of a mystical presence of the Lord in their midst, and a vivid expectation of his return according to the Scriptures. All this belongs to the experience of salvation, to the experience of being the Church.

At the end of his little book, *The Gospel and the Church*, Alfred Loisy writes: "Jesus foretold the Kingdom, and it was the Church that came."[4] He eventually concluded that the Church should not have come. Yet as it emerges through the Synoptic Gospels, the Church is no other than the group of those who expect the kingdom announced by Jesus. They read the signs of its coming in their commemorative Eucharistic meals, in the preaching of the good news to both Jews and Gentiles, in the joy of faith and baptism. The earliest Church was, as Luke put it, the group of those who "remained faithful to the teaching of the apostles, to the brotherhood, to the breaking of bread, and to the prayers" (Acts 2:42). This community stands in continuity with Jesus' preaching of the kingdom. It forms the historical link between the beginning of salvation and its fulfillment in the expected kingdom.

The Johannine Writings

Neither in the Gospel of John nor in the first two epistles does the word, *ecclesia*, occur. In the third epistle, it designates the community to which Gaius, the addressee, belongs and where a conflict opposes two leaders— Diotrephes, who rejects "the elder" and his envoys, and Demetrius, who "has been approved by everyone" (2 John 9 and 13).

At any rate, the communities that owe their origin to "the disciple whom Jesus loved" are profoundly aware of being the Church. Their members have an "Advocate with the Father, Jesus Christ, who is just" (1 John 2:1); they have been "anointed by the Holy One" (2:20); having "the anointing" (2:27), they also know the truth (2:21); since they acknowledge the Son, they also have the Father (2:23), and the Spirit is to them "the other Advocate" (5:6);

[4]Alfred Loisy, *The Gospel and the Church* (Philadelphia: Fortress Press, 1976), p. 166; originally published in 1902.

they are "children of God" (3:10; 4:6) and from God (4:4). The heart of their faith is that Jesus Christ "is the sacrifice that takes away our sins, and not only ours, but the whole world's" (2:2). This implies acknowledging that "Jesus Christ has come in the flesh" (4:2) or, equivalently, that "we believe in the name of his Son Jesus Christ, and that we love one another" (3:23).[5]

Several "antichrists" have left the community (2:18). They were "false prophets" (4:4) who pretended to a special knowledge of God while failing to "keep his commandments" (2:3-4). They were "deceivers, refusing to admit that Jesus Christ has come in the flesh" (2 John 7). Their departure marked them out as false brethren who did not really belong. They are "of the world" (1 John 4:5), and "the whole world lies in the power of the Evil One" (5:19). They taught some form of the docetic heresy, possibly under the influence of some form of Jewish gnosticism. Yet the Johannine insistence on the antithesis between the community and those who have left it evokes the sectarian mind of a group that is self-contained and self-righteous and whose missionary spirit is stifled by a basic anxiety to preserve its purity, keeping away from "the world" (2:16-17) and shunning all contact with the "Evil One" (5:18) who "was a sinner from the beginning" (3:8).

The perspective of the Gospel is more universal. It emphasizes the privileged position of those who are addressed as "you" in Jesus' discourses and who may stand both for Jesus' direct disciples and for the members of the community to whom the Gospel is destined and also for those who are designated by "we" ("we saw his glory" [John 1:14]; "from his fulness we have all received, grace upon grace" [1:16]). Yet the Gospel also evokes the broad picture of those who "through their word will believe in me" (17:20). On this occasion, the believers' community is defined in theological terms: "that they may be one in us" (17:21). Their unity is encompassed in the oneness of the Father and the Son. Further, the community of the Beloved Disciple is shown to have begun at the cross when the dying Jesus spoke to his mother and to the Disciple, "And from that moment the disciple made a place for her in his home" (19:27). Yet one point remains unsettled. Is the unity in question that of the Johannine community only? Or does it encompass a wider fellowship of communities, some of which would owe their origin to one of the Twelve or to any one of many missionary preachers, among whom Paul was the most prominent? It seems reasonable to argue that the Johannine communities are aware of sharing a unique ecclesiological fulness. On the one hand, the Beloved Disciple was closer to Jesus than anyone else. The key to being the Church does not lie in apostolic origin but in the perfect discipleship that is exemplified in the only disciple who did not abandon Jesus at the cross. On the other hand, these communities' doctrine and life are grounded in a "higher" Christology than that of other believers in those

[5] Raymond Brown, *The Community of the Beloved Disciple: The Life, Loves, and Hates of an Individual Church in New Testament Times* (New York: Paulist Press, 1979).

times when doctrinal orthodoxy was still in its early formative stage. This was the Christology of the Fourth Gospel: Jesus is the preexisting Word of God who "was made flesh" (John 1:14).

In these conditions, one may wonder if the Twelve still hold a special place or have a specific function in the Church. The clearest answer is provided by the Apocalypse of John. The author, who does not rank as an apostle but as a prophet (Rev 22:9), sees the messianic or eschatological City of God. There is no temple—no church—in it because "the Lord God almighty and the Lamb" are themselves the temple (21:22). The new "Jerusalem, the holy city, coming down from God out of heaven" (21:10) has twelve gates made of twelve pearls; its foundations are covered with twelve precious stones. These are identified with the apostles: "The city walls stood on twelve foundation stones, each of which bore the name of one of the twelve apostles of the Lamb" (21:14). In other words, the apostolic function is strictly eschatological. In the last days when the New Jerusalem comes down from heaven, the Twelve will be the foundation stones of the City of God. The writings of the Johannine communities do not tell us whether the Twelve have a function in the interim between their original witness, or *martyrium*, and their eschatological task. One may presume that when the last days, the *eschaton*, break out upon the world, the Churches of the Twelve will have accepted the Johannine communities' understanding of the Word made flesh.

The Later New Testament

In most of the New Testament, the awareness of being the Church is identical with the knowledge and experience of salvation through Christ. Yet new accents emerge in the later writings. One should distinguish, however, between the more theological lines followed by 1 Peter and the letter to the Hebrews, and the more institutional orientation of the pastoral epistles.

While it is influenced by Pauline thought, especially as expressed in the letter to the Ephesians, the first epistle of Peter introduces a non-Pauline perspective when, starting from Paul's idea of Christ as the cornerstone, it sees the believers in the same line. Like Christ, the "living stone, rejected by men but chosen by God," they themselves are "living stones making a spiritual house" (1 Peter 2:4-5). Speaking, it would seem, exclusively to a group of Gentile Christians, the author further affirms: they are "a chosen race," as under the Old Covenant, "a *basileia*" (that is, an Imperial Palace, the palace of the *Basileus* or Emperor), "a priesthood, a consecrated nation, a people set apart" (2:9).[6] In sum, they are "the people of God" (2:10) "called" by God "out of darkness into his wonderful light" (2:9). They are a people

---

[6]John Hall Elliott, *The Elect and the Holy: An Exegetical Examination of 1 Peter 2:4-10* (Leiden: E. S. Brill, 1966).

on pilgrimage. Having been promised an "inheritance" that is preserved in heaven (1:4), they are on the way, "guarded by God's power through faith, until the salvation that has been prepared is revealed at the end time" (1:5).

That the Church is on pilgrimage is heavily accented in the letter to the Hebrews. Christ is the Son, "the radiant light of God's glory and the perfect copy of his nature" (Heb 1:3). Through him, God "made everything that is." Salvation lies in following Christ, the "leader" (2:10), into the heavens, above the angels (1:4), where he has entered once for all, thus becoming "the high priest according to the order of Melchisedek" (5:10). Jesus alone is "the apostle and the high priest of our religion" (3:1). Along with the Apocalypse of John, Hebrews stresses the liturgical quality of the experience of being the Church: "You have come to Mount Zion and the city of the living God, the heavenly Jersusalem, where millions of angels have gathered for the festival, with the whole Church in which every one is a first-born and a citizen of heaven" (12:22).

The First Letter to Timothy identifies the "house of God" with "the Church of the living God, which upholds the truth and keeps it safe" (1 Tim 3:15). The Greek word, *oikos*, means both house and household (family). Truth is the right belief and doctrine about Jesus, a "deposit" (1 Tim 6:20) that Paul has entrusted to Timothy. In the Church as God's house there must be a person in charge, a leader or head. If this person is not Paul, because he is too far away or more probably because he is dead, it is Titus or Timothy on whom the apostle imposed hands (2 Tim 1:6) in the rabbinic gesture of the transmission of knowledge. Timothy and Titus are themselves to appoint presbyters or *episcopoi*. These should be married and the fathers of children with a good reputation (Titus 1:5), "trustworthy men, capable of teaching others" (2 Tim 2:2). They are to designate deacons who should also be married and good governors of their children and household (1 Tim 3:8).

The pastoral epistles presumably originated in Pauline communities that were eager to maintain their link with the apostle of the Gentiles in the face of growing institutionalization. It is even attractive to think that at one moment of their redaction they constituted the Third Book of Luke.[7] In any case, these writings show the reaction of some believing communities to the emergence of a Christian gnosticism. The Johannine communities faced this challenge when several "false brethren" affirmed that Jesus is not of God in a unique way or that he has not come in the flesh or that the resurrection has already taken place for believers. In the Pauline and other communities, this took the form of "empty speculation" about the Law (1 Tim 1:6); there have been "false teachers . . . with a craze for questioning everything and arguing about words" (6:3). The heart of the true faith is that, just as there is one God, "there is only one mediator between God and humankind, himself a man, Christ Jesus, who sacrificed himself as a ransom for them all" (2:5). In him,

---

[7]See Stephen G. Wilson, *Luke and the Pastoral Epistles* (London: SPCK, 1978).

"God's grace has been revealed, and it has made salvation possible for the whole human race" (Titus 2:11). Any teaching at variance with that is false.

The reactions are diverse. The followers of the Beloved Disciple simply expel dissidents. In the Pauline communities, the organization is streamlined and strengthened, bringing the elders' authority closer to that of the great apostle himself. In both cases, however, the concern about true doctrine hinges on the experience and understanding of salvation and forgiveness of sins. The Church is still defined in soteriological terms, and it is the safeguard of the integrity of salvation that sets the pace and determines the orientation of Christology. In turn, the experience of salvation and the reality of Christ, who is God's agent for the salvation of all, determine the churches' self-understanding. They are essential to the believers' awareness of being the Church.

Ecclesial Awareness

The awareness of being the Church is born of the experience of being saved through faith in Christ. There are two levels of this experience, the individual and the corporate or collective. At the individual level, the believers formulate their faith in a set of personal beliefs; they profess it publicly; on occasion they feel a certain warmth and spiritual security and comfort in their faith. This is expressed in the credal statement that Jesus Christ lived, died, and rose again "for us and for our salvation," an emphasis that became central to Martin Luther's insistence on the *pro me* ("for me") purpose and effect of Christ's work and of all of God's gifts.[8]

The personal appropriation of faith has a necessary sequel in service. The believer is called to shed all selfishness. The faithful know their life to be transformed from common human self-centeredness when they live, not for themselves but for others, not for human satisfaction and achievement, but for the fulfillment of God's creative purpose. And following St. Paul, they understand this transformation to imply that they live not in themselves but in Christ their Redeemer.

As Pope Paul VI analyzed the "act of ecclesial awareness" (ES, n. 23) that prevails in the Roman Catholic Church, he noted a number of points. The Church is "both instrument and expression" of that interior communication of the Word of God that is perceived "by listening to the message of salvation" and in "the act of faith which . . . is at the beginning of our justification" (ES, n. 19). This is the principle of a "renewed discovery of her vital bonds of union with Christ" (ES, n. 35). It implies participating in the "mystery of the Church" in such a way that this mystery "is not a mere object of

---

[8]Martin Luther, *Small Catechism,* part 2; James M. Kittelson, *Luther the Reformer: The Story of the Man and his Career* (Minneapolis: Augsburg, 1986), p. 217-20.

theological knowledge; it is something to be lived, something of which the faithful soul can have a kind of connatural experience, even before arriving at a clear notion of it" (ES, n. 37).

This may be summed up as follows. The awareness of oneself as a member of the Church or, in the inclusive sense of being-with, as being the Church along with all those who also are the Church, is experienced in three dimensions. There is awareness of self as not belonging to oneself but to Christ, of sisters and brothers who are epiphanic images and actuations of the salvific work of Christ, and of those who remain outside the Church's visible boundaries yet who share internally, though unknowingly, the reality of the Church as the realm where divine grace is channeled and received through Christ and where spiritual freedom is given in the Holy Spirit. These also are waiting, along with the whole universe, for the full revelation of the children of God. Part IV of this book will further investigate this universal dimension of Church-awareness when one discovers, so to say, the Church beyond the Church.

At the corporate level, the believers formulate their faith in common. This is the purpose of the traditional creeds. Yet the adoption of a creed is no warrant of authenticity. No group can be the Church until the service for which Christ came into the world molds its corporate life. This is the service of salvation that is given, along with justifying grace, in the self-revelation of God through Christ. The traditional marks of the Church, as they are formulated in the central Nicene-Constantinopolitan creed, include unity, holiness, catholicity, apostolicity: "One, Holy, Catholic, and Apostolic Church." This will retain us at length in chapter 6. Yet a few indications may be noted now. Apostolicity denotes both the Church's grounding in the original apostolic mission and the permanence of this mission through the ages by the Church's agency. Apostolicity derives, as was well perceived at Vatican Council II, from the mission of Jesus Christ, the Word made flesh, sent by God the Father to bring salvation to sinful humanity. In the recent recovery of ancient categories, *diakonia* stands for that service of humanity by the Church through which Christ's fundamental mission is pursued. The messianic task of the Savior did not stop at his own generation. It is through the continuing community of his disciples that it can reach later generations.

The service offered by the Christian community has naturally varied according to the needs of different places and times. This service starts in the preaching of the gospel to bring others to salvation. It branches out in many forms of spiritual and corporal healing, in the assistance of the poor, in the practice of the traditional works of mercy and the advocacy of justice and peace, in the promotion of religious and technical education and information, in the guidance of the city when secular authority is found wanting, in the protection of the weak and powerless, in the defense of minorities and the victims of oppression and prejudice. As secular society takes over many of these tasks, the Christian community looks for new ways of service, for instance in cooperating with and supporting official agencies and unofficial initiatives, in participating in movements of liberation, in urging protestors to non-violence, in encouraging dialogues between rival points of view and competing interests.

Yet the *diakonia* of the Christian faithful and of their communities is not to be confused with the human philanthropy that is practiced, often with great generosity, by many non-religious or quasi-religious organizations. Even when it is totally unselfish, which it often is, the inspiration of such groups is limited to a purely human horizon. Nor should Christian *diakonia* be identified with the religiously motivated services that are urged by other religions, although it may have many things in common with them. Christian love of the neighbor is not the same as, for instance, Buddhist compassion or the almsgiving that is one of the "pillars" of Islam or Jewish philanthropy. The difference does not lie in what is done and not even in the strictly religious inspiration of the purposes that are pursued and the deeds that are done. It lies in the doer's inner attitude. The *diakonia* of each religion is modeled on the focus of its beliefs. Christian *diakonia* therefore has a Trinitarian structure. Radically tied to the salvific purpose of the incarnation, it is also dependent on the gifts of the Holy Spirit, and it is oriented toward the perfect offering of spiritual sacrifices to God the Father through Jesus Christ.

For Further Reading

Emile Mersch, *Theology of the Mystical Body* (St. Louis: Herder Book Co., 1951).

Yves Congar, *The Mystery of the Church* (Baltimore: Helicon, 1960).

Giovanni Battista Montini (Pope Paul VI), *The Church* (Baltimore: Helicon Press, 1964).

Rudolf Schnackenburg, *The Church in the New Testament* (New York: Herder and Herder, 1965).

M. J. Le Guillou, *Christ and the Church: A Theology of the Mystery* (New York: Desclée, 1966).

Michael Richards, *The Church of Christ* (London: St. Paul Publications, 1982).

George Sabra, *Thomas Aquinas' Vision of the Church* (Mainz: Mathias-Grünewald Verlag, 1987).

John N. Collins, *Diakonia. Re-interpreting the Ancient Sources,* New York: Oxford University Press, 1990.

3

Life in the Spirit

The salvific purpose of Christ in his Church cannot be fulfilled by human efforts, achievements, or works even when these are grounded in the Christian faith. The commitment of faith would not bear fruit unless the Holy Spirit, sent by the Father, were active in the hearts of Christians. The believers participate, by faith, in the life of the Spirit. Without this participation, faith could not, in St. Paul's words, "work out through love" (Gal 5:6). It would be dead like the faith of demons of James 2:19. The present chapter will therefore explore the fundamental ties of the Christian community with the Holy Spirit.

The Biblical Source

The writings of the New Testament allude many times to the Spirit of God. Yet in most cases what they say of the Spirit is hardly distinguishable from what was already written in the Old Testament. The Spirit of Christ can then be identified with the Spirit of God according to the meaning of this expression in the Jewish tradition. It is *rouach Adonai*, "spirit of the Lord," meaning not the Spirit that is effective in the Lord, in God, but the spirit that has been sent by the Lord and is active on earth. God is believed to send both the good spirit and the bad spirit according to the divine purpose and the receiver's capacity. In such a perspective, the spirit is no other than God's influence in the hearts and minds of the people. In the more remote biblical times, this conception of the spirit of the Lord favored the notion of collective retribution according to which "God punishes the faults of the fathers on the children, grand-children, and great-grand-children of those who hate him" (Deut 5:9).

The critique of collective punishment by the prophet Ezekiel in chapter 17 and his advocacy of personal responsibility did not suffice to do away with the belief that God's spirit is good or evil according to its good or bad mission. This remains the most common connotation of the term in the New Testament, yet with two major qualifications. First, the bad spirit, if not entirely done away with, is mostly ignored. Second, from then on it is through the Word incarnate that the good spirit is given to the faithful as the fruit of the Lord's death and resurrection. Further reflection on the experience of God's gift in faith was bound to lead to the conviction that the spirit given by God, the *pneuma*, was supremely at work in Jesus Christ.

Taking one more step, the Christians would soon discern that "spirit," as it is active in Jesus Christ, is not what was meant in the Old Testament. It is not tantamount to God's general influence on the structure and the course of nature or even to God's specific influence on particular persons as in prophetic inspiration. Rather, the Spirit that is manifest in Jesus is already alive in God before being sent: spirit is now Spirit, Holy Spirit, *the* Holy Spirit, or, in the older English vocabulary, the Holy Ghost. The process of specification is already completed in Paul's letter to the Romans: "the Spirit of God has made his home with you. . . . Unless you possessed the Spirit of Christ you would not belong to him. . . . The Spirit himself and our spirit bear united witness that we are children of God. . . . The Spirit comes to help us in our weakness. . . ." (Rom 8:9-26).

The Great Controversies

Further reflection on the Spirit flourished in the wake of the Christological controversies of the first centuries of Christianity. As discussion about who Jesus was brought about a new conceptualization of belief in God, the controversies shifted from Christ to the Trinity. This process was brought to a head in 325 when the council of Nicaea endorsed an affirmation that was to be basic to all later formulations of the Christian faith: the Logos of God, who took flesh as Jesus the Christ, is *homoousios* with the Father. The Word and the Father are one in all their being. Thus the central principle of Trinitarian theology was established.

Yet among the bishops and theologians who recognized the *homoousia* between the Father and the Logos, some doubted that this *homoousia* also included the Spirit of God. The extension of divine *homoousia* to the Spirit was the main achievement of St. Gregory Nazianzen (327-390) in the "Theological Discourses" that he delivered at the church of the Anastasis in Constantinople in 380. Gregory's efforts were soon crowned by the council of Constantinople I in 381 when it made some additions to the creed of Nicaea: the Spirit is "coworshipped and conglorified" with the Father (*simul adoratur et conglorificatur*).[1] If the Spirit is so honored, this can only be because the Spirit is one in being with the Father and thereby with the Father's Word. At the level of official formulation, the Trinitarian development seemed thus to be over. Yet what consequences this entailed for the Church's structure and life remained a moot question. The ecclesial dimension of Trinitarian doctrine needed to be made explicit. This in turn would manifest the full originality of the Christian experience of the Spirit.

Spirit and Church

"The Spirit and the Bride say, Come" (Rev 22:17). In context, the Bride is represented by "the one who hears, . . . the one who thirsts, . . . the one who desires, . . ." and who receives "the water of life, at no cost." In other words, the Book of Revelation, and thereby the New Testament as a collected corpus of writings, end on a remarkable suggestion: the Spirit of God and the Church of Christ stand in a bridal relationship. What several Old Testament prophets had described as a bridal relationship between *Adonai* and Israel is now effective in the Christian Church. The Spirit now stands for *Adonai*, for the Lord. And the vocation of Israel has been passed on to the community of Christian believers, the Church.

The Spirit, however, is given and received through the only Mediator, Jesus Christ. It is no longer anonymous, a symbol for the divine activity. The Spirit, manifest in the life of Jesus, was released to his disciples in his death and rising. This is obviously relevant to the nature of the Christian Church. For the Christian life also, modeled on that of Jesus, is inspired by the Spirit. Consequently, the place of the Spirit in God's Trinitarian life reached paramount importance in patristic theology. What the Spirit does in and for the faithful flows from, and reflects, what it is in God. In the course of the doctrinal development concerning the divine Trinity, the Holy Spirit came to be called the "Third Person" in God. That the Spirit is, like the Father and the Logos, a divine Person, followed from the theology of the Cappadocians and from the creed of the first Constantinople council. That divine personhood, however, is not univocal but covers three distinct ways of being a Person, will be basic to the later developments of Trinitarian doctrine.

The recognition of full divine dignity to the Third Person implies that no discrepancy, contrariety, or disharmony can be conceived between the Church's ties to Christ and its relation to the Spirit. Having received in Christ the divine revelation that brought the Old Covenant to its fulfillment, the Christian community finds itself radically dependent on the historical events

[1]St. Gregory Nazianzen, *Five Theological Orations* (*Nicene and Post-Nicene Fathers*, 2nd series, vol. VII, 1894, p. 284-328).

through which Jesus lived, died, and rose again for human salvation. It keeps the memory of this past in what is called the tradition. To this memory, the Church must always be loyal if it is to remain the Church of Christ.

At the same time, the bridal relation of the Spirit and the Church turns the community to the future. For the Church looks in hope toward the fulfillment of God's promises and toward undefined divine gifts to be expected in the future as God's design for the creaturely world progressively unfolds. This design will not be entirely fulfilled until the season of the end of time when the early Christian expectation generally projected the second coming of Christ. The Church's outlook on further gifts of the Spirit would not be complete without a deep desire for the return of the Lord and an eager watching for signs of the ultimate harvest of salvation.

There can be no disharmony between the Lord and the Spirit. These two divine Persons structure God's eternal self-expression. The theological tradition has commonly referred to the Word as being spoken by the Father in the Holy Spirit and also to the Spirit as linking together the Father and the Word who, through the Spirit, returns to the Father. In my own attempt to formulate Trinitarian doctrine with the help of modern linguistics, I have presented the Word as eternally spoken by the Father to the Spirit so that all those creatures who are capable of hearing the Word do so only in the Spirit.[2]

In any case, the Father of all is, as it were, hidden behind the Second and the Third Persons, acting and communicating through them. Their manifestations on earth, in what St. Augustine called their missions, are strictly complementary.[3] In spite of what are often mistaken appearances, there may therefore be no contradiction between the Scriptures that embody the givenness of the Word of God in the incarnation and the traditions that, guided by the Spirit, hand on the Church's memory from generation to generation. Nor can there be any discrepancy between the signs of Christ's presence and those of the Spirit's action, between word and sacrament, between fidelity and inspiration, between remembrance of the past, renovation of the present, and hope for the future. As the whole life of the Church is Christlike, so is it Spiritlike. It is lived through Christ, in the Spirit, "to the glory of God the Father" (Phil 2:11).

The Christian believers' salvific relation to Christ does not detract from their bridal relation to the Spirit. Nor does this bridal relation replace or render obsolete their relation to the Savior. The one is given in baptism and lived in faith. The second is symbolized by confirmation and lived in love. Christ gives the Spirit, and the Spirit leads to Christ. Christ reveals and the Spirit empowers. In the full sacramental system that developed in patristic

[2] *The Vision of the Trinity* (Washington: University Press of America, 1981), p. 119-140.

[3] St. Augustine, *On the Trinity*, bk IV, ch. 20, n. 27-29 (*Nicene and Post-Nicene Fathers*, 1st series, vol. III, 1905, p. 83-85).

times and the early Middle Ages, baptism includes a desire for confirmation and for the Eucharist. Conversely, the Eucharist and confirmation affirm and make effective the grace of conversion (*metanoia*) received in baptism. As each believer's relation to the Spirit builds up the Christian life through a progressive reception of spiritual gifts, it tends to maximize the relationship to Christ that is at the heart of the Christian faith. Thus, great saints have believed that they were great sinners. So overwhelmed were they by undeserved spiritual gifts that they were the more convinced of their fundamental and permanent need of salvation.

Pentecost

As was noted by Vatican Council II, the Church started, according to the patristic tradition, with "Abel the just. . . ." (LG, n. 2). Yet the event of Pentecost as narrated by Luke (Acts 2:1-42) has generally become a symbol of the Spirit's active presence in the Church. Pope John Paul II sums up this part of the tradition in his encyclical on "the Holy Spirit in the life of the Church and the world," *Dominum et vivificantem* (1986): "The *era of the Church* began with the 'coming,' that is to say with the descent of the Holy Spirit on the Apostles gathered in the Upper Room in Jerusalem together with Mary, the Lord's Mother" (DVif, n. 25). At Pentecost, the Church was "publicly manifested to the multitude" (AG, n. 4). The first perspective is more interior. The Church is seen as the realm of justice, that is, of faith and of love, on the model of the promised kingdom of God. In the second perspective, the interiority of the Church that is present in the hearts of the believers takes visible shape in the social and political arena; the Church of Christ is seen as an organized institution.

Yet one need not hold to the historicity of Pentecost, which is unknown to the gospel of John, to recognize that the interior and the exterior aspects of the Church are inseparable. In the Johannine Gospel, it is on the Cross that the Spirit is released for the believers by the death of Jesus in the symbolic form of water and blood poured from the side of the crucified Lord (John 19:34). And it was on the evening of the day of resurrection when he appeared for the first time to his disciples that Jesus "breathed" on them and gave them the Spirit (John 20:19-22). That Thomas, one of the Twelve, was absent at the time shows that the Spirit is given first to the community rather than to the individuals who make it up. Coming from God, sent through the risen and ascended Christ, the Spirit transforms the small group of frightened disciples into the *ecclesia* of God, heir to the promises.

The "Institution" of the Church

This is the proper place to take a look at an old formulation that is usually taken for granted: Jesus Christ, in the power of the Holy Spirit, instituted the Church on earth. He did it gradually as when he selected the Twelve (Matt 10:1-4); when he proclaimed Cephas "the Rock" (Peter), announced that on this Rock he would "build his Assembly," and promised to Peter "the keys of the kingdom of heaven" (16:18-19); and when, after the resurrection, he confirmed what he had previously said by sending them "to all nations, baptizing them into the Name of the Father, the Son, and the Holy Spirit, and teaching them to keep all that I have commanded you" (28:19-20).

This institutional model of the Church remains Christocentric since Christ was the author of the institution, and it is also pneumatocentric because the disciples were promised the Spirit's assistance. But if this model has been given priority in the mind of Christian believers, it is vain to speak of the Church "from Abel the just" or of the Church being born at Pentecost when the Spirit was received in the Upper Room and publicly manifested in the streets (Acts 2:1-13). There is a problem of ecclesiological consistency that has never been entirely solved in Christian reflection. Nor does it vanish when diverse models of the Church are considered complementary and logically compatible. This problem is compounded today by the growing consensus of biblical scholars that the explicit Christology of the gospels is the fruit of reflection about Jesus but cannot be attributed directly to him. If it was not totally eschatological, projected by Jesus himself on the popular expectation of the imminent "Day of the Lord" when the mysterious figure of the "Son of Man" would come from heaven, the Christology of Jesus of Nazareth was, at the most, implicit in his actions, not in his words.

In this case, however, the selection of twelve apostles, if it actually took place, may have been a prophetic gesture with eschatological significance, but it was not tantamount to creating an Assembly that was to last for millennia and still less to initiating what was to become the sacramental structure and the hierarchic organization of the Christian Church. The idea that Jesus "instituted" his Church is therefore to be taken with a grain of salt. What the expression should convey is simply that the Church became what it is as the disciples and their successors faithfully reflected on the memory of the life and teaching of Jesus in light of their continuing experience of the Spirit's guidance and of the presence of the risen Lord in their midst.

Two Views of the Spirit

As theologians of later centuries reflected on the Trinitarian mystery, they spoke, though chiefly in the West, of an "opposition of relations" between the divine Persons: each is defined by its face-to-face relationship to the other two. But these face-to-face relationships in God were differently perceived in the East and in the West at the end of the patristic period. In the East, at least since the time of Photius (patriarch, 858–867 and 877–886), the Spirit was believed to proceed from the Father only: originating directly in the

First Person, the Spirit is face to face with the Father only, even though he reposes upon the Son. This was thought to be substantially conveyed by the credal expression of the council of Nicaea, "who proceeds from the Father." *From*, in this context, means that there is no other source of the Spirit.

In the West, however, the Spirit was said by St. Augustine, who has been commonly followed in the Latin tradition, to proceed "from the Father and the Son (*Filioque*) as from one principle."[4] The eternal source of the Spirit is the first two Persons acting together as one. This is not the place to examine the rather subtle arguments in favor of either position. But one should realize that these two theologies of the Holy Spirit have had far-reaching consequences in ecclesiology.

Rather than in the life of individual believers who, whether they are Greek or Latin, rely equally on divine grace and the Spirit, the divergent views of the Spirit have made a difference in the very functioning of the Churches. Where the Spirit is believed to proceed from the Father and the Son as from one principle, the Church tends to underline the presence of the Second Person, the incarnate Word, in the community of his disciples. And since this presence is signified through certain traditional symbols (sacraments and sacramentals), it tends to stress the centrality of these symbols in the Church's daily life. Some of these symbols being identified with actual persons, the ordained ministers, the representativeness of ministry has been strongly underlined. Ordained ministers not only "stand in the presence and serve" God (as is said in the contemporary third canon of the Roman Mass). They also "act in the person of Christ" (*in persona Christi*) when they preside over the Eucharist. The phrase, *in persona*, borrowed from the legal system of ancient Rome, means that ministers "stand for, in the stead of," the one whom they represent, who is seen to be juridically present through them. When this representativeness is seen at the episcopal level of the ministerial hierarchy, acting in the person of Christ is easily extended to all the authoritative decisions that are made by bishops for the good of the community. From this also came the notion of authority that was eventually embodied in the primacy of the bishop of Rome: "successor of Peter," "vicar of Christ." The Spirit, given by the Father through Christ, testifies to Christ and brings the faithful to him and his representatives. All in the Church are then subordinated to those who represent the Lord incarnate.

Where the Spirit is believed to proceed from the Father alone, the Spirit's presence and action confirm the memory of the Lord's saving deeds and words. They also build up the contemplative knowledge of what the Word has done, said, and given. Whence the Church's tradition is not only memory but also contemplation and reflection (*gnosis*). As the Father sent the divine Logos into the world through the incarnation, so does he now send the Spirit into the Church. The Spirit enables the faithful to live their multi-

[4]St. Augustine, l. c., bk XV, ch. 17, n. 28-29 (l. c., p. 215-16).

sided relationships in the world as indeed the *koinonia* of the disciples. The Spirit is not more in the hierarchy than in the communion of the faithful. And so Christian authority can never be that of one person over others. It is always—in fact as well as in principle—synodal, conciliar, or collegial (all fundamentally equivalent terms).[5] As the Spirit is received and its understanding is conceptualized, so is the *koinonia* experienced. Further, the distinction between priest and people that is functional chiefly in the Holy Liturgy never becomes a distinction between clergy and laity as two classes or castes in the people of God.

Two Styles of Communion

Two styles of Christian life have therefore marked the Christianity of Eastern Europe where Orthodoxy has been normative, and that of Western Europe, dominated by Catholicism. For Orthodox Christianity, historically identified with the Byzantine empire and the modern nations that grew out of it, the Christian *koinonia* is the domain of the Spirit. The sacraments, sacred actions performed in the power of the Spirit, stand at the high point of Christian life as moments when the Spirit flows into the hearts of the faithful. Everything in the Church is subservient to this mystical reception of the Body and Blood of Christ in which all comes from the Father through Christ and is given by the Spirit.

Accordingly, the task of the ministers of Christ in the liturgy and the community is to free the faithful so that they may be led by the Spirit in newness of thought no less than in holiness of life. Newness of thought does not depend on scientific discoveries and technical achievements. It takes place apart from human progress and technological civilization. The Christian life consists in living on earth as though we were already with the saints in heaven. It is at the service of humanity to bring to all peoples the word of God, the presence of Christ, and the action of the Spirit. But it should leave to human initiative the choice of modes of government, the selection of social systems, and the promotion of social advancement. Action is for the sake of contemplation, body (*soma*) and mind (both as *psychè* and as *nous*) for the sake of spirit (*pneuma*).

On the other hand, the Christianity of Western Europe, identified with the Latin world and with the nations that grew out of the Carolingian empire or that were converted by its missionaries, has had a different understanding of the Spirit. From Augustine's theology of the *Filioque*, certain sociological consequences have been drawn. The action of the Spirit and the believers' forward-looking anticipation of divine gifts to be received in the future have taken second place, being subordinated to the Church's memory of Christ

[5]See below, chapter 6.

and to its preservation of the deposit of faith. The hierarchy has acted as the trusted keeper of the deposit, hence a more authoritative conception of hierarchy, a more systematic regulation of episcopal authority, a more centralizing trend in organization, a tendency to bring unity close to uniformity, a desire for clarity of formulation in defining and teaching the Christian faith and for uniformity of liturgical language and of canon law, a submission of theological speculation to the process of decision-making, a subordination of contemplation to action, a domination of ministerium by magisterium.

Soul of the Church

This expression is occasionally found in the Latin Middle Ages where it was used by analogy with the human soul: the Holy Spirit is "the soul of the Church." In itself, the expression is generally intended to refer to the Spirit and his work in the community of the disciples and in the hearts of the faithful. Yet nuances in interpreting the analogy could vary according to underlying anthropologies. Soul implies a contrast with body. And there are many conceptions of the relations between soul and body. Hindu theories of the illusionary nature of body and Buddhist conceptions of no-soul had no influence on Christian developments. Rather, these were marked in different degrees by Platonic, Aristotelian, or Stoic philosophies, all of which had their own understanding of the soul's nature and function.

Firstly, Platonism gives a negative slant to the connotation of body, for it sees the human soul as confined in its body as in a temporary jail. Transposed in ecclesiology, this would emphasize the primacy of interior life at the expense of external ties between the faithful; it would favor contemplation over action, worship over service, the monastic life over lay commitments, intention over realization, theory over practice. At the limit, life in the Spirit would be more essential to the Christian life than witness to the person and teaching of Jesus. Conversion would be an interior experience beyond all regulation from the community. The Communion would be in danger of fading away into total invisibility.

Secondly, the philosophy of Aristotle maintains the togetherness of soul and body in such a way that the two of them coexist as dovetailing principles of being. The one cannot be without the other. The soul is the form and the body the matter animated ("informed" is the technical term) by the soul. Were this the proper model for the relation of Spirit and Church, then every aspect of the Church's institution would be guaranteed by the Spirit. Every decision of its ministers would carry the weight of God's truth and revelation. Bishops would be heard like divine oracles. The way would be open to innumerable delusions and uncontrollable abuses of authority.

Thirdly, the analogy was also influenced by Stoicism: here, the point of comparison is less the human soul than what was taken to be the "soul of the world" which the Stoics called *Logos, Ratio*, "Reason." This is, one may say, the inner intelligibility of all that is. In this analogy, the outside, visible aspects of the Church have an intrinsic meaning that is to be gathered not from external appearances but from an interior logic that is ultimately from God and is attributed or appropriated to the Holy Spirit. The Stoic analogy is in fact the most enlightening regarding the nature and function of the Church.

Yet neither approach should be exclusive. Above all, that the Spirit is the "soul of the Church" is not to be taken literally. There is no identity between the Creator and the creature, the Spirit and the Church. The expression was highly favored in the Counter Reformation, though not always for the right reason. It helped to discriminate between the people who are of both the body and the soul of the Church, those who are of the body but not of the soul, and those who are of the soul but not of the body. The first were often identified as Roman Catholics who had both faith and charity, the second as Roman Catholics who might have faith but lacked charity, the third as any human persons who had charity even in the absence of faith.

The value of the expression lies in the light it throws on the Church as communion. Since, in Trinitarian theology, the Spirit is itself a permanent and total relationship within the substance of God, the Spirit in the Church is like a soul that gives life to the interrelationships of the body's members or, in the Stoic perspective of the world-soul, to the interrelationships of the many parts of the cosmos. Its presence is at the heart of the Church as the community of all believers. The Spirit itself is the source and the model of the communion between and among all the faithful of Christ, the warrant and the promise of their mutuality.

Breaks in the Communion

Yet there have been breaks of communion. These are not only contradictions of the prayer of Christ for the oneness of his disciples. They are, in addition, veils that hide the presence of the Spirit in Christian life and thought, that hinder the recognition of the Church as God's prophetic institution for the world. All breaks of communion imply that the disciples have not been faithful to the Spirit who lives at the heart of the Church.

The council of Florence, in 1439, tried to find a formula that could reconcile the Orthodox and the Catholic conceptions of the Holy Spirit. The attempt was well meant. For given the close ties between the theology of the Spirit and the Church's structure, such an agreement should help restore the communion, making sure that the diverging ecclesiologies of East and West stop short of separation. The council, however, failed. The solution that was chosen was not able to stand the test of time. It declared identical in their ultimate meaning two distinctive formulas. The standard Western formula, derived from Augustine's teaching that the Spirit proceeds from both the Father and the Son as from one principle, stands behind the three-fold statement of faith in "the Father, *and* the Son, *and* the Holy Spirit" that is frequently featured in Latin liturgies. The other formula that was widely used in both East and West went back at least as far as Tertullian: the Spirit proceeds *from* the Father *through* the Son.

In so doing, however, the council of Florence took little account of the diverging senses of this expression in the theologies of East and West. In the East, as we have seen, it was commonly understood in the light of the Trinitarian theology of Photius: the credal wording, "from the Father," means "from the Father alone." "Through the Son" conveniently refers to the gift of the Spirit to believers through the incarnation of the Logos of God. The doctrine of Photius allowed no equivalence with the Latin view. But at Florence, "from the Father through the Son" was taken to mean "from the Father *and* from the Son" even when one insisted, with Augustine, that the Father and the Son act as one principle, and, with Thomas Aquinas, that being source of the Spirit is itself the Father's gift to the Son.[6]

One may presume that these divergent theological traditions of Orthodoxy and of Latin Catholicism have their origin in distinctive spiritual insights that may well both be correct. But in the absence of proper research into such insights, the attempted conciliation was bound to fail. The paper agreement of Florence was not followed by the ecclesiological consequences that were expected from it. The divergence actually widened as it became a mutual schism.

The further breaks in communion that shook the complacency of Latin Christianity in the sixteenth century had themselves their roots in medieval developments. The Reformers attempted to recover the proper place of the Spirit in Christian life. As Luther insisted, the Spirit cannot be experienced outside of the believer's relationship to Christ that is effected by grace alone and is known in faith alone. Hence the Lutheran concern for one's personal appropriation of salvation, given *pro me* ("for me"), and the primacy of Scripture over ecclesial traditions, for Scripture embodies the earliest forms of the word of God concerning the Redeemer.

Going further, Calvin, who took his cue from Augustine, taught that the effect of the Spirit in the life of faith is to open believers to the true knowledge of God and of self.[7] As the true knowledge of God and of self gains ground in society, there must follow a radical transformation of social relationships in the image of the expected kingdom of God. And since it is the Spirit that

---

[6] *Decree for the Greeks*: DS, n. 1300-1302; Paul Evdokimov, *L'Esprit Saint dans la tradition orthodoxe* (Paris: Le Cerf, 1969); *Summa theologica* 1, q.36, a.2, ad 2.

[7] *Institutes of the Christian Religion*, bk I, ch. 1.

leads the disciples, the Spirit's testimony in the reading of Scripture is normative for the community. The Spirit does not reveal, for Christ is the revealer. Yet the Spirit affirms and testifies to Christ. Neither the letter alone nor the ecclesial traditions can be the norm of thought and conduct, whether in reading Scripture or in organizing the Christian community as one Church. Both are subordinate to the Spirit.

The Pentecostal Strain

Following the classical Reformers' concern for the Spirit, the sundry groups that constitute what is often called the "Spiritual Reformation" shifted the accent from the interior action of the Spirit to some inward and outward signs of that action. This was not entirely new. From time to time at all periods of the Church's history, some believers have taken the interior testimony of the Spirit to be an additional revelation. Following what they identified as the testimony of the Spirit to themselves, they have at times contradicted the collective stance of the community and even the biblical data. Thus the Montanists or Cataphrygians, in the second century, accused the larger Church of being unspiritual because it did not recognize the Spirit in the sayings of Montanus and his ecstatic followers. Thus also a number of medieval sects—the Cathars or Albigensians being the largest—claimed to constitute a small remnant, the Church of the pure, opposed to and persecuted by the larger body that had fallen into the unspiritual ways of the world. Thus, the first Reformers were themselves condemned as insufficiently reformed by the Anabaptists and by other radical sectarian movements, and the Church of England was said by the Puritans to be an "interimistical" Church, imperfectly reformed.

From time to time in the history of Christianity, would-be prophets have claimed that they had received from or through the Spirit an additional revelation destined to supplement or even to supersede the revelation given in Christ. Thus, Emmanuel Swedenborg (1688-1772) published the revelations that he believed he had received during numerous journeys to heaven made in the Holy Spirit. Or Joseph Smith (1805-1844), in 1830, started the movement that led to the establishment of the "Church of Jesus Christ of the Latter-day Saints" or Mormons. Or Mary Baker Eddy (1821-1910) promoted a novel interpretation of the healing message of Christ that she expounded in her *Science and Health* and *Key to the Scriptures* (1890). Thus, the Rev. Sun Myung Moon, the Korean founder of the "Holy Spirit's Association for the Unification of World Christianity," believes himself to be the herald of the Second Coming that is projected for our own generation, as is explained in the basic book of his movement, *Divine Principle*.[8]

---

[8] *Divine Principle*, HSAUWC, 5th ed., 1977.

This is also the proper perspective from which to look at a number of modern sects that have mushroomed in Europe, at the numerous Independent Churches that have emerged in Africa, and at several more or less prophetic Christian conventicles that have multiplied among immigrants in the larger cities of America and Great Britain. In a syncretism that mixes Christian insights with ideas borrowed from the monistic religions of Asia, "New Age" literature shows what confusion can be bred when the trust that the Spirit "renews the face of the earth" is not controlled by solid theology. In most of these movements, the sense of the universal community of believers is reduced to a minimum. The "Great Church" that Augustine placed against the separate community of the Donatists has been replaced by conventicles. Each believer or initiate is like an atom of belief, but the atoms are no longer linked by the overall structure of the *Ecclesia.*

Even apart from belief in a new revelation, pentecostal strains have agitated the Churches. In the American Protestantism of the second half of the nineteenth century, several new Churches came into existence because the classical Churches did not promote the kind of spiritual experience that they believed to be normative according to the Scriptures, such as extraordinary motions of the body, being caught in a trance, "shaking," speaking in tongues, being "slain in the Spirit." In spite of the intrinsic improbability that the Spirit of God would commonly signal his presence through such corporeal signs, the Holiness and the Pentecostal Churches have in turn influenced the classical Churches. In the Churches issued from the Reformation and in the Catholic Church itself, "charismatics" have regarded experiences of the Holy Spirit as supplemental to hearing the word and receiving the sacraments, and this against one of the traditional principles of the discernment of spirits, namely, that whatever phenomena may have a natural or ordinary explanation should not be attributed to supernatural, praeternatural, or extraordinary causes.

The Spirit is undoubtedly at the forefront of contemporary Christian concerns. It is to a recovery of the sense of the Holy Spirit in Catholic life that one owes the recent interest, even outside of scholarly circles, in the writings of Meister Eckhart (c. 1260–1328) and in such medieval visionaries as Hildegard of Bingen (1109–1179) and Julian of Norwich (d. after 1416). Feminist theology likes to dwell on the fact that the Hebrew term for Spirit, *rouach,* is of the feminine gender and that, following the genius of their language, the Syriac Fathers spoke of the Spirit in the feminine. As a matter of fact, however, the assumption that this is significant ignores a datum of modern linguistics: there is no connection between grammatical gender and the sexuality of men and women.[9] Yet the underlying concern points to the urgency for the contemporary Church to construct not only a more adequate an-

[9]See my essay, "Sexist Language in Theology?" in Walter Burghardt, ed., *Women, New Dimensions* (New York: Paulist Press, 1977), p. 124–146.

thropology but also a more developed theology of the Spirit of God, and above all to arrive at an agreement on the matter of the *Filioque*.

The Question

The pentecostal movements in all their forms raise a major query: does the Spirit ever speak in contradiction to the message of Christ in the Scriptures or to the tradition through which the Catholic and the Orthodox Churches believe themselves to have been guided by the Holy Spirit? The very formulation of the question implies the only answer that can be given in Catholic theology: personal inspirations that may well come authentically from the Holy Spirit never can contradict the testimony that was given by the Spirit in the past, whether in written form in the normative Scriptures or as orally conveyed in normative traditions. Both Luther and Calvin argued from this principle against the *Schwärmer* or "fanatics" of their time. As for those who do not share this basic conviction, there is little that stands in the way of mistaking all kinds of psychic experiences for the voice of the Holy Spirit. Modern psychology can explain away most of such experiences. Common sense can act as a brake that will block the drawing of hasty conclusions from vivid impressions, whether these are internal, visual, or auditive. Yet in an unfriendly world, neither common sense nor psychology, and not even the supporting ties of communion among the faithful, can shield from all confusion the many who find solace in superficial or sensational experiences and in the ensuing delusions.

The Reintegration of Unity

This is the title of Vatican II's decree on ecumenism (*Unitatis redintegratio*) that fulfilled one of the purposes assigned to the council by Pope John XXIII: to contribute to the reconciliation of separated Christians. When he called for a council, Pope John followed what he considered a sudden inspiration of the Spirit. When he referred to what the council should be and do, he liked to speak of "a new Pentecost."[10] Thus, he believed that the Church was in need of reviewing and renewing its relationship to the divine Third Person. He perceived the scope of this renovation to include an *aggiornamento*, an updating in the light of certain "signs of the times" that were elicited by the Spirit in the context of the modern world. The bishops at the council partly answered the Pope's challenge in the conciliar constitutions on the Church (*Lumen gentium*) and on the Church in the Modern World (*Gaudium et spes*): the work of Christ must be seen against the backdrop of the divine pur-

[10]See below, chapter 13.

pose of creation in which, precisely, the Spirit of God is at work. The function of the Christian Church is to bring the world to the point where it can be identified with the communion of the disciples. In ultimate analysis, the Church of Christ must become this communion of the whole people of God as they fulfill their secular tasks under the guidance of the Spirit.

The council also pursued the vision of John XXIII in a more traditionally ecclesial direction. Because they have lived in disparate communities for many centuries, the Christian believers have generally lost sight of their wholeness. They are more concerned about the identity of their smaller communities and distinctive movements than about the universal *koinonia* that should embrace them all. The trees hide the forest. The individuals hinder the corporation. The atoms have lost—or they are gradually losing—their organic interrelations. Hence the council's appeal to all Christians toward a reintegration of unity and its attempts to establish acceptable structures for such a reintegration, to formulate realistic groundwork rules for an ecumenical dialogue of the separated Churches, and to inspire theological research and prayerful emulation in anticipation of future reconciliations. It placed this work under the aegis of the Spirit. This will be examined further in chapter 13.

For Further Reading

Henri de Lubac. *The Splendour of the Church*. 2nd ed., New York: Paulist Press, 1963.

Georges Florovsky. *Bible, Church, Tradition: An Eastern Orthodox View*. Belmont, MA: Nordland Publishing Co., 1972.

Avery Dulles. *Models of the Church*. New York: Doubleday, 1974.

Rosemary Haughton. *The Catholic Thing*. Springfield, IL: Templegate, 1979.

Louis Bouyer. *The Church of God*. Chicago: Franciscan Herald Press, 1983.

John Meyendorff. *Catholicity and the Church*. Crestwood, NY: St. Vladimir's Seminary Press, 1983.

4

The Glory of God

In the awareness of being the Church, the confession of personal salvation in Christ by faith and the conviction of the Spirit's dwelling and acting in one's heart through love are reached in two moments. These are not separable since the Word is not separated from the Spirit. Nor are they complete in themselves, for they lead to a third moment that coincides with the first two. Even in what they unveil, there remains a hidden depth. Just as within each divine Person there is the common *ousia* (substance, essence) of the Three, so the missions of the Son and of the Spirit have their root in the First Person from whom they receive the divine *ousia*. Christ is known as the incarnate Word of the Father and the Spirit as the Spirit of God. As such, they have their subsistence, not in themselves solitarily, but organically in the one in whom they originate—the first by filiation, the second by procession. What they then convey in revelation and communicate in the grace that is apprehended by faith is their identity, received from the Father, as his Word and his Spirit.

This statement is of course made in the light of the mystery of the First Person that was formulated in the developed theology of the Trinity. Yet the insight that was eventually conveyed in more fully developed Trinitarian formulae was already present in the beginnings of the Christian community before the theological language had been honed out of its semitic and Greek matrices. That an unfathomable depth yawns beyond the Word and beyond the Spirit was suggested in the early Church by the vague yet rich concept, borrowed from the Old Testament, of the glory of God. The meaning that was recognized in this term by the early Christians was related to the salvation that they experienced in faith and to the guidance of the Spirit that was evident in their life. Glory evoked the believers' joy as they caught glimpses of a halo around the image of Jesus Christ that was more than Jesus, and of a radiation from behind the Spirit that was not the Spirit itself. Both the Word incarnate and the Spirit share a glory, the glory that was depicted in some way by the Old Testament prophets who perceived the presence of the *kabod Adonai* in the Temple.

The Glory

The concept of the Glory of God is not found in the tradition of the patriarchs. It emerges with the Mosaic revelation and appears in the early Hebraic community on the way to Mount Sinai: the *kabod* of the Lord is in the cloud that leads the people, a cloud of fire by night and of darkness by day (Exod 16:10). In its origin, the term is metaphorical, taken from the perceived radiance of the sun and the stars that are particularly striking in the arid landscapes of the land of Sinai. The glory remains with the people and dwells in the tabernacle (Num 14:10). Moses himself radiates the divine glory as he descends from the mountain with the tables of the Law. The glory is a light that radiates in the clouds from a source that is itself light but cannot be seen precisely because of the brilliance of its radiation. It connotes at the same time communication and hiddenness, light and darkness. The light makes known, though indirectly, the darkness of God.

The prophet Isaiah briefly described what happened in the temple around the year 740 B.C.E. when he was presumably fulfilling his priestly duties: "I saw the Lord seated on a throne, high and exalted, and the skirt of his robe filled the Temple" (Isa 6:1). What Isaiah depicts, however, is not the Lord but the seraphim that were all around: "Each had six wings; one pair covered his face and one pair his legs, and one pair was spread in flight" (6:2). They sang to one another, "Holy, holy, holy is the Lord of Hosts: the whole earth is full of his glory" (6:3). This, at least, is the Greek formulation in the Septuagint. Following the Hebrew text more literally, one could say, "Fullness of all the earth, his glory!" The *kabod* of the Creator is the plenitude of creation. Without it, the earth would miss its fullness. Were the acknowledgement of this glory by the creatures missing, creation would not be true to its purpose. But the very fact that the Lord chooses a prophet who will see the glory in a special vision indicates that the glory of the Lord is normally hidden. The universe is not seen as divine glory by the average onlooker. Neither the man in the street nor the man in the laboratory, the technician, perceives the divine glory. The one whom John Courtney Murray called the "man of the theatre," the artist, has some inkling of the glory.[1] But only the man in the Temple has both an inkling and a knowledge of the transcendent source of the glory that pervades the world. Yet not even then is the glory as such seen. Rather, the

[1] John Courtney Murray, *The Problem of God* (New Haven: Yale University Press, 1964), p. 102-103.

seraphim reveal to those who hear their spiritual chant that there is glory of God in the fullness of creation and that this fullness is part of the Creator's glory. The people may "listen" and "look," but they "will not understand" and they "will never know" (6:9) unless they believe the prophet. The divine glory is manifested through the seraphim to the prophet and by the prophet to the people. It is evident only to faith.

In the year 580 B.C.E. during the exile in Babylon, the prophet Ezekiel also perceives the glory of God, this time in a vision of heaven. The vision is complex and frightening. In a storm, in the fire of lightning, seraphim are seen, having four faces of a man, an ox, a lion, an eagle, and four wings. They move straight in all directions. There are also moving wheels under them and a vault "like a sheet of ice" above them. The noise is tremendous, "like the noise of an armed camp" (Ezek 1:24). Above the vault, the prophet perceives a noise, "a sapphire in the shape of a throne," and "upon the throne, a form in human likeness" (1:26). The form is like fire, and it radiates like a rainbow in dark clouds. "It was like the appearance of the glory of the Lord" (1:28).

The glory of the Lord is thus a radiance, the source of which is not visible. The seraphim, who are under the hidden source of light, prepare the human seer for it. Yet the glory should not be confused with the seraphim's fantastic appearance. It is above and beyond them, in utter transcendence. It calls not for curiosity and speculation but for adoration. "When I saw this, I threw myself on my face. . . ." (1:28). If it fills the temple in Isaiah's vision, it fills the universe in that of Ezekiel. The implication is the same in both cases. Both the temple and the universe have an invisible dimension, the dimension of the glory of God. But the task of the prophets is not to analyze the glory; rather, it is to invite the people to bow down and worship in the presence of the glory.

In Jewish history, these passages have been of importance in *shekhinah* mysticism, the mysticism of the divine presence.[2] The presence of God is at the heart of the glory perceived by prophets in the Temple and in the universe, and by mystics in their heart. As they symbolically ascend the ten *sefîrôt*, or divine attributes at work in creation, the mystics build up the *knesset Yisrael*, the true community of Israel, that embodies the kingdom of God here below. It is undoubtedly significant that, whatever the originality of their experience and of its formulation, the mystics of Israel are not, like some of the Christian mystics, hermits living in isolation. They cluster in schools and synagogues, forming small communities within the great community of Israel.

If the meditations of the Jewish kabbalah are in continuity with their biblical source, then one should accept the principle that the prophetic visions of the divine presence implicitly contain an ecclesiological principle. In less esoteric terms than those of the kabbalists, one may say that it is in the cult,

[2]Gershom Scholem, *Major Trends in Jewish Mysticism* (New York: Schocken Books, 1946); *Kabbalah* (Jerusalem: Keter Publishing House, 1974).

whether external worship in the Temple or internal ascent in the heart and soul of the devotees, that the divine presence is perceived. In either case, the perception of the presence is inseparable from the community that is publicly recognized by its fidelity to Torah, the God-given Law.

Glory in the New Testament

The Greek term used in the New Testament is *doxa*. It can be generally translated as brightness, splendor, radiance, magnificence, fame, glory. The Hebraic conception of God's glory persists in the New Testament. Yet the divine glory that is now discerned is always tied to Christ. Christ is the one through whom God's glory is manifested. St. Paul is particularly emphatic on this point. Since it shines with special radiance in the "divine dispensation of the Spirit" (2 Cor 3:8), the glory of God is tied to the person and action of Christ through whom this dispensation has taken place. And it far outshines the glory that was manifested in the gift of Torah to Moses. Paul in fact reverses the common Jewish perspective. Instead of the *kabod Adonai* he speaks of *Adonai kabod*, the Lord of glory (1 Cor 2:8). In his Lordship, the risen Christ is the very glory of God, the radiance of the Father. This glory is incarnate as Jesus. Jesus therefore rose from the dead in the "glory of the Father" (Rom 6:4). The disciples, that is "those who are justified," are destined to share the glory of Christ (Rom 8:30).

In the Johannine writings, the glory that is mentioned in the book of Revelation is similar to that of the prophetic visions of Isaiah and Ezekiel. But in the gospel, the divine glory is manifestly present throughout the life of Jesus to the point that John affirms, "we have seen his glory" (John 1:14). This glory is given by the Father to the Son (14:13) and promised by the Son to the disciples (17:22). The unique manifestation of Christ's glory in the cross and resurrection is a precondition for the gift of the Spirit to the disciples (12:16).

In the Synoptic Gospels, too, the coming of Christ shows forth the divine glory. It is perceived by the shepherds as light shining in the night over the universe (Luke 2:9) and by the Magi in the form of a guiding star (Matt 2:2). Jesus himself will sit on the throne "in celestial glory" (Matt 19:28). This glory is shared with Elijah and Moses and manifested to the three apostles on Mount Tabor (Luke 9:29-36). Yet there is a paradox. For as Luke points out, it is by way of his passion that Jesus will enter into his glory (Luke 24:26).

Whatever translation one adopts for *doxa*, this term in the New Testament always refers ultimately to the depths of God that are hidden by their very radiation in the created world. The Old Testament belief that one cannot see God and live (Exod 30:20) is now taken in the sense that the depths of God are simply not communicable to the creature: even the most endowed mystical insight does not do justice to God.

The Light of God

The theme of the divine glory is often couched in terms of light. This is even at the center of patristic thought. Theology is doxology. The Nicene Creed includes in the Christian faith the belief that the divine Logos is "God from God, light from light, true God from true God." Like the glory in the Old Testament, the *lumen* of the Creed is borrowed from human experience. The natural light, the light of the sun in the world, the lighting of fire to warm oneself and to cook, the light of candles and lamps in the home are indispensable to life. Likewise, the divinity that is within and around all that is, makes it to be. Like the light that shines on a multitude of objects, God the Creator is radically self-giving. The light is one, yet shared by the many. As it gives itself fully in an endless series of gifts, it is never exhausted. The first gift is the Word; the second is the Spirit; and the third, spread out in innumerable particular gifts, can only be the creaturely world.

At each level, there is divine light which is uncreated and equal to the Father in the Word and the Spirit and is created, derived, and therefore graduated in the creatures. The light of God is reflected by all creatures on earth.[3] But it can be truly shared only by intelligent creatures who refer to God their awareness of the divine light in and around them. Since, however, the light originates in the Father and knowledge of the Trinitarian life of God derives from God's self-revelation in Christ, there are special ties between the Christian community, the light, and the glory of God.

Not by accident did Christian reflection about God among the Fathers of the Church often take the form of a theology of the light. The visions of Isaiah and of Ezekiel; the prophecy of the Son of Man coming on the clouds of heaven in the Book of Daniel; the episode of the transfiguration in the Synoptic Gospels; the assertion of the prologue of John, "He was the true light come into the world, that enlightens every human" (John 1:9); the descriptions of heaven in the Johannine Apocalypse; the incipient theology of light in the First Epistle of John: such passages and others conspired to create a vision of the Church that identified the Christian community with the realm in which the radiation of God's light in the creaturely world is perceived in faith. If the whole universe is the created horizon of the divine glory, the Church is the focus in which the rays of divine glory, concentrated in Christ and the Spirit, are seen to illumine the world.

In the first Christian centuries, the image of the light permitted the strains flowing from the Old Testament and from the Jewish roots of the community to converge with other currents of thought and imagery that were familiar to the pagan world. The theology of the glory of God, derived from Judaism,

---

[3] Jaroslav Pelikan, *The Spirit of Eastern Christendom (600–1700)* (*The Christian Tradition: A History of the Development of Doctrine*, vol. 2) (Chicago: University of Chicago Press, 1974), p. 258–269; Marie-Madeleine Davy and Jean-Pierre Renneteau, *La Lumière dans le christianisme* (Paris: Le Félin, 1989).

spread in the Roman empire just when the cult of Mithra was popularizing the image of God as *Sol Invictus*, "Unconquered Sun." This is Apollo whose head is, in painting and sculpture, surrounded by a halo of shining rays. A theology of the light was therefore eagerly pursued in patristic times, both in the numerous conventicles that scholars have grouped under the general name of "gnosticism" and in the Great Church. In the Church, it developed in both the East and the West in ways that were not identical. St. Augustine of Hippo gave it a highly intellectual content as he placed it at the heart of his doctrine of knowledge by divine illumination. In the East, however, it followed a more spiritual orientation, being closely associated with the soul's interior ascent to God. Christ is the light that never fails, shining in the darkness of the world and of sin. As Simeon the New Theologian (949-1022) was to write in his Hymn n. 43, "I see you like a sun, / I bear you in my bosom like a pearl, / I look at you like a lamp that is lit inside of a vase. . . ."[4] The Oriental point of view on the divine light was embodied in the painting of icons. And when, in 782, Nicaea Council II endorsed the art of the icon painters, it did not simply admit the validity of certain artistic activities. Rather, it promoted a certain type of painting as being intrinsically religious, and it taught that the works thus produced, the icons, truly reflect the divine light and are proper sacraments of worship.

Theological reflection on the light that shines in the darkness of the world soon leads to the remark that light at its fullest is both illuminating and dazzling. Its rays blind those who would look straight into it. This confirms the belief of all religions that the depths of God are unfathomable. It fits the insight that the *ousia* of God lies hidden in the One whom Christians call the Father, the source of the Word and of the Spirit, the Creator of all things visible and invisible.

If, then, the Church of Christ is the focus of the divine light on earth, the Church as community—and all its members individually—must stand in a very special relation to the depths of God. This special relation may be looked at from three complementary points of view.

Negative Theology

The first view has to do with the negative character of all human knowledge of the First Person and the ensuing catechetical requirements. Since God the Father communicates only through the Word and the Spirit, one cannot speak directly of him. As the Russian Orthodox Sergius Bulgakoff asked at the end of his investigation of *The Word Incarnate* and *The Paraclete*, "The Father. . . . What can one say of Him, who is Silence, Mystery,

[4]Simeon the New Theologian, *Hymn* n. 42 (SC, n. 196, 1973, p. 45).

Transcendence, even in the bosom of the Holy Trinity?"[5] Starting from the sense of awe that is inspired by contemplation of the unseen powers at work in the universe, the religions of the world have spoken of a *mysterium tremendum* which is also, by the same token, *fascinosum*, both awesome and mesmerizing. Beneath the surface of reality, there lurks a "mystery" that is frightening yet fascinating. Mystery, in this context, has the original meaning of the term: it is that in which one enters by secret initiation, of which the initiates may catch a glimpse in the darkness of this world, thus receiving the promise of a more thorough contemplation of it in the next world.

Philosophers, theologians, and mystics of all major religions have tried to enter this mystery. They have named it. Images of descent have been used for this purpose. The mystery is "ground of being," "being itself," "eternal being," "the soul of the world," "divine nothingness," *Ungrund* and *Urgrund*. Images of ascent have also been used. The mystery is symbolically located beyond the top of a mountain after the ways of ascent have become "noway;" it is, as Vladimir Soloviev, who took his cue from the kabbalah, called it, *Ain-Sof*, the Utterly Transcendent, the Unnamed because Unnamable.[6]

The Christian faith places this mystery in the recesses of the divine essence characteristic of the First Person, the Father. As the Father does not act in the world except through the two that Irenaeus of Lyon metaphorically called his "hands,"[7] the Word and the Spirit, likewise the Father is unknowable, except in the Word and in the Spirit. Human creatures may reach the conviction that there is an eternal Father of the universe, a Creator. But they have no knowledge of God as *the* Father, except by faith in the Word incarnate and the Spirit of Christ. While the great religions locate the mystery that is frightening and fascinating in the divine being or essence, the Christian faith sets it further still from the human level, in the First Person, the Unbegotten.

Yet even the Christian faith does not know the Father directly, but only indirectly as reflected in the Christ and the Spirit. It cannot speak of the Father in direct speech, but only by analogy and, at one more remove from the reality that is intended and aimed at, with recourse to metaphors. As the Church proclaims its faith, it should therefore give primacy to negative theology. That is, whatever the catechisms need to affirm about the historical life of Jesus Christ and about the diverse manifestations of the Spirit in the

[5]Sergius Bulgakov, *Le Paraclet* (Paris: Aubier, 1946), p. 343 (under the significant title, "Epilogue, also to be used as prologue"). The writings of Louis Bouyer present a counter-test: there is a separate volume, *Le Père invisible* (Paris: Le Cerf, 1976), besides the volumes *Le Fils éternel*, 1974, and *Le Consolateur*, 1980; but this volume on the First Person speaks less of the Father in the Trinitarian revelation than of natural perceptions of God, pagan religions, and philosophical deviations.

[6]D. Strémooukhoff, *Vladimir Soloviev and his Messianic Work* (Belmont, MA: Nordland Publishing Co., 1980), p. 54-55.

[7]Irenaeus of Lyons, *Adversus Haereses*, V, 6, 1 (SC, n. 153, 1969, p. 73).

Church, they also must deny that anyone, be it the most impressive theologian or the greatest saint, ever penetrates the transcendence of the Father. This is the originating and ultimate Abyss. Abysmal knowledge can only be put in the negative form. The positive form would be misleading. Yet the negative form cannot be entirely negative if God indeed has manifested himself, whether in nature or in the religions. If "I know" says too much, "I know not" says too little. "I fail to know" is correct in that it implies both a desire and an attempt to know. There is a dimension of knowing God that is necessarily agnostic, yet only partially so.

This is not, however, an admission of ignorance. It is an enlightening invitation to know God beyond the intellect, to enter, through love, the realm of doxology, and there to taste God through the soul's spiritual senses. From the times of St. Gregory the Great (590-604) through the Middle Ages, theologians spoke of love of God as being true knowledge of God. William of St. Thierry (c. 1080-1149) wrote in his commentary on the Song of Songs: "In the vision of God, love alone is at work." More didactic, St. Bonaventure affirmed: "Knowledge is not perfect without love," and "When the intellect fails, love goes on. . . ." Or in the language of an anonymous English mystic of the 14th century, the mystical knowledge of God takes place in a "cloud of unknowing." At the Renaissance, Nicholas of Cusa (1401-1464) identified the knowledge of God as *docta ignorantia*, a "learned ignorance."[8] At the Reformation, Martin Luther repeated time and time again that God is primarily *Deus absconditus*, the hidden God. For this reason God is not known by reason, but by faith; and there is no valid "theology of glory" that is not first of all a "theology of the cross."[9]

Facing the primordial mystery of the First Person, the effective knowledge of the Father is both faith alone, for science fails, as well as worship and adoration; for love goes beyond knowledge, the heart further than the mind. Worship determines the nature of the Christian community in light of the primordial mystery. Worship, however, has two fundamental dimensions. There is a communal worship of God that is collective and external and an internal worship in the hearts of the faithful. Each type throws light on the basic nature of the Christian Church.

[8]William of St. Thierry, *Exposé sur le Cantique des Cantiques* (SC, n. 82, 1962), p. 296; Bonaventure: "There is no perfect knowledge without love" (George H. Tavard, *Transiency and Permanence: The Nature of Theology according to St Bonaventure* [St Bonaventure, N.Y.: Franciscan Institute, 1954], p. 80); *The Cloud of Unknowing* (*The Classics of Western Spirituality*) (New York: Paulist Press, 1981); Nicholas of Cusa, *Of Learned Ignorance*, ed. by W. Stark (New Haven: Yale University Press, 1954).

[9]See theses 19-21 of the Heidelberg Disputation; Bengt R. Hoffman, *Luther and the Mystics: A Re-examination of Luther's Spiritual Experience and his Relationship to the Mystics* (Minneapolis: Augsburg, 1976).

Liturgeia

This is the second point of view. The communal worship of God involves the entire Church in the perception of the divine presence and glory. The prayer of the whole people of God is then appropriately called the "common prayer." In the Church's liturgy, the people of God are carried into the divine light. The dimension of glory burns at the heart of Christian worship. The Church is never as much what it is called to be as in the liturgy. Then, common prayer is also, as in the usual oriental expression, "divine liturgy."

In its secular use in Greek, the word, "liturgy," denotes any kind of motion, but especially a recurring motion. Likewise, the religious use of the term designates the movement of the Christian community toward God in worship. The faithful get together from the four corners of the city. They enter a room that has been adorned with symbols of adoration. This place is described by the Fathers of the Church as being already filled with an invisible throng of angels who have also come to worship. The believers offer to the Father the sacrifice of praise. They use the inspired psalms of the Old Testament, and they let the Spirit, who "through our inarticulate groans is pleading for us" (Rom 8:27), suggest fresh prayers in their hearts. They sing hymns "to Christ as to a God" as the Roman author Pliny the Younger (62-113), governor of Bithynia, reported it to Emperor Trajan (98-117).[10] Pliny could not know that, whatever their forms of words, the hymns are addressed to the First Person to whom they are presented through Christ, the only Mediator, and in the power of the Holy Spirit who "comes to the aid of our weakness" (Rom 8:26).

As it was organized in the first centuries of the Church by transformation of the *berakôth* or "blessings" of the Jewish worship in the synagogues, the sacrifice of praise was sustained by the commemoration of the sacrifice of Christ. The Greek word, *eucharist* (thanksgiving), was originally translated *berakah*. But Christian usage and interpretation added a Trinitarian dimension to the original *berakôth*. The Eucharistic worship followed from the start a Trinitarian structure. The faithful present to the Father, along with their blessing of God for the beauties of creation, their thanksgiving for the redemption brought through Christ and for the pentecostal gift of the Spirit. The account of the Last Supper, when Jesus offered himself, ties together the perspective of the heavenly glory that pervades the universe and the acceptance of human life that is shared with Christ the Savior. The Holy Spirit who is invoked to "transform" the gifts of bread and wine into his body and blood unites the participants to the risen humanity. For Christ has now entered the Holy of Holies in heaven with the blood of his sacrifice (Heb

---

[10]Pliny the Younger, *Letter X* (to Trajan), quoted in Henry Bettenson, ed., *Documents of the Christian Church* (New York: Oxford University Press, 1953), p. 3-5.

9:11-16).[11] His eternal acceptance by the Father shines forth in the sacramental presence of his risen humanity.

Not by accident does the word *communion* designate both the reception of the sacramental body and blood of Christ at the end of the "great prayer" and the community of the faithful. The chief sign that there is a community of the faithful is precisely their participation in the liturgy of which the Eucharist is the climax. The Church is made of those who gather together to share the Eucharist. In a sense, it comes into being at the moment of this sharing, for until then the participants, though united in faith, have worked separately at their diverse tasks and functions and have lived separately, sometimes even in rivalry and hostility, in the confines of their families, clans, tribes, and nations.

Yet it is not the gathering of the faithful that makes the Church, as though this were a merely human grouping of believers. The faithful would not come together in the first place unless they were led by faith, in the power of the Spirit, through Christ to the Father. Their being drawn to the Savior is itself a pure gift. And the gift, since it comes from God, is made in advance. It pre-exists those who receive it. This gift is the Church. *Liturgeia* thus brings out the nature of the Church as *koinonia*. And the *liturgeia* cannot take place outside of the *koinonia*. If these are two gifts from God, the gifts are inseparable. They cannot be contrary to each other. One may, indeed one should, look at each from the standpoint of the other. The best way to understand the liturgy is to know the community, and the best way to understand the community is to know the liturgy. Thus Vatican Council II declared: "The liturgy is the summit to which all the Church's action tends, and also the source from which all its power derives" (SC, n. 10).

By the same token, a group of discontented believers can no more set up a separate worship than they can create a new Church. It is God who creates the Church through Christ and who in the Holy Spirit initiates the conditions for worship.

Interior Worship

The true knowledge of God is totally given in faith. That is, faith is more than belief. Belief refers to statements about God that can be itemized, classified, analyzed, and compared to statements about the entire field of human knowledge; it is the acknowledgement that those statements are true, that they correspond to undoubted facts. Faith, however, implies a personal commitment, not to the perceived correspondence of propositions with facts,

---

[11]George H. Tavard, "The Meaning of Melchisedek for Contemporary Ministry," in Earl E. Shelp and Ronald H. Sunderland, eds., *The Pastor as Priest* (New York: Pilgrim Press, 1987), p. 64-85.

but to the facts themselves. Beyond the credal statements, or articles of faith, about the Father, the Word incarnate, and the Spirit, faith links the believer personally to the three Persons. It implies confidence, acceptance, self-giving. The three virtues that St. Augustine distinguished in his *Enchiridion on Faith, Hope, and Love* are aspects of the one fundamental stance before God that Paul identified as *pistis* (the Greek term he used). This is "faith that works through love" (Gal 5:6).

What the Eucharist or common prayer is to the community of the faithful, faith is to each of the believers. It is the point of contact with divine grace, the place where "all good giving and every perfect gift" are received "from the Father of the lights of heaven" (Jas 1:17). It is the level at which one knows oneself as the child of God redeemed by Christ, the dwelling place of the Holy Spirit. Since this is a profoundly personal and interior happening, one may speak of an "interior Church," an "invisible Church," a "Church in the heart," of an experience of being one with the Word, begotten of the Father in him, and one with the Spirit, carried in the eternal procession from the Father.

From time to time, Christian mystics have described such an experience. They have spoken of being "caught up as far as the third heaven" and "into paradise," of hearing "words so secret that human lips may not repeat them" (Paul in 2 Cor 12:2-4), of seeing "a rift in the sky" (Stephen in Acts 7:56), or "a gate open in heaven" (John in Rev 4:1), of climbing to God up the ladder of perfection, or up the degrees of divine love, or up the slopes of a mountain, whether this be called Mount Sion with Bernardino de Laredo (1482-1540) or Mount Carmel with John of the Cross (1542-1591). Conversely, they have spoken of descending to the center of one's being where, as Augustine wrote in the *Confessions*, God is *intimior intimo meo*, "interior to my interior."[12] They have adapted from the Old Testament the analogy of a marriage between the Lord and Israel: they have been betrothed to God; like Teresa of Avila (1515-1582), they have entered into spiritual marriage with God; with St. Bernard (c. 1090-1153), they have received from God the kiss of the mouth.

These metaphors attempt to suggest impressions of God's grace. They should be read in keeping with the principle of negative theology. They are windows into doxology. No more than words do images provide a handle to get hold of God or even to trace what St. Bonaventure called *itinerarium mentis in Deum*, "the soul's journey into God."[13] It is God who, through Christ, takes hold of the elect in the Holy Spirit, beyond all human imagining

---

[12]The text continues: "*et superior summo meo*" (*Confessions*, bk III, vi, 11): "More inward than my inmost self, and superior to my highest being" (John K. Ryan, ed., *The Confessions of St Augustine* [New York: Image Books, 1960], p. 84). Two translations are possible: "interior to . . ., superior to . . ." (my choice), or "more inward than . . ., higher than . . ."

[13]This is the title of Bonaventure's classic: Lawrence S. Cunningham, ed., *The Mind's Journey into God* (Chicago: Franciscan Herald Press, 1979).

and telling. In the process, God creates an interior Church in the hearts of the faithful. There, in their inner sanctuary, each of them communes intimately with God by grace and in faith. It is for the sake of that interior Church that Christians are gathered by the Holy Spirit in their worshiping assemblies and that they have communion together, thus being made into one ecclesial communion. The exterior Church is at the service of the interior Church.

The Church as Priesthood

At the period of the Reformation, the "spiritual Reformers" condemned the exterior Church whether "evangelical" with Luther, "reformed" with Calvin, or traditional with the supporters of the bishop of Rome. They endeavored to restore what they felt to be the true Church, a community of the elect that is both exterior and interior. Yet they made two mistakes. In the first place, the Church cannot be built by human hands and not even by the striving of a few toward holiness. In the second, interior and exterior do not denote different Churches. There is no dichotomy between the inside and the outside. Even when holiness does not seem visibly to prevail, there is only one Church, living at two levels. This one Church may be called, equivalently, the Church of God, the Church of Christ, the Church of the Spirit. Referring to the marks of the Church in the creed of Nicaea, one could argue that the Church is *one* because it is of Christ, *holy* because gathered in the Spirit, *catholic* because made by the Creator of heaven and earth, and *apostolic* because it perpetuates the mission entrusted by Jesus to his apostles as to the instruments of its institution.

Another way of stating the unicity of the Church of Christ is opened in the First Epistle of Peter: "You are a chosen race, a royal palace, a priesthood, a holy nation, a people set apart by God. . . ." (1 Pet 2:9). If race designates a social entity, the fact that it has been chosen is spiritual. The royal palace, as building, is external, yet it has internal dignity as being the sovereign's. Likewise, the holy nation and the people set apart are at the same time external and visible, internal and invisible. In the lingering perspective of the levitical priesthood that stands in the background of the Epistle of Peter, the priesthood is corporate, entrusted to the tribe of Levi, and it is spiritual by virtue of its purpose and functions. When this twofold dimension is transferred to the Church of Christ, it becomes clear that the Christian people are priestly, yet not as individuals. They are priestly insofar as they are, together, the Church. In the traditional theology of the sacraments, the believers are incorporated into this ecclesial priesthood by the regenerating waters of baptism.

The Church as God's Purpose

The ties between the Church and the doxological purpose of creation have from time to time prompted theologians and spiritual authors to venture into bold language when speaking of the Church. It is said in the *Shepherd of Hermas*, a writing of the second century, that the author, in a vision, saw the Church under the features of an elderly woman. As he wondered why she looked so old, Hermas was told: "Because she was created before all. . . . It is for her that the world was created."[14] Likewise, St. Epiphanius wrote in the fourth century: "The Holy Catholic Church is the beginning of all things." This theme was frequently commented upon in medieval sermons and biblical commentaries. Even though it has been largely lost—with some notable exceptions—in modern theology, it looms behind the sometimes astonishing images that have been applied to the Virgin Mary in Catholic parlance. The very notion that the Church is given by God to humankind as the community of salvation calls for special emphasis on those members of the Church who, in the eyes of the generality of the faithful, best exemplify the divine predestination, justification, sanctification, and salvation. These are of course the saints, and above all, the Holy Mother of God.

To most Christians today, both Protestant and Catholic, mariological language and marian devotion often seem to be extravagant in the strict sense of being outside the norm. This impression is right if, on the one hand, the norm is identified as Christ alone and if, on the other, the selfhood of the saints and of Mary is seen as a symbol of total catholicity. One may indeed admit that the great majority of the faithful do not commonly distinguish between the reality of a person (the saint, the Virgin Mary) or of an association of persons (the Church) and their symbolic meaning as images. Yet if the world and humanity find their ultimate purpose in their doxological destiny, then the principle holds that that which best expresses the Father's glory embodies in itself the purpose of creation and the reason for which the world was made. Since the world is a theophany, there must be someone who can read it as the script of the divine glory. For Christian believers, this reader of God's design is no other than Jesus Christ, the "perfect adorer."[15] Yet it is also the community of the women and men who, through Christ, in the Holy Spirit, give glory to God the Father. And this community is, precisely, the Church.

---

[14] *The Shepherd of Hermas*, vision 1, IV, in Kirsopp Lake, tr., *Apostolic Fathers*, vol. 2 Loeb Classical Library (Cambridge: Harvard University Press, 1965), p. 25; Epiphanius: *Panarion*, I, 1, 15 (PG, 41, 181).

[15] Such expressions as "Perfect Adorer," "Special Adorer," are applied to Jesus Christ in the French School of Spirituality, especially by Bérulle. See Michael J. Buckley, "Seventeenth-Century French Spirituality," in Louis Dupré and Don E. Saliers, eds., *Christian Spirituality: Post-Reformation and Modern* (New York: Crossroad, 1989), p. 42, 53.

Liturgeia, koinonia, diakonia go together. The Church is a communion in which common prayer and common service imply each other. The liturgy is the work of the community. It is *opus* (the task, the service), *opus Dei* (the service of God) as it is called in the Rule of St. Benedict. The faithful are prepared by it for their service of God and neighbor. The community, in which they share all spiritual gifts and, in turn, place their own goods at the disposal of the needy, is equipped and strengthened for mutual service by the Eucharistic liturgy that is at the heart of its life and by the mystical communion with Christ that the faithful experience in their heart. The liturgy—the worship of God "in spirit and in truth" that is offered to the Father through Christ in the Holy Spirit—gathers the faithful into one as communion with the sacramental Christ associates them in mutual communion. Thus is the ecclesial community built up for service by worship.

The Church is at worship before the Father, recognizing his glory and reflecting it back to its source. It is built as a communion by the Spirit. Through the mediation of Christ, it shares the service of word and sacrament that enables it further to serve the sick and the poor, offering reconciliation and peace to the world. Thus the three basic dimensions of the *Ecclesia* relate the members of the Church to the three divine Persons from whom they and it derive: coming by creation from the Father through the Son in the Holy Spirit, they return by grace in the Holy Spirit through the Son to the Father.

Thus did Vatican Council II declare:

> The liturgy, through which, especially in the divine sacrifice of the eucharist, the "work of our redemption is done," brings it about that the faithful express by their life and show to others the mystery of Christ and the genuine nature of the Church. It is proper to [the Church] to be both human and divine, visible and endowed with invisible qualities, fervent in action and occupied in contemplation, present in the world and yet on pilgrimage, in such a way that the human in it is ordered and subordinated to the divine, the visible to the invisible, action to contemplation, the present to the future city which we seek (SC, n. 2).

The Kairos

The course of human life is punctuated by moments of awareness. In a life, in a year, even in a week or a day, one may, like John at Patmos, find a gate opened into heaven and discern something new in the mystery of God. Thus is the Christian message gospel, that is, good news. Such moments are brought about by the emergence of a "revelatory situation," a situation that is suited to receiving new insights into the revelation given once for all in Jesus Christ. At such moments, the Spirit takes by the hand those who have been chosen and, in keeping with Jesus' promise in the Gospel of John, leads them into all the truth (John 16:13).

Vatican Council II was such a moment for the Church as a whole, both inside and outside of Roman Catholicism. What was perceived—by participants and by those who followed the debates from the outside—reached much further than the superficial matters of organization that made the headlines, such as the formation of National Episcopal Conferences. It reached further than the theological questions that were debated, like the sacramentality of the episcopate or the proper relations between the episcopal college and the bishop of Rome, the bishops and their people, the laity and their clergy. The sense of the *kairos* of 1962-1965 was much closer to the meaning of the Church and to the heart of the gospel than any such peripheral problem: it had to do with the communion of believers as their participation in the inner communion (in technical language, the "circumincession") of the divine Persons.

As things happened, much of the ecclesiological reflection that followed Vatican Council II was more occupied with the periphery than with the center. This is understandable. The high pitch of mutually reinforcing expectation and achievement that was generally maintained at the council itself could not be kept up once the bishops had returned to the routine of their ordinary existence. They were then taken up by practical problems of local administration and liturgical updating. Priests, most of whom had never even been close to the action of Vatican II, were occupied by demands of homiletics and catechetics, by the new pastoral concerns that followed the sudden thrust of society into the computer age and the spread of public and legal permissiveness in regard to sexual behavior. Theologians were busy facing queries and questions that emerged from the new ecumenical spirit, from the latest trends in biblical studies, and from the more or less utopian and often contradictory perspectives of a Church-wide freedom of the Spirit and a world-wide liberation of the oppressed. Professors were engaged in the reshaping of courses according to the spirit of the council and in the formulation and defense of conciliar theses. The people at large, and notably the women, were excited afresh by the rediscovery that they too are the Church in their own right, and not only by way of obedience. Then the *kairos* of Vatican II was mostly stifled in the ensuing bustle. The result is now patent: despite the beginning reform of Church institutions and especially of the Roman curia that was initiated by Paul VI, the Catholic Church has not yet acquired structures consistent with the spirit of Vatican II.

None of these concerns, legitimate though they be, can open shortcuts to the Church of tomorrow. Only by returning, not to Vatican II as to an intriguing event of yesteryear, but to the core of what was then found, shall we have access to the spiritual dimension of being the Church: unanimity of minds and hearts in Christ and the Holy Spirit, for the sake of the glory of God in creation. The Scriptures give us a hint: "In this we have known love, that he lay down his life for us, and we too should lay down our lives for the brethren" (1 John 3:16). And one may dream of the song of St. John of the Cross being taken up by the whole Church:

> Oh, fire lamps,
> in whose splendors
> the deep caves of sense
> hitherto dark and blind,
> with strange beauties
> warmth and light shed near the Beloved![16]

For Further Reading

Dietrich Bonhoeffer. *The Communion of Saints.* New York: Harper and Row, 1960.
Avery Dulles. *The Dimensions of the Church.* Westminster: Newman, 1967.
Louis Bouyer. *Eucharist: Theology and Spirituality of the Eucharistic Prayer.* Notre Dame: University of Notre Dame Press, 1968.
Archbishop Joseph M. Raya. *The Face of God: An Introduction to Eastern Spirituality.* Denville, N.J.: Dimension Books, 1976.
Geoffrey Wainwright. *Doxology: The Praise of God in Worship, Doctrine, and Life.* New York: Oxford University Press, 1980.
Henri de Lubac. *The Motherhood of the Church.* San Francisco: Ignatius Press, 1982.

---

[16]This is the third stanza in John of the Cross' poem, *The Living Flame of Love;* see Kieran Kavanaugh and Otilio Rodriguez, *The Collected Works of St. John of the Cross* (Washington: ICS, 1973), p. 718 (with a different translation of the poem).

PART TWO

TRADITION

The awareness of being the Church is structured around the experience of servanthood for the sake of God and of neighbor (*diakonia*), of communion in faith and love with the other believers (*koinonia*), and of pilgrimage in hope toward the glory of God that is present in the twofold sanctuary of the Church and of the soul (*liturgeia*). Such an awareness has not been lived out and expressed in the same way throughout the centuries that separate us from the time of the incarnation. Whether by its members or by the world, the Church of Christ has not always been seen in the same light. It has been recognizably one, yet with evolving features through successive centuries. Depending on one's cast of mind and on the point of view one has adopted, the Church has seemed to be unchanging and constant, a rock in the ebb and flow of human societies, a monolith untouched by the prevailing erosion all around it. Or on the contrary, caught in the flux of temporality, tossed around by the waves of progress and decay through which it has tried to steer, the Church has seemed to flutter at every wind of change. The impression of "variations" that struck Bossuet when he studied the history of Protestant churches may well be conveyed also by the history of the Catholic Church, whether taken in the universal sense or as the name of the Roman Catholic Church. The Christian community has passed from its early hesitant days in Jerusalem and Antioch to the conversion of the Gentiles and its Constantinian flowering, and thence to the conversion of the barbarians and the construction of European nations, to missionary expansion in the Americas and finally in Asia, Africa, and the islands of the Pacific ocean. Sociologically, the Church has been many things. It has been the religious dimension of the Roman Empire, the pacifier and guide of the Germanic tribes, the sponsor and arbiter of kings, the associate of the conquistadors, the critic and the ally of the modern age. At each age, the believers have pursued an ideal picture of the Church, and they have also struggled with the opposite caricature that was drawn by its detractors.

The sequence and the eventual coexistence of different ideas of the Church have suggested that several "models" of the Church have been at work among the faithful and their leaders. The Church has molded itself on several models. Without trying to be exhaustive, Avery Dulles has analyzed some such models: the Church has been seen as Institution, as Mystical Communion, as Sacrament, as Herald, as Servant, as the Image of God's Kingdom, as the Depository of divine revelation. There has usually been one predominant model favored by external circumstances and cultural evolution. Such predominant models have varied. With the evolution of mentalities, they have replaced one another. Even then, however, models of the Church have coexisted, as the central model of each period could not do away with the partial effectiveness of the others. But they have often coexisted in tension or conflict.

The writings of the New Testament provide the starting point for all historical models of the Church. Yet they do not really put forward models, blueprints, or even ideals. Instead, they employ a multitude of appellations, and they designate the Church with numerous symbols and images. We will therefore begin with a survey of the biblical images of the Church (ch. 5). We will continue through the two rather general models that have been most prominent in history—the patristic model, focused on conciliarity (ch. 6), and the medieval one, dominated by the monastic ideal, that has persisted in various forms into the modern age (ch. 7).

5

Images

At the beginning of the constitution on the Church, Vatican II issued an invitation to contemplate the "mystery of the Church" (ch. 1). From there it went on to speak of the people of God (ch. 2), the episcopal structure (ch. 3), the laity (ch. 4), the call of all members to holiness (ch. 5), the place of religious orders (ch. 6), and finally the "eschatological character of the Church" (ch. 7) and the place of the Virgin Mary "in the mystery of Christ and the Church" (ch. 8). In this sequence the "mystery" is at the beginning and at the end, the middle chapters finding their place in relation to the mystery of the Church. In other words, the essence of the Church, that which makes it what it is in God's eyes, is not the visible structure or even the members of it with their various and complementary functions, their human talents and achievements, their spiritual yearnings and experiences. It is mystery, a spiritual reality hidden within the structures.

The Way into Mystery

Not by rational and philosophical consideration can mystery be reached. It is not expressed in univocal terms strung together according to the rules of Aristotelian logic. It falls neither under the knife of historical analysis nor under linguistic rules of verification. Like the glory of God in which it shares, mystery, by its very nature, must be grasped in an internal vision or intuition. Without such an insight, it degenerates into a problem, a miracle that cannot be accounted for in rational ways, or a conundrum that remains for the time being beyond the capacity of the human mind. When Vatican II opened its ecclesiology with the mystery of the Church, it could do no better than to confront its readers with the multitude of New Testament images that correspond to what it is to be the Church of God.

As it originates in the creative purpose of God, the Church includes "all the just since Adam, from Abel the just to the last of the elect" (LG, n. 2). It finds its highest manifestation in the inauguration of the kingdom of God on earth through the advent of the Word made flesh. And it is sanctified by the Spirit "who dwells in the Church and in the heart of the faithful as in a temple" (n. 4). Through the death and rising of Jesus who was then manifested by the events of the Passover as "Lord and Christ and Priest for eternity" (n. 5), the Church has inherited the mission of announcing the kingdom. And as the kingdom is itself not a reality of this world but of the divine glory, it can best be designated when the languages of this world accede to their poetic and imaginative dimension: "As in the Old Testament the revelation of the kingdom is often proposed under images, so the inner nature of the Church is suggested to us with various images, which, taken from pastoral life or agriculture, or from the art of building or even from the family and marriage, are outlined in the prophetic books" (n. 6). The council thus opens an indirect way, but the only possible one, to the heart of what it means to be the Church.

The mystery of the Church is suggested by the biblical images. Yet it will be fully unfolded only at the end of history when the eschatological nature of the Church is finally unveiled and the Church is totally assumed in the kingdom of God. Yet the Church that is on pilgrimage is already, throughout its journeying, united to the heavenly Church that has entered into the glory of God. This, precisely, is eschatology. The eschaton, the end time of the world and of the Church, is not destruction but perfection, not withering but flowering. After the exile comes the return home; after captivity, liberation. If the present life is compared to walking in the valley of death, the Church already carries the promise of the resurrection. All along its pilgrimage, it dreams of the shrine to which it goes. It keeps in its heart the image of the kingdom as an internal telltale by which to tell where the wind blows and how to steer. And however darkly, it contemplates the reflection of the divine glory in the Virgin Mary, icon of the Church both in the humility of the handmaiden and in the crowning of the bride, in the turmoil and struggles of the present life and in the consummation to come.

Biblical Images

As the disciples of the risen Jesus began to branch out of Jerusalem into the countryside and the diaspora, the idealistic description of the earliest community that is given by Luke could no longer apply: "The whole body of believers was united in heart and soul. Not one of them claimed any possessions, but everything was held in common. . . ." (Acts 4:32). Whether the Jerusalem community was itself as Luke describes it, is of course a moot point. In any case, the diversities of urban and other surroundings and the growing distance between clusters of believers made such unanimity impossible. The communities began to organize themselves around elders, prophets, teachers, and other officers. As they did so, each one knew that it was not alone and that other communities also preserved the memory and kept the memorial of the Lord. But their theological conceptions of the Church could be no less diverse than their understandings of the Christ certainly were.

Yet the Christians of many locations were aware of sharing a spiritual unity in Christ. Indeed, various inspired prophets assured them that they were not just a new kind of synagogue. As the *ecclesia* of God, they were the "sheepfold" of which Christ is the only gate. One image drawing another, they were also "the flock" of which God is the shepherd. This line of ovine imagery underwent significant developments in paleo-Christian art. Whether painted in a fresco or sculpted on a sarcophagus, the Shepherd of the catacombs is represented in imitation of several pagan shepherd-gods often shown carrying a lamb over their shoulders. But as wealthy Christians, aware of their mortality, designed the adornment of their tombs, the Shepherd was the divine Shepherd of the universe, Christ the Word of God, supporting all human nature on the shoulders of his divinity. As bereaved Christians and their friends gathered in the catacombs and at the tombs of the martyrs to celebrate the memory of the dead, it was not separation and sadness that prevailed; it was trust and hope, for the dead were seen as "orants" celebrating the Good Shepherd, as lambs drawn to the Shepherd from Bethlehem and from Jerusalem. Even the Shepherd was himself often depicted as sharing the nature of a lamb, indeed, as "the Lamb of God, who takes away the sins of the world."

If the Church can be the sheepfold and the flock of Christ, it also is the "field of God." Like the ovine images, the agricultural image is Christocentric. In the field of God, there has been planted and grown "the tree," whether an olive tree or a vine, which is Christ. As the olive tree, Christ has brought about the reconciliation of Jews and Gentiles in their common faith in him. Being the vine, he gives "life and fecundity" to all branches and twigs, "that is, to us, who remain in him through the Church, and who can do nothing without him" (LG, n. 6).

The Church knows itself also to be "God's building," erected on the stone that Christ is. In the light of this basic architectural image, the Church soon becomes the "house of God," the "dwelling of God in the Spirit," the "tent of God among humans," the "holy temple," the "holy city, New Jerusalem." In the *Shepherd* of Hermas, the building is a tower, the stones that go into it being the Christian faithful.[1] It took about two centuries for Christians to be allowed to build modest churches for their worship. And they waited until

---

[1] Hermas, l. c., vision III, ii, 4ff, l. c., p. 30–32.

the conversion of Emperor Constantine for the building boom during which great churches were erected by the emperor, especially in Rome, in Jerusalem, and in Byzantium. In fact, the absence of Christian temples in the first centuries made it all the easier to imagine the Church under the features of a heavenly temple, more grandiose than the great temple of Jerusalem, more beautiful than the many pagan shrines that graced the cities of the Roman Empire.

In this case, however, it was an interior building, the Church in the heart, that was the true Temple of God. Or with the apocalyptic image of New Jerusalem, the Church was the city, and God himself the temple in it. Just as the Church has no high priest but Christ, it has no temple but God (Rev 21:22). It is the internal sense of being the Church that has guided the hands of those who, through the ages, have built the churches of Christendom— from the imperial cathedral of Hagia Sophia in Constantinople, erected by Emperor Justinian (d.565), and the great Romanesque and Gothic cathedrals of the West, to the humble country churches of all Christian lands. And it still is not rare for Christian believers to be overwhelmed by the sense of being the Church when they enter with faith the buildings of worship. This image bore noteworthy fruit in the sacramental theology of Hugh of St. Victor (c. 1096–1141) who identified the dedication of a church as the first of all sacraments.[2] As appears from the hymns and prayers of its ritual, the dedication of a church represents the interior dedication of the soul as the dwelling place of God, the sounding chamber of the Word, the repository of divine Love.

Following the associative logic of images, Vatican II links New Jerusalem with motherhood: New Jerusalem, the "Jerusalem from on high," is, in Paul's words, "our mother" (Gal 4:26). Such an association, in fact, has a long history. Already in the Old Testament, womanhood is related to Temple worship, even though women are not admitted to the inner courtyards. Whoever selected the week of seven days and the month of twenty-eight days as patterns for the liturgical calendar did, wittingly or not, model the temporal structure of worship on the bodily rhythm of women. And this in turn, in the first chapter of Genesis, provided the framework for the creation of the universe. Thus woman, in the Hebraic tradition that stands behind the New Testament, is already the symbol of the Mother. This is not the "Great Mother" of some Middle Eastern religions that thus identify Mother Earth as the embodiment of nature. She is rather a preexisting Mother coming down from heaven, the divine Wisdom. As this line of symbolism passes into Christian thought, the Church, New Jerusalem, easily becomes "the immaculate bride of the immaculate Lamb" (LG, n. 6), the Mother of all believers, expressions which a later semantic shift will apply to the Virgin Mary.

---

[2]Hugh of St. Victor, *De Sacramentis*, bk II, part V (PL 176, 439–442).

This image also stresses the centrality of Christ. For Christ "loved [her] and gave himself up" for her (cf. Gal 2:20). And again, it is pregnant with eschatological possibilities. The pilgrim Church, exiled on this earth, longing for her full encounter with the Bridegroom, aspires to the heavenly realities. In her longing, she already gets a foretaste of heaven, in that her "life is hidden with Christ in God" (Col 3:3).

This is the basic reason why the Nicene-Constantinopolitan Creed designates "the holy Catholic Church" as *communio sanctorum* (saints in the neuter gender)—the sharing of the holy things that are given by God to the Church—which is also *communio sanctorum* (saints in the personal gender)—the communion of those who are saints, having been made *sanctae* and *sancti* by Christ through faith and baptism. And it is not indifferent that, in the Creed, the articles of the Church immediately follow those of the Holy Spirit and lead to the evocation of the eschaton, "the life of the world to come." Imbued with the Spirit who guides it and inspires its members, the Church looks forward in hope to the ultimate fulfillment of all the promises of God. The vision of a new heaven and a new earth belongs to the sense of being the Church of God and of Christ.

The Body of Christ

Many other images of the Church are found in the New Testament such as the sheepfold, the flock, the field, the family of God, the temple, the Jerusalem from on high, the Israel of God, salt of the earth, light of the world, leaven in the dough, column of truth, fullness of Christ. The Catholic tradition has particularly favored the image of the body: the Church is the body of Christ. In Catholic reflection, this has in fact become more than an image, something like a definition of what the Church is. The source of this image, and of the corresponding line of thought, is found in the letters of Paul.

Scholars have drawn attention to the use of the symbolism of the body in the genuine Pauline letters. The mental picture of the erection of a building evokes, as it were naturally, a growing body. In the Greek culture that was known to Paul, society was familiarly compared to a body, the diverse limbs of which stand for the different and complementary social functions of the members of society. Thus Paul was not loath to use the image of the body for the Church made of many people who are one in faith. But the originality of his approach lay in bringing together the metaphor of the body and the community's experience of baptism and of the Last Supper.

All the believers have been made one by their baptism into one body (1 Cor 12:13). They have plunged into the death of Christ and have risen with him from the dead (Rom 6:4-5). They have shared his body and blood in the breaking of bread at the Eucharistic meal (1 Cor 11:23-27). They are one body. And this body is no other than that of Christ. Crucified and buried

as a physical body, it is now risen from the dead in the form, otherwise unknown, of a spiritual body: "Because there is one loaf, we, many as we are,
are one body, for it is of one loaf of which we partake" (1 Cor 10:17).

The image of the body is far from univocal. At one level, it is a mere sociological truism which, incorporated in a political argument against secession
by Agrippa Menenius Lanatus (consul in Rome in 503 B.C.E.), was familiar
to the Roman and Greek world: a body, though it has many limbs, is one.
At a second level, the body that is equated with the community of Christian
believers draws its unity from Christ's human, but now risen, body into which
the believers are assimilated through baptism and the breaking of bread. In
Paul's thinking, this implies that the community is itself the body of Christ
animated by his Spirit. At this point, the trajectory of the image easily divides
along two different lines. One line of vision follows in reverse the Eucharistic
perspective of sharing in the body and blood of Christ. Instead of starting
from the believing community to go to Christ, it begins with Christ to arrive
at the community. Then Christ himself is the body that includes his disciples,
the Christian believers (1 Cor 12:12). His Spirit is their spirit. His life is their
life. Another line which seems to predominate in the post-Pauline letters to
the Colossians and the Ephesians evokes the Lordship of Christ over the
disciples. The faithful are the body, and Christ is their head. From him alone
they draw sustenance and obtain direction (Eph 1:22-23).

Another level still is reached in these letters. "In Christ the fullness (*pleroma*)
of the deity dwells bodily" (Col 2:9). And since the fullness of the deity pervades the cosmos, it follows that "the body of Christ which is the Church"
(LG, n. 48) embraces the whole universe. It is the means by which God fulfills his creative purpose for the cosmos and its inhabitants. Christ has been
placed by God at the head of "the Church which is his body, the fullness of
the one who fills all in all" (Eph 1:22-23).

When they reflected on the body of Christ, early medieval theologians
were led to distinguish between three bodies of Christ or, better, three states
of his body. There was the historical body of Jesus living in Palestine: by his
rising from the dead it has now become his spiritual body in heaven. There
is his sacramental body, with which the faithful commune in the Eucharist.
As this takes place in the liturgical mystery, it was commonly called the mystical body in the earlier Middle Ages. And there also is the "body of Christ
which is the Church," itself the fruit of redemption. Since it is signified and
effectively nurtured through the sacraments, and chiefly through the Eucharistic liturgy, the adjective *mystical* has generally been reserved to the ecclesial body since the twelfth century.[3]

That the Church is the Mystical Body of Christ has been a favored image
in the Roman Catholic ecclesiology of the twentieth century. It provided the

[3] Henri de Lubac, *Corpus Mysticum: L'eucharistie et l'église au moyen âge* (Paris: Aubier, 1944).

topic for Pope Pius XII's encyclical, *Mystici corporis* (1943).[4] The perspective of Pius XII, however, was primarily institutional. The Mystical Body of Christ was seen in its social dimension as "the social body of Jesus Christ." The Church of Christ, a social body of which the Holy Spirit is the soul, was practically identified with the Roman Catholic Church. That this body is mystical meant that its unity is neither physical nor merely moral; it is given by Christ and is animated by an "internal principle," the Holy Spirit. In his eagerness to affirm the close ties that unite Christ and the Church, Pope Pius, however, ventured to use uncommon language. To the traditional idea received from St. Augustine that the head and the body, Christ and the Church, are not two, but one, and may be called *totus Christus*, "the total Christ," the pope added a more hazardous notion: from the first moment of the incarnation, in the beatific vision that he enjoyed even in his Mother's womb, the Redeemer already embraced all the members of his mystical body. Furthermore, Pius XII understood the *pleroma* of Paul to be the fulfillment and completion, in the Church, of Christ and his works. He therefore ascribed to the Church the dignity of being "the fullness and completion of the Redeemer."

Taking one more bold step, Pope Pius prolonged but modified an earlier tradition. Tertullian had called each Christian "*alter Christus*" (the other Christ). Enlarging the horizon, Augustine had seen Christ and the Church as *totus Christus*. Bossuet (1627-1704) had spoken of the Church as "Christ spread out and continued."[5] For Pius XII, the Church is "the *alter Christus* [who] bears his person on this earth." Indeed, Christ so lives in the Church "that she stands out, so to say, as the other person of Christ (*quasi altera Christi persona*)." Pius XII identified Christ and the Church in some mysterious way: together they form "the new man."

Paradoxically, Pope Pius' mystical identification of the Church with Christ was tied to empirically verifiable conditions of membership. Positively, there must be baptism and the profession of the true faith; negatively, one must not have left the body or been expelled from it by legitimate authority. Legitimate authority belongs exclusively to the bishops "under the authority of the Roman Pontiff."

Vatican II and the Mystical Body

Vatican Council II also gave great importance to the biblical image of the Church as the body of Christ. It closely associated it to reception of the Spirit

---

[4] *Acta Apostolicae Sedis*, 1943; the citations are respectively on pp. 235, 267, 217, 202, 211.

[5] Tertullian: in baptism, the neophyte is anointed by the Spirit, like Aaron and Jesus (*Christus* means "anointed"); see *De baptismo*, VII (*The Ante-Nicene Fathers*, vol. III, 1903, p. 672); Bossuet's vision of the Church is both Trinitarian and Christocentric: see Yves Congar, *L'Eglise, de saint Augustin à l'époque moderne* (Paris: Le Cerf, 1970), p. 397-400.

of Christ: "By communicating [to them] his Spirit, he [Christ] mystically constituted his brethren, called from all nations, as his body" (LG, n. 7). It is the life of Christ himself, given to the faithful especially in Eucharistic communion, that makes them his body.

From the image of the body of Christ, the council drew the implication that the Church exists on two planes. As "the community of faith, hope, and love," it is an organized hierarchic society, visible and earthly (LG, n. 8). As Christ's body in mystery, it is a spiritual community endowed with goods from heaven. There are not two Churches, but one. The question, however, is how the two aspects are related.

Pope Pius XII had simplified the solution: he took it for granted that the invisible Church, the Mystical Body of Christ, is the Roman Catholic Church. But this was done at the cost of ecumenical reality. For in other churches, too, the believers have the experience of being the Church. Vatican II, however, kept its distance from Pius XII on several points. It did not follow the Pope's reading of St. Paul's image of the *pleroma*. The fullness of Christ does not derive from the Church. Rather, it fills the Church: "'Since it is in him that all the fullness of the divinity dwells bodily,' with his gifts he fills the Church, which is his body and his fullness, so that it itself may grow and reach all the fullness of God" (LG, n. 7). Likewise, the Church is not now called "the other person" of Christ. Moreover, instead of simply identifying the Roman Catholic institution and "the body of Christ which is the Church," the council wrote:

> The one Church of Christ . . . constituted and organized as a society in this world, subsists in the Catholic Church, that is governed by the successor of Peter and the bishops in his communion . . . (LG, n. 8)

"Subsistence in" implies that the Church, which is the body of Christ in mystery, now lives in a hidden state. It is invisible to the eyes of the flesh, and therefore its existence and nature as the Church are empirically unverifiable. Yet being constituted and organized as a society, it also is an organic body, the members of which relate to one another according to some effective norms. By confessing that this Church subsists in the Roman Catholic institution, the council indicates that it knows where the Church is. Yet it also teaches that the Church of Christ is invisible, lying where it is in a hidden state that may not be recognizable to all Christian believers. And the council says nothing for or against the possibility of its also invisibly subsisting in other ecclesial institutions and other visible churches. Logic would seem to make this contention acceptable in the problematic of Vatican II.

Yet many different readings have been made of the ecclesial image of the "body of Christ." The evolution of that image into the more recent one of the Mystical Body, and what may be called the materialisation or institutionalisation of it in the writings of Pius XII, raise certain questions regarding the proper use of images. What is the scope of the biblical symbols of the Church?

Have they an ultimate meaning? Before examining these questions, we should consider the image that stood out at Vatican II.

The People of God

In the constitution *Lumen gentium*, special attention is paid to this image derived from the Old Testament. God selected a people, Israel, to which he promised to send a Redeemer for all of humankind. When the resurrection of Jesus from the dead was recognized and confessed by his disciples, God's choice shifted from the old Israel according to the flesh—the people of the preparation, made of the descendants of Abraham—to the "messianic people," the "new Israel" according to the Spirit, comprising those who by faith and baptism confess the resurrection of Christ. In their faith, they have become one with the Redeemer. Certainly, the image of the new people of God is inspired by the Bible. Yet the immediate appeal of it at Vatican II and its continuing popularity are undoubtedly due to contemporary political and social concerns about "the people."

Most of the modern nations are governed according to constitutions that set the seat of power in the people, the people delegating authority to its elected representatives. Opposite conceptions of representation inspire liberal democracies and "popular democracies." In the unrest of the 1960s, there arose such demands as "Power to the people." Even in the world of commerce and business, one finds "People's Banks" and "People's Drugs." Political movements have made the referendum, *l'appel au peuple*, an instrument of government. And politicians of all colors appeal to the people for their votes and claim to speak for them. There are socialist parties that claim to put the needs of the people above all else and communist parties which identify the proletariate as the vanguard of the people. Even one slogan of Hitler's National Socialist Party began with *Ein Volk* (One People), and it continued with *ein Reich, ein Führer*!

The biblical origin of the ecclesial image of the people of God does not protect it from profound ambiguity. On what model will the people of God be seen by the people in the Church? Shall it be on the biblical model of the people that lived by the Law in expectation of the coming of the Messiah? Shall it be on the reinterpretation of the Old Testament model that is delineated, but not fully developed, in the letters of Paul and the Acts of the Apostles? Or shall it be on a modern political model?

Vatican Council II tried to eschew the political pitfall as it gave a Christian content to the Old Testament image. Using the Christological analogy of the *triplex munus* (the threefold task) which goes back to Eusebius (c. 260–339) and was systematized by Calvin (1509–1564), the council explained ecclesial peoplehood as a collective participation in the kingship (LG, n. 9), the priesthood (n. 10–11), and the prophethood of Christ (n. 12). The people of God shares the kingship or Lordship of Christ insofar as it lives in a state of "dignity and freedom" and it looks forward to the Kingdom of God (n. 9). It shares the priesthood of Christ in the sacraments (n. 10). It is a "sacerdotal community" nurtured by the Spirit in the same sacraments (n. 11), and its institutional structure is based on two ways of sharing in the priesthood of Christ—the way of all the people and, in addition, that of the ordained clergy: these two ways, in the words of Vatican II, differ "in essence, and not only in degree" (n. 10). The Church is finally a prophetic people in that the faith of the people of God "cannot fail." Its "sense of faith" (*sensus fidei*) implies a "consensus concerning what pertains to faith and morals" (n. 12) that is protected from error by the Holy Spirit. The people of God is potentially universal, all the peoples of the world being called to the Kingdom which the "Church or people of God" inaugurates (n. 13).

Ambiguity has not been avoided in this exposé. Because it evokes the people of the Old Covenant, the ecclesial image of the people of God brings up the question of the status of the Jewish people and religion in the official beliefs of Christians. Was the Covenant with Moses abolished by its fulfillment in Jesus the Messiah? If it was not abolished, then what normativity pertains to the Christian faith? Such questions will occupy us in chapter 12. In any case, the image of the people of God is, if not confusing, profoundly ambiguous. For it not only evokes the chosen people of the Bible; it also evokes modern political theory and the practice of democratic government "of the people, by the people, and for the people." The image of the Church as the people of God is in fact largely responsible for much of the turmoil of the post-conciliar years with their largely uncontrolled experimentation in all directions and the mistrust of authority that is one of the unalienable rights of all peoples whatever their political system. This turmoil in turn provoked the reactionary stance of Archbishop Lefèbvre and his "traditionalist" followers who behave as though the tradition of the people of God stopped when Pope Pius V (1566-1572) promulgated the post-tridentine liturgy of the Latin mass, replaced by that of Paul VI after Vatican II.

Like the various interpretations of the body of Christ, the equivocation that now surrounds the image of the people of God raises a fundamental query. What is the scope of symbols and images? What should they mean in a balanced ecclesiology?

Images and Symbols

One may speak of a language of images, since images do communicate meaning and language is evidently the most employed means of communication. But language—of any type—is either univocal, analogical, or equivocal. Now, the language of images is not univocal. One image does not denote one meaning. And it often happens that what seems to be one image is in fact a cluster of related images. Largely because of this, theology, in its dogmatic and systematic forms, has long been prejudiced against the recourse to images, even when such images are drawn from the Bible.

Never univocal, the language of images is rarely, if ever, analogical. Classical theology at least is at home among analogies. It recognizes that all human discourse about God is analogical. That is, such discourse—theology in the etymological sense of the term—does correspond to what God is, even if there is no agreement whether the central analogies of God-talk (Creator, Father, Trinity, Nature) are analogies of attribution or analogies of proper proportionality, that is, no agreement on how human discourse corresponds with what God is. St. Thomas Aquinas himself seems to have wavered on this question. But if it is neither univocal nor analogical, language can only be equivocal. Equivocity means that an expression or image may have diverse or even contradictory senses. The fear is then legitimate that ambiguity may so invade theological expression and conceptualisation that no conclusion can ever be reached with certainty.

In addition, there runs a thin line between images and metaphors. In metaphors, terms are distorted from their customary empirical meaning and applied imaginatively to what, taken to the letter, they cannot mean. The allegorical reading of Scripture, with which both patristic and medieval theologians were familiar, gave pride of place to metaphors. But it has lost its status in modern theology. It has fallen under a twofold critique. On the one hand, Thomas Aquinas, followed by the Reformers, admitted only the literal sense of Scripture in theological argumentation.[6] On the other, the scientific study of the Bible, whatever school it follows, is equipped to deal only with the historical context and the literal meaning of the texts. Thus allegory and metaphors have been ruled out of modern systematic theology and of the critique of doctrinal formulations that is now recognized as one of the main tasks of theology.

In the meantime, piety, prayer, liturgy, and contemplation have continued to feature other means of expression than the commonplace use of terms. The language of images has continued to dominate the reflection on the Christian experience that has been made by Christian mystics. Admittedly, authors in the Calvinist tradition have often distrusted mystics and mystical theology. For they have believed their writings to be vibrant with more or less distant echoes of the Gnostic heresies. Yet the Catholic tradition and Martin Luther himself, the editor of *Theologia Deutsch*, have granted a legitimate status to the expression of Christian experience by the mystics. At times, this has been couched in terms of sight and visions, as with the popular Mother Julian of Norwich (d. c. 1416) or in the now rediscovered Hildegard of Bingen (1098-1179).[7] It has been perceived as spiritual hearing

---

[6] *Summa theologica* I, q.1, a.10, ad 1.

[7] Edmund Colledge and James Walsh, eds., *Julian of Norwich, Showings* (New York: Paulist

and locutions that were carefully analyzed by St. John of the Cross. The mystical experience of grace has also found subtle modulations in the dance of words, sounds, and rhythms that characterizes poetry, including the hymnody of the Protestant churches, as immediately appears from a look at the hymns of Martin Luther or of John and Charles Wesley. And also, beyond sight, hearing, and speaking, at a further remove from the clear affirmative language, mystical insights have taken refuge in the apophatic perception of God as *Deus absconditus*, the hidden God. Since the days of Pseudo-Dionysius (fifth-sixth century) this has been typical of Eastern Orthodox piety and theology. Yet the sermons of Meister Eckhart (c. 1260–c. 1327) and the distichs of Angelus Silesius (Johann Scheffler, 1624–1677) are notable Western instances of the apophatic approach.

What then does it mean that the Church has been felt and described as a sheepfold, a flock, a field, a house, a tower, a bride, and whatever else the New Testament authors and their successors have considered appropriate images? It can only mean one thing: from time to time in the history of the Church, some or many of the faithful have known themselves intimately to be really led, or carried, by the divine Shepherd. Or now and again, like St. Augustine telling the tale of his conversion, the faithful have wandered in spirit in the garden of God. They have seen the Church as God's organized field or garden in which both space and time are controlled by the divine Gardener, the weeds of this world are sorted out, seeds of grace are sown, plants are watered and they grow, wild beasts are tamed, and the creation accedes, through redemption and grace, to the level of its intended beauty. Or also, some of the Christians have felt themselves so guided by Divine Providence in the external and internal happenings of their lives that God was truly the artist shaping them, who built them up in order to make his dwelling with them. Or yet, and perhaps more frequently, the faithful have so loved God and above all so known themselves to be loved by God that the language of courtship, wedlock, and sex came spontaneously to their mind. What the Church truly is in the authentic experience of any of the faithful, it must be in itself, even though others need not resonate uniformly to the images and language that have been used to express such an experience.

The images and similes by which the Scriptures of the New Testament designate the Church are other than metaphorical depictions or allegorical interpretations. They are symbols, in the true sense of the Greek word *symbolon*: something that brings two realities together (*sym*, or *sun*, meaning *with*), a verbal hyphen or copula. The symbols of the Church that were favored by the early Christians reached beyond a description or delineation of what the Church is. They expressed what the disciples perceived through the eyes of faith: God coming to them through Christ, in the Holy Spirit, as

Press, 1978); Hildegard, *Scivias*, (Santa Fe: Bear and Co., 1986); John of the Cross, *The Ascent of Mount Carmel*, bk II, ch. 19-32 (Kavanaugh-Rodriguez, l.c., p. 163-213).

their Spouse, guiding them as their Shepherd, shaping them as their Builder or Painter, nurturing them as their Gardener.

The thrust of such symbols is to open a window onto the interiority of the Church. There, the Church is the communion of God with the creatures, achieved through the redemption of humanity by the Word incarnate. Known in faith by interior experience, this dimension of the Church remains invisible to the outsider. It may be an object of awe to sympathetic observers. It frequently is patronized by the amused contempt of the "cultured despisers" of Christian beliefs.

There is an order between the exterior and the interior, the surface and the depth, the visible and the invisible. And this order is irreversible. Primacy belongs to the inner reality. The adage of the New Testament applies here: "The letter kills; but the Spirit gives life" (2 Cor 3:6). This is as true of the Church as it is of the Law and the Scriptures. The entire purpose of the impressive organization of the Church—in its institutions, rules, liturgies, in the instructions of its clergy, the pastoral letters of its bishops, the encyclicals of its popes, in its regulation of theology, formulation of doctrine, and definition of dogma—is to promote the interiority of the Church. Failing to do so, the external aspects of the Church would become oppressive. The chief task of *ecclesia docens* in its teaching is to promote the spiritual freedom and flowering of its members so that *ecclesia discens*, in its learning, may share the life of the images—seeing, tasting, and touching their truth.

The best formulation of this concept in the documents of Vatican II is found in the Constitution on the Liturgy:

> It pertains to the Church to be both human and divine, visible and yet endowed with invisible gifts, fervent in action and given to contemplation, present in the world and yet on pilgrimage, in such a way that in it the human is ordered and subordinate to the divine, the visible to the invisible, action to contemplation, and the present to the future city that we seek (SC, n. 2).

The Mystery and the Koinonia

The ultimate meaning of the ecclesial images that abound in Scripture is suggested in Vatican II's treatment of the eschatological nature of the Church. On the one hand, chapter I of *Lumen gentium* places the biblical images under the heading of "the mystery of the Church." On the other hand, in chapter VII, the Church heralds and prepares the kingdom of God, without ever being itself the kingdom. "The Church . . . will have its perfection only in the heavenly glory. . . ." (LG, n. 48). The heavenly glory is another expression for the eternal kingdom of God. But as the glory is anticipated by faith in the gift of divine grace, so is the kingdom anticipated in the intimate

experience of being the Church that the symbols connote. The spiritual reality that is pointed to by the images of the Church has its proper locus between the mystery of the kingdom of God and the experience of the *ecclesia*
as communion.

The kingdom of God of Christian theology derives from the *kabod* and
the *shekinah* of the Old Testament. It is the ultimate epiphany of God's Lordship over the created world. God is indeed present in it (*shekinah*) and the
divine creative energies pervade the universe. When this is perceived in faith,
then the presence is reached and the glory (*kabod*) manifested. It remains
for the prophets to have recourse to a multitude of symbols to communicate
the awesome reality of the glory of the Lord. Then, those who discern the
glory become its witnesses. As they testify to the Word of God, they also
edify the community, sharing its worship and adoration. The prophet Ezekiel begins by seeing the glory in the temple (Ezek 1:2), and he ends, during
his exile in Babylon, by measuring and describing in minute details the future
temple yet to be restored (Ezek 40:48) where perfect worship will finally be
offered. This future temple is, in Christian eyes, the mystery "hidden for long
ages and through many generations . . . but now disclosed to God's people"
(Col 1:26-27). In this sense, the mystery is not an obscure point of theological
speculation or an event that escapes scientific and rational explanation. It
is an inkling of the hiddenness of God.

As the Christian faithful grasp something of the mystery that is revealed
in Christ, they are themselves caught in it. The glory of God dwells in their
heart, and at times it radiates through them. They echo the sounds of the
Word that resonate in the Church's memory. They become links in the living
chain that connects the present and future community with the apostles'
gathering in the Upper Room and with the foundational events of the death
and resurrection of Christ. The memorial of the Lord and their interior vision
converge. At the breaking of bread, they recognize him in their sisters and
brothers. In their mutual *koinonia*, the disciples stand face to face with the
redeeming presence of the Lord.

The Openness of Images

Since scholastic theology replaced monastic theology in the schools of
the thirteenth century, systematic theologians have been reluctant to rely on
images. Partly under the influence of the striving for precision that is characteristic of canon law, partly for the sake of the self-identity of communities
that define themselves by their confession of faith, partly also because the
geometric mind functions best with clear and distinct ideas, theologians have
often aspired to the ideal of univocal language. This, however, has been at a
high cost. The nature and function of analogy in expressing the knowledge
of the Triune God that is given by the revelation in Christ have been mis-

understood or ignored. Nonverbal theologies have been neglected, abandoned to the iconic spirituality of the Orthodox Church, to the passing moods of religious fashion, and to the idiosyncracies of individual artists.

Yet in their daily life, people communicate with body language no less than with words. Likewise, the convictions of faith and the insights into the divine realities that are given by the Holy Spirit can be expressed nonverbally—as in the painting of icons, in the building and adornment of churches, in the composing of plain song and of music, in the playing of instruments and the ringing of bells, in the processions and *tableaux vivants* of liturgical solemnities.

Images are rooms in the memory palace of the Christian tradition. In them, the Church has stored up the precious experiences of the first Christians who discovered themselves to be part of one *Koinonia* with God through Christ in the Holy Spirit and who thus knew one another to be, in the eyes of God, one body, the body of Christ. Functioning as symbols, the same images acquire a heuristic role. They open up the eschatological future. As the faithful read and listen to the Scriptures with faith, they become sensitive to the inner testimony of the Spirit. They follow the way of images into the mystery that is revealed in them. Thus is the tradition passed on.

Several lessons could have been learned from the New Testament. This set of writings, which against all reasonable expectations came, in Christian eyes, to replace the Old Testament as the heart of the biblical revelation, ends with the Book of Revelation which is entirely structured around images. From this, one could have learned, first, that the New Testament as such is not closed, even if no new book may be added to it: it cannot be closed because images are essentially open. One leads to another by a process of association whose oneiric logic escapes all the theories that try to encapsulate it in a formula. It follows that the nature and structure of the Christian Church, as these are seen in the closing images of the Apocalypse (the New Jerusalem, the Jerusalem from on high), can be neither properly described in the categories of any single theological system nor adequately limited by canonical legislation. Both rational speculation and law reach their limit before the openness of images. The "spirit of geometry," as Pascal mused, is not commensurate with the "spirit of finesse."[8] While speculative and canonical categories are by nature determinate and exclusive, images are indeterminate and inclusive: they may not be exactly pinpointed, and unlike theological statements and canonical rules, they need not deny their contrary. There never is a last and final image: past and present images breed new images for the future.

It follows, and this should be a second lesson, that the Church—as a cluster of New Testament images that have been enriched in the Christian tradition—is of the nature of poetry, of song, and of dance. Because the ex-

[8] *Pensées*, n. 21 (*Oeuvres complètes* [Paris: La Pléiade, 1954], p. 1091-1093).

perience of worship has associated it with basilical, romanesque, gothic, baroque, and modern buildings, the Church is, for theology as for the popular mind, more frequently seen on the model of architecture. The Middle Ages, in fact, knew better than that: architectonic constructions, the product of intensive labor and more or less advanced techniques, were only the context. The text was the pictorial "Bible of the poor" that was featured on the walls in frescoes and mosaics, in the windows by stained glass, in and around the building in statues. Both context and text came from the pretext that this was the mystery of the divine presence in the heart of the Church and in its people of believers.

There is a third lesson: if the Church is a cluster of images that is better understood poetically than rationally, then it should be approached and explained as the realm of the divine Beauty. In the modern popular mind, the Church and its teachings are commonly identified with ethical and moral issues, esthetics being relegated to art studios and museums. But this has immeasurably impoverished the Christian imagination. In fact, the Old Testament and the Jewish tradition have known better: the *shekinah* of God is a thing of transcendent beauty. Patristic and medieval theologies themselves included elaborate perspectives on physical and spiritual light as it radiates from the divine Beauty. Eastern Orthodoxy is incomprehensible outside of a theology of iconic light and beauty, in which ways to and from the divine Light and Beauty are opened. From time to time, as Hans Urs von Balthasar has shown, Christian theologies have been inspired by perceptions of the Glory of God. They have struggled to convey such perceptions in their explicit reconstructions. And one may still find in these theologies and in the Church itself hidden sources of beauty that are simply waiting to be tapped.[9]

For Further Reading

Lesslie Newbigin, *The Household of God. Lectures on the Nature of the Church,* London: SCM Press, 1953.

Bernard Lonergan, *Insight. A Study of Human Understanding,* New York: Philosophical Library, 1957.

Hans Küng, *The Church,* New York: Sheed and Ward, 1967.

Jean-Marie Tillard, *The Eucharist, Pasch of God's People,* New York: Alba House, 1967.

John W. Dixon, *Art and the Theological Imagination,* New York: Seabury, 1978.

Raymond Brown and John P. Meier, *Antioch and Rome. New Testament Cradles of Catholic Christianity,* New York: Paulist Press, 1982.

[9]Hans Urs von Balthasar, *The Glory of the Lord: A Theological Aesthetics* (San Francisco: Ignatius press, vol. 1, 1983, vol. 2, 1984, vol. 3, 1986). George H. Tavard, *Juana Inés de la Cruz and the Theology of Beauty* (Notre Dame: University of Notre Dame Press, 1991).

6

Conciliarity

One image stands out among those that were passed on to subsequent ages by the Church of the first centuries: the Church is a gathering of otherwise isolated and disparate people and peoples. In the Christian Church, what the Old Testament identified as the two sections of humanity, Jews and Gentiles, have become one. The Gentiles were called into the Church along with the Jews who recognized Jesus as the Messiah. But soon, the Christians of Jewish origin were the minority, and the Church became, for all practical purposes, a non-Jewish organism. The Jews who did not recognize Jesus as the Messiah formed the continuing Judaism that was reconstructed by the Pharisees after the destruction of the temple and of Jerusalem. Focused on the Talmud and on later tradition no less than on the Bible, this is the Judaism that has coexisted, often painfully, with the Christianity of Eastern and Western Europe as it has also coexisted with Islam in the Near East and in Northern Africa. Its very existence has served, by way of contrast and of opposition, to strengthen the Christian social identity as the people that have been gathered from the nations.

In the cities where they live, the Christian faithful gather together for worship and mutual support. Their presbyters meet as a presbytery around the bishop. The bishops themselves gather in local and regional synods to discuss their common problems and to determine the formulation of right doctrine as various Gnostic movements push forward interpretations of the Christian texts that threaten the historical specificity of the gospel. As early as the third century, like-minded Christians, wishing to flee the allurements of wealth and comfort, live in the deserts of Egypt and Palestine and in the forests that still cover the greater part of Europe. The churches that are built after the peace of Constantine are modeled on Roman basilicas, buildings where the people of the Roman empire hold civic and other meetings. Thus, seen sociologically, the Christian movement takes the shape of a systematic reorganization of society.

Yet in its essence, it is primarily interior and spiritual. Christian communities emerge at several levels: local (house-churches), city-wide, diocesan (the diocese being a subdivision of the Roman empire), inter-diocesan or regional, more or less following the borders of the imperial provinces. When, in 325, Emperor Constantine calls a universal council of all the bishops to answer the questions raised by the Arian controversy, the Church discovers itself to be ecumenical. It is coterminous with the *oecumene* (related to the Greek word, *oikos*, "house, home"), that is, with the known civilized world, the Roman empire. Yet it has already crossed the Roman borders from Syria into Persia and from Egypt into Ethiopia. From southern Europe and Gaul, it is beginning to spread into Germanic lands north of the Danube and east of the Rhine, and from Gallo-Roman Gaul beyond what will be later known as the Channel, it is gaining ground among the Celtic tribes of Great Britain.

Local and Universal

The coexistence of several sociological levels of the Christian community raises an important question regarding the self-understanding of the Church and its members. To put it in simple terms, one may ask when the faithful know themselves most fully to be the Church of Jesus Christ. Is it when, through the bishops who represent them, they somehow participate in a provincial, regional, or ecumenical council? Is it when, personally or through their deacons and presbyters, they take part in a synod of their diocese? Is it when, gathered for Sunday worship around their bishop—or in larger dioceses, around a presbyter—they form what St. Paul called "the *ecclesia* of God" in a given location? In more theological terms, one may wonder if the Church of Christ lives its life most fully as a local assembly of believers or in what unites local assemblies over a broader geographical territory or in the universality of the Churches of God in all cities.

Theologians have often noted that the Church of Christ has usually been identified by Greek and Eastern Christians as the local community that is gathered under the leadership of a bishop, whereas it has been commonly identified by Latin and Western Christians as the Church spread all over the *oecumene*, now taken in the sense of the whole world. In the first perspective, the Church is experienced as local even when it also connotes the universality of the Churches. It is sensitive to concrete circumstances of time and place, and it easily takes on regional or national characteristics. The model of the Church is local. In the second perspective, the Church is experienced as universal even in its smaller gatherings. The connection of the believers in each place with those in all other places becomes more important to them than their own local or national customs and traditions. The model of the Church is universal. In light of these distinctive points of reference, it is self-evident that the sense given to a universal primacy among all the Churches was bound to vary considerably in the East and in the West.

Each model has its drawbacks, as history abundantly shows. By encouraging local identification, the first model is open to a fusion of the sacred and the profane and to the ensuing confusion of powers between the Church and the Empire or State. It becomes difficult to sort out the respective responsibilities of emperor, king, or prince and of bishop. When the head of the State takes it as a duty to protect and promote the Church, the danger of political domination and of manipulation of the sacred for profane purposes is patent. The Church is often uncritically equated with the nation, and the universal Church may be rent asunder by national projects, rivalries, jealousies, and prides.

Yet as it tends to identify each believer with the universal Church, the second model is open to no less threatening possibilities. As they lose the sense of belonging to a Church in one place, the faithful easily fall into the competing individualism that is a mark of occidental countries. In fact, the sense of belonging to the universal Church is not always able to counterbalance the divisive effects of self-assertion. Hence the Western need for strong episcopal leadership and for a powerful primacy in the universal Church that will be able to escape control by the political power of nations and governments. But a strong primacy can easily override the proper subsidiarities and usurp power through a growing centralized bureaucracy.

Theologically, either model is acceptable as long as it does justice to the primacy of the Eucharistic assembly among all Christian gatherings. The sense of being the *ecclesia* of God arises from the Eucharistic experience. It must be nurtured by recurrent encounters with Christ in word and sacrament. The Scriptures, in fact, offer two complementary perspectives. On the one hand, the disciples gather to hear the word of God and to recognize Jesus in the breaking of the bread: this is the local Church of God. On the other hand, the Pauline communities in Macedonia and Achaia send offerings to the saints in Jerusalem, thus acknowledging them as brothers and sisters in Christ and creating links that the saints in Jerusalem cannot ignore: this is the universal Church. Whether the ethos and mentality of the believers orient them toward a local or toward a universal loyalty, it is only in the discipleship of Christ that the people exist as the people of God and as the body that is the Church. The Church, therefore, stands at all levels where the faith is expressed, where the commitment to others is extended to them in love, and where the ensuing sense of community is experienced. All levels of this communion have equal validity and importance.

The Church of the Creed

As they met in Constantinople in 381 under the leadership of St. Gregory Nazianzen for what was to be the second ecumenical council, the bishops formulated what has remained the fundamental statement on the nature of the Church: "We believe . . . in one, holy, catholic, and apostolic Church. . . ." (DS, n. 150). The Greek form of the creed, which is of course the original one, uses the same word, "in" (*eis*), that has already been used in relation to the Father almighty, to Jesus Christ, and to the Holy Spirit: "We believe in. . . ." Yet there have been subtle differences of interpretation at this point. Can one believe "in" the Church just as one believes in God?

The earlier Creed of the council of Nicaea (325) included no article on the Church, the credal formula ending with "in the Holy Spirit." Before the Creed of Nicaea, several forms of the creed professed in baptism were in use. They generally correspond to "the Apostles' Creed" that is still recited at baptism among Western Christians. Now, the baptismal creed, in its most common form, had another form of words regarding the Church: "I believe in (*eis*) the Holy Spirit in (*en*) the Holy Church." That is, as they entered the Church through baptism, the catechumens did not confess faith in the Church. Rather, they confessed faith in the Father, the Word, and the Spirit, who are, and therefore who are to be found, in the Church. The faith was that the Church is the realm of the divine presence of the Three Persons. There was no article of faith in the Church. But the threefold faith confessed in baptism included membership in the Church, for that is where the Father, the Word, and the Spirit are to be found.

As they reflected on this fundamental point, Western theologians compared the two basic creeds, baptismal and "Nicene," that were known to them. From the time of St. Jerome (c. 348–420) and St. Ambrose (c. 340-397), they interpreted the second in the light of the first. And the form of the baptismal creed in turn influenced the Latin translation of the Nicene Creed. As a result, the Western Nicene Creed has existed in two forms. The one strictly follows the Greek wording: "We believe in . . ., and in the Church . . ." The other makes the difference explicit between the Three Persons and the Church: "We believe in . . ., and [we believe] the Church. . . ." Whatever form was in use locally, all medieval theologians insisted, with Bruno of Würtzburg (d. 1046): "I believe the Holy Church, not in it, because it is not God, but it is the convocation or congregation of Christians and the house of God."[1] Thomas Aquinas himself preferred the simple form without "in" for the same reason. And the Catechism of the council of Trent, in 1566, took the same position:

> The Three Persons of the Trinity, Father, and Son, and Holy Spirit, we believe, in such a way that in them we put our faith. But now the manner of speech changes: we profess to believe *the*, not *in the*, Holy Church, so

---

[1]St. Bruno of Würzburg, *Commentarium in symbolum apostolorum* (PL, 142, 560); Thomas Aquinas, *Summa theologica* II II, q. 1, a. 9, ad 5; *Catechismus ex Decreto Concilii Tridentini* (Regensburg, 1883), part I, ch. 10, n. 23, p. 83. The present theme is studied in Henri de Lubac, *La Foi chrétienne. Essai sur la structure du Symbole des apôtres* (Paris: Aubier, 69).

that through this different manner of speech, God, the Creator of all, is distinguished from what is created, and all the marvelous gifts we have received, that are given to the Church, we attribute to the divine goodness.

Not the Church, but only God, is the object of faith. The Church is the place where one believes and trusts in God. By the same token, but in another sense of the word, "believe," the Church is believed by the faithful when it transmits and teaches the faith. As it does so, it may well be called "Mother of the faithful" in keeping with a tradition that has roots in the Old Testament prophets who described Israel as a woman wooed by God. Indeed, the theme of "Mother Church," *Ecclesia Mater*, is common to Christian preaching and writing from the second century on, to Martin Luther and John Calvin themselves. But the Church teaches the faith and mothers the faithful by pointing beyond itself to God and Christ who are known in the Holy Spirit.

This sense of the Church tends to be lost with the contemporary vernacular translations of the Creed which generally say: "We believe in God, the Father Almighty, . . . and in One, Holy, Catholic, and Apostolic Church. . . ." The impression is thus given that faith in God and faith in the Church are one and the same thing. Yet strictly speaking, the faithful do not believe in the Church. They believe in God from the midst of the Church. Or they, in the Church, believe in God, and they also believe the Church and its teachings.

The Church is One

The Church in which faith in God, in the Word made flesh, and in the Holy Spirit is born and nurtured, receives four qualifications in the creed of Constantinople: "We believe [in] One, Holy, Catholic, and Apostolic Church." These are the Church's fundamental "marks" or essential characteristics, that the faithful also attribute to their gathering.

In the formative period of patristic theology, the belief that the Church is One was, like most of the articles of the Creed, directed against specific doctrinal deviations. As already appears from the New Testament, the Pauline Churches had to struggle with the question of their oneness. The many who came to believe in the Messiah could not abandon their prejudices and customs immediately upon receiving baptism. The previous division between Jews and Gentiles could easily have been perpetuated as a rivalry between Judeo-Christians and Gentile-Christians; that between Palestinian Jews and Hellenistic Jews of the diaspora could have continued among Judeo-Christians; those between Levites and ordinary members of the people, between Zealots, Pharisees, Sadducees, Essenes, and other political or religious groups could have been perpetuated as soon as members of these groupings joined the Christian movement. The division of Hellenistic society between masters and slaves threatened the liturgical unity of the faithful as the body of Christ. The distribution of tasks and responsibilities between male and female that was regulated by custom in Judea, in Greek lands, or in Rome endangered the communities by introducing in worship and leadership a distinction that St. Paul had declared abolished in Jesus Christ. For it was part of Paul's gospel that the partition walls of humankind have been brought down by "putting on Christ" in baptism: "There is neither Jew nor Greek, neither slave nor freeman, neither male nor female. But you are all one in Christ Jesus" (Gal 3:27-28).

The oneness of the Church was threatened early. Already the letter to the Hebrews warned against being drawn to "strange and varying doctrines" (Heb 13:9). These were presumably the gnostic strains of late Judaism. Precisely, gnostic interpretations of the Scriptures and of the gospel inspired numerous extravagant theologies in the second century. They spread through apocryphal writings that claimed apostolic authorship. Irenaeus and Tertullian wrote extensively against them. But gnostic sectarianism ended up breaking the unity between those who recognized Christ as the Savior. With Marcion and his followers, the opposition of Jews and Gentiles became a contradiction between the Old Testament and the New. A charismatic emphasis on the Holy Spirit which characterized Montanism ended up by forming separate sects in opposition to the main Church. Faced with the doctrines of Arius, defended by many bishops against many others, the Church at the call of Emperor Constantine exemplified its oneness in the ecumenical council of Nicaea (325) and protected it by its dogmatic and disciplinary decisions.

The oneness of the Church is twofold since it resides in the existence of one universal gathering of believers and in the teaching of one doctrine. This twofold oneness was affirmed by the confession of One Church in the creed of Constantinople. It implies the sacramental union of all believers in the body of Christ and thereby their societal communion with one another under their bishop as the local Church of God. In turn, whether the bishops are gathered in synods or exchange news and views by mail or simply pray and care for one another, their mutual communion expresses and warrants the unity of all the Churches of God. The communion of all believers in space, as they live year after year, brings about their communion in time as generations of believers succeed one another. Since the third century when agreement was reached in identifying the writings of the New Testament, the oneness of the Church has been embodied in the Christian attitude toward the Scriptures: the written word of God is one, and all the Churches of God recognize it together. By the same token, it is also embodied in the principle of tradition. For as the word of God is transmitted from age to age by word of mouth and in writing, this transmission is consistent and faithful to itself. It expresses the oneness of the Church in time.

The conviction that the Church is one was instrumental in the addition of *communio sanctorum*, the communion of saints, to the articles that are confessed at the end of the Apostles' creed: "I believe . . . the Holy Catholic Church, the communion of saints. . . ." This addition appeared in the course of the fifth century and was accepted in Rome by Pope Nicholas I (856–867). The original meaning of the phrase is not certain. Was it the "communion of holy things" in the Eucharist (*sanctorum* as neuter) or in the sacraments in general or the "communion of saints" as holy persons (*sanctorum* as masculine, implying also the *sanctarum* or holy women)? and if these, was the accent placed on the dead saints now in heaven or on the living saints still on earth?

In the course of time, the communion of saints has come to mean both the communion of the saints in the "Church triumphant" in heaven, the communion with them of the faithful who are the "Church militant" on earth, and the mutual communion of the two in their sharing of the holy things given by God to the Church. In other words, the oneness of the Church is not univocal. Rather is it multifaceted. It connotes the unity of God's purpose as the whole of humanity is redeemed by Christ and guided to ultimate salvation by the Holy Spirit. But this unity of purpose is embodied in a multitude of spiritual gifts that are available in the Church.

It follows that the article, One Church, has a further connotation. For God's purpose regarding those who believe is at one with the divine purpose in creating the universe. It is for this reason that medieval authors frequently stressed the analogy between the macrocosmos of the world and the microcosmos of the human creature, the Church being the place where this correspondence is best manifested. Indeed, the architectonic structure of medieval cathedrals expressed this cosmic dimension of the unity of the Church: it was based on the "golden symmetry," a mathematical measurement of the symmetry of the human body that itself was taken to be the very measure of the cosmos, the "golden number." Thus the very church building showed forth the oneness of the Church while the contrasting colors of its windows illustrated the infinite varieties of gifts in the one Church and, following the course of the sun in the sky, the constant change of hues and moods of its interior vividly translated the waxing and waning of life among the innumerable peoples. Thus the fundamental belief was highlighted that the Church is one in diversity like the world itself and like the divine revelation which is spoken in the one Word of God and is successively received by the prophets and apostles.

The Church is Holy

Holiness is an essential mark of the Church. This follows from the belief that holiness does not result from human achievement but from God's gift. Baptism implies, for the neophyte, the erasure of the inherited or original sin, the forgiveness of personal sins, the introduction into the realm of God's gracious friendship; and it is completed in the course of Christian initiation by the reception of the Holy Spirit (sealing, confirmation). Medieval theologians identified the gifts of God to the baptized as not only all the gifts of the foundational "virtues" or spiritual powers of faith, hope, and love but also the seven "gifts of the Holy Spirit" that were understood to have been bestowed on the Messiah: "the spirit of wisdom and intelligence, the spirit of counsel and fortitude, the spirit of knowledge and piety," and finally "the spirit of the fear of God" (Isa 11:2-3). Christ, as Head of the Church that is his body, received them for his disciples no less than for himself. In the theology of Thomas Aquinas, these seven gifts of the Spirit were considered to be the chief means of sanctification. Other theologians such as Bonaventure added that baptism includes a still higher gift from God: participation in the twelve Beatitudes that itemize complementary aspects of the summit of holiness.

Although such a systematic analysis of holiness has become obsolete, this theology at least points to two basic aspects of the Church. On the one hand, the call to conversion that is communicated by the preaching of the Christian gospel contains an invitation to holiness. Thus Vatican Council II described "the universal call to holiness in the Church" (LG, ch. 5). In this perspective, the accent lies on the holiness of the faithful who are, in the language of Paul, "the saints." Yet part of their holiness resides in the confession of their unworthiness, even of their sinfulness. The holiness of which they partake is not theirs; it is Christ's. It does not reside in them even when they receive it as God's gift, for it resides in Christ. And it is only insofar as they are in communion with Christ that they share his holiness. Indeed, there is plenty of room in Christian life for desiring and striving, for improvement and progress, for penance and conversion. But whatever is obtained or achieved through meditation, prayer, and human effort is itself God's gift. In the theology of grace that derives from St. Augustine, when God rewards the good deeds of the elect, it is his own gifts that he crowns.

On the other hand, the holiness of Christ is given to the Church, his body. In the life of struggling Christians who walk along the pilgrimage of the present life confronted with temptation and sin, the gift has all the appearance of an "alien" holiness, a justice or righteousness that does not belong to them. Yet this justice of God is really given, in Christ, to what the Book of Revelation calls "the New Jerusalem" (Rev 21:2). This is the "Heavenly City, Jerusalem" of medieval hymnody that will be manifested at the end of time. And already the Church on earth has some features of the Heavenly Church. This was in the mind of the patristic and medieval authors who presented the Church on earth under the symbol of the Moon. After waxing into the glory of the Full Moon, it wanes into the hiddenness of the New Moon. Yet it always shines, even when its light has become invisible, with a radiance that does not belong to it but to the Sun which is Christ.

Such is the holiness of the Church. Yet because the faithful on earth are still prone to sin and stand in constant need of forgiveness, the Church as communion of saints is also a communion of sinners. It shares their imperfections and suffers from them. In the language of Luther, the Christian is *simul justus et peccator*, just and sinful at the same time. Vatican II concurred: "The Church, that includes sinners, that is at the same time holy and in need of purification (*sancta simul et semper purificanda*), ceaselessly practices penitence and self-renewal" (LG, n. 8).

The Church is Catholic

The third mark of the Church has been called catholicity, universality, ecumenicity, and, as in the Slavonic rendering of the creed, *sobornost* (the Church being *sobornuju*). Each of these terms connotes certain nuances in the basic assertion that the Church of Christ is catholic.

As is indicated by its etymology in the Greek language, catholicity is primarily a matter of wholeness. What is "catholic" is patterned "on the whole" (*catholicos*, from *cath'olou*). If the wholeness in question is not fully achieved, it is at least potentially present. To affirm that the Church is catholic is therefore to say that it is destined by God to embrace the whole of humanity. In God's eyes, it already represents the whole of humanity qualitatively, however small the quantitative size it has actually reached. In other words, the application of this term to the Church is grounded in the doctrine of the *pleroma*: as in Christ "all the fullness of God dwells bodily" (Col 1:19), so the Church is "his body and the fullness of him who fills all in all" (Eph 1:23). The term, "catholic," has been explicitly used as an adjective qualifying the Church since the letter of Ignatius of Antioch to the Smyrneans.[2] From the third century to the time of St. Bernard (c. 1090–1153), it also functioned as a substantive: the *catholica* is the Church. It is clearly distinguished from sectarian groups, heretical conventicles, separated bodies, whose doctrine or structure betray human narrowness of mind and soul, whereas the *catholica* shows forth the fullness of Christ and the wholeness of redemption. The "Great Church" of patristic times was the *catholica ecclesia*, in contradistinction to the gnostic circles and, under the pen of St. Augustine, to the North African separatism of the Donatists. In the Roman tradition, the bishop of Rome sends his blessing *urbi et orbi* to the city (of Rome) and to the orb or sphere of the whole earth, for he does so in the name and for the sake of the *catholica*.

This sense of catholicity as the wholeness of the Church according to God's design has been, so to say, a *leitmotiv* in the history of the Church of Rome

---

[2]Ignatius: *Letter to the Smyrneans*, n. 8 (*The Apostolic Fathers*, vol. I [Cambridge, MA: Harvard University Press, 1952], p. 261). The four marks of the Church are studied at length by Yves Congar in *L'Eglise, une, sainte, catholique, et apostolique* (Paris: Le Cerf, 1970).

which called itself, precisely, at Vatican Council I, *sancta catholica apostolica Romana Ecclesia* (DS, n. 3001), the "holy, catholic and apostolic Roman Church," or, in brief, "the Church." Yet catholicity is also affirmed each time Christians of whatever denomination proclaim the Nicene Creed. And the assertion of catholicity as potential wholeness can be properly made in whatever church or denomination Christians experience the wholeness of Christ's grace and love. Even when Luther, rather unwisely, advocated altering the Creed by substituting the word, "Christian," for the word, "catholic," he did so because of his profound conviction that the catholicity of the Church is none other than that of Christ.

It would be a mistake, however, to understand catholicity only in the corporate sense and to pin the catholic label exclusively on the entire community of believers. Indeed, each one of the faithful may be no less catholic than the whole Church. As St. Gregory the Great explained, "That which we say generally of the whole Church, we now mean specially of each soul."[3] In its qualitative dimension, catholicity is the principle of Christian contemplation. "The contemplative soul," Bonaventure wrote, "contains a picture of the whole world, and of every spirit that has the whole world depicted in itself, and of the Supersubstantial Radiance that contains both the whole world and every spirit."

Universal

If the fundamental meaning of catholicity denotes fullness or wholeness, the word soon acquired in Christian eyes the connotation of geographic extension. The Church is universal in that the gospel is to be preached and has already been preached, as even was believed in the fourth century, in the whole world. This sense is grounded in the scriptural injunction, "Go, make disciples of all nations. . . ." (Matt 28:19). As it is understood in Christian usage, this is not simply a factual assertion concerning the actual geography of the faith. It is above all the expression of a mission. The Church must go to all nations. It must send its evangelists everywhere, as opportunity arises. Not by superfluous generosity is the Church missionary, but by essence. It has been given the task of bringing the wholeness of Christ to all men and women everywhere. In this, the two meanings of the word, "catholic," are intimately related.

The missionary dimension of the Church's catholicity remains imperative even today when Christians have become aware of the profound religiosity expressed in myths and mythologies all over the world, even outside the "Religions of the Book." God, in fact, did not wait for the incarnation of the divine Word to send the Holy Spirit to all lands and all cultures. The

---

[3]St. Gregory the Great, *In Canticum*, I, n. 3 (PL, 79, 479); Bonaventure, *Collationes in Hexaëmeron*, XX, n. 8.

Spirit inspired the many prophets who from time to time in many parts of the world have opened new ways of interior life and of devotion. Here is precisely the point regarding universality as the Church's task and obligation. There are experiences of divine grace in all religions. Several religions have even produced an impressive prophetic or mystical literature concerning the experience of God. That this is part of the mystery of the Church as the people of God was willingly admitted by Vatican Council II (LG, n. 16).

Yet this need not mean that God has sent different Saviors to different regions or countries or that God deals with humanity according to several parallel covenants or that the Christ has been present in other forms and under other names outside of the biblical realm. Rather, as was already believed in the first centuries of Christianity, the Holy Spirit was sent from the earliest days of humankind to prepare the way of the Savior in the hearts of men and women. The religious myths of humanity are no other than artistic reconstructions of what St. Paul described as the basic creaturely experience of the Spirit: "The creation waits with eager expectation for God's children to be revealed. . . . We know that the whole creation groans as in childbirth until now. . . ." (Rom 8:19, 22). Far from having come to a dead end, the missionary injunction now turns the Church's attention to the possibility of a dialogue with the many religions of the world in order to discover the ways of the Spirit in them. But the Spirit always leads, be it in the long run, to God through Christ (AG, 2-5).

Ecumenical

In its fundamental meaning, ecumenicity expresses the feeling that the Church of Christ is spiritually, if not physically, identical with the known civilized lands, the *oecumene*. Admittedly, the Fathers of the Church could not be acquainted with the five continents. They had a certain awareness of Africa—Christianity reached Ethiopia in the third century—and of Asia at least as far as India—where the armies of Alexander the Great had penetrated. They knew of the unchartered lands of central and northern Europe, tribes from which filtered in growing numbers through the borders of the Empire. But the Greeks made a marked distinction between themselves and the barbarians. The temptation was strong, after the conversion of Constantine, to identify the Church with the Empire. In Old Testament terms, Adam, "male and female," made "in the image and likeness" of God (Gen 1:27), is entrusted with the care of the cosmos and its inhabitants (Gen 1:28). In line with this, the Christians could equate the Church of Christ with "the whole world" (*orbis terrarum*) and see it, in the broad vision of Ambrosiaster, as "an epitome of the whole, of what is in heaven and on earth."[4]

---

[4]Ambrosiaster, *Commentarium in Epistolam ad Ephesios*, ch. 1, verses 22-23 (PL 17, 398).

Yet, as he reflected in his book, *The City of God*, on the fall of Rome to the Ostrogoths of Alaric on 24 August 410, Augustine perceived that there are in fact two cities on earth, and only two. The "most glorious City of God, living by faith, is on pilgrimage through the ages among the impious" (XIV, 28). Grounded in "the love of God reaching to contempt of self," it is "the heavenly city," "the city of the saints," "the city of those who wish to live in the peace of the spirit" (XIV, 1), the Church. But the city of this world, the "earthly city," that is built "on the love of self reaching to contempt for God" (XIV, 28), is not separated from it empirically. The two cities are mixed. The second is alive and well within the confines of the first, so that, as it goes on its pilgrimage, the City of the Saints is in fact a mixed body of saints and sinners. Each one of the saints can even experience the sinner within.

Ecumenicity is that aspect of catholicity by which the Church is perceived by faith as the pure and spotless City of God, whatever film of selfishness and sinfulness may still cover its purity. To the basic notion of wholeness it adds the note of holiness. To the extended notion of cosmic universality, it adds the quality of grace. God's creative action made the cosmos. The Creator's care made nature. In the society that humans have built with the capacities of their human nature, the Redeemer's grace has now introduced a new power, the power of God's love and of unselfishness. As grace impacts the realities of this world, the small company of believers slowly becomes the *oecumene*.

It is among the Greek Fathers and their successors in the Orthodox Church that the sense of ecumenicity has been the stronger. Latin Christianity has been attentive to both basic wholeness and geographic extension. Yet the breakdown of the Roman world, the slow construction of Christian Europe, and the modern deconstruction of its Christianity have not favored the perception of the City of God in the features of the Church. Greek Christianity, on the contrary, has been marked by the impact of the Church's wholeness upon the Byzantine Empire. As the Empire was holy and the Emperor acted as the Church's "exterior bishop," the patriarch of Constantinople was—and is still—called the Ecumenical Patriarch. When the Byzantine Empire was conquered by the Turks with the fall of Constantinople in 1453, the sense of ecumenicity fell back upon the Church itself: this is a gate opened onto the Divine Energies. Those who enter it taste heaven while still on earth. Indeed, the Church is heaven on earth. Ecumenicity is symbolized by the icons of Christ and of the saints and is actualized in the divine liturgy.

Sobornuju

The understanding of catholicity as ecumenicity stands behind the rendering of the Creed in Old Slavonic. The Church (*Cerkov*) is *jedinu, svatuju, sobornuju i apostolskuju*. The experience of the heavenly Church of God in the divine liturgy does not remain an exception. In the life of Christian believers, it continues through the perception of the glory of God that shines on the face of Christ and that pervades the sacramental life. In the ongoing existence of the Church, it inheres in its collegial structure. As the bishops who visited the court of the Byzantine Emperor constituted a "permanent synod" (*synodos endemoussa*) that could be called into consultation and action at any moment, so the whole Church of God may be compared with a universal synod. Its life is marked by the meeting of councils. Its doctrine is formulated in the seven ecumenical councils, from Nicaea I (325) to Nicaea II (787). Its bishops rule in harmony with their diocesan synods and with one another. One may speak of a "conciliarity" of the Church.

This was vividly sensed by those who took part in Vatican Council II. The conciliar experience brings the participants directly into touch with the catholicity of the Church. The Church gathered in council seeks for the wholeness and the healing power of God's grace. To take part in the council provides participants with an experience of the Church's universality: bishops converge into one from the far corners of the globe. It is an experience of its ecumenicity as the council strives to express the totality of the Christian vision in the light of the signs of the times. In the language and the theology of Vatican II, the collegiality of the episcopal college flows from the conciliarity of the Church when it is understood with the specific nuances of *sobornuju*.

Conciliarism

Neither catholicity, ecumenicity, or conciliarity, nor *sobornost* or collegiality is identical with conciliarism, which is a political conception of the government of the universal Church when there is a conflict between the bishop of Rome as universal primate in charge of the Petrine ministry of unity and the majority of the bishops. Conflicts of various levels of seriousness between the pope and a number of bishops, or the pope and a number of priests, were frequent in the ancient Church and in the Middle Ages up to the time of the Reformation which started as such a conflict. Nobody was especially upset by such events until the conflict took the form of a split among the electors of the pope—the cardinals—one group electing one pope, another group electing another pope. As we have seen, this papal schism occasioned the first systematic treatment of ecclesiology. Strictly speaking, conciliarism was the theory that was then devised to force an end to the schism. Simply, the theory was that a general council of bishops has authority over all bishops, including the pope of Rome.

Acting on this principle, the council of Constance (1415–1418) was able to bring the papal schism to an end by obliging two popes to resign and electing another in their stead. This was the work of the fourth and fifth sessions. The council decreed:

> [This holy Council], lawfully gathered in the Holy Spirit, being a General
> Council, and representing the Holy Church Militant, has its authority di-
> rectly from Christ, and everyone, of whatever status or dignity, be it papal,
> is bound to obey it in what pertains to faith and to the destruction of the
> said schism, and to the general reform of the said Church in its head and
> members (Decree *Haec Sancta,* 6 April 1415).

In addition, the council of Constance decreed that there should be one
general council every ten years (decree *Frequens*, 9 October 1417). The new
pope, however, Martin V (pope, 1417-1431), eventually rejected the legitimacy of these conciliaristic decisions, in spite of their temporary efficacy in
restoring papal unity.

In its essence, conciliarism is therefore the theory that an ecumenical council is superior to the bishop of Rome. This doctrine was still taught by the
bishops at the second session of the council of Basle in 1432 after Martin V's
successor, Pope Eugene IV (pope, 1431-1447), in the bull *Quoniam alto,*
decreed the nullity of this council and convoked another in the town of
Bologna. Eugene IV, however, retracted his decision (bull *Dudum sacrum* in
1433) and generally recognized the ecumenicity of the first twenty-five sessions of the council. He later obtained its transfer to Ferrara in 1438, then to
Florence (1438-1442), and finally to Rome (1442-1445). Even so, in 1447 in
the bull, *Ad ea ex debito*, Eugene IV explicitly acknowledged the authority
of the council of Constance and its decree *Frequens*. Meanwhile, a dwindling
group of bishops hung on in Basle for some years and, on the basis of the
conciliarist theory, denied the legitimacy of the papalist council in Florence.
But the work they did—including a definition of the Immaculate Conception of Mary at the thirty-sixth session in 1438—had little audience, and it
was never received as Catholic doctrine by the Church at large. Little by
little, most of the bishops and Churches that held to the conciliarist decrees
withdrew their support. In 1460, in the bull *Execrabilis*, Pope Pius II (pope,
1458-1464), who—as Cardinal Aeneas Silvius Piccolomini—had argued for
conciliarism, outlawed all appeal from a pope to a future ecumenical council.[5]

Conciliarism, however, lingered on in some places, chiefly in France, in
the mitigated form of Gallicanism. Some of the doctrine of Basle passed into
the Pragmatic Sanction of Bourges that was given force of law by King
Charles VII in 1438: the superiority of the council over the pope was affirmed.
It was maintained, in conjunction with some traditional "freedoms" of the

---

[5]On the problem of conciliarism and gallicanism, see Küng, l. c.; Aimé-Georges Martimort, *Le
Gallicanisme de Bossuet* (Paris: Le Cerf, 1953); Olivier de la Brosse, *Le Pape et le Concile. La
comparaison de leurs pouvoirs à la veille de la Réforme* (Paris: Le Cerf, 1965); Margaret O'Gara,
Triumph in Defeat: Infallibility, Vatican I, and the French Minority Bishops (Washington:
Catholic University of America Press, 1988). The fundamental question of conciliarism and
gallicanism relates to the experience of *communio* and to the relations between ministerial call
and magisterial responsibility; see below, chapters 8 and 9.

Church of France, in the Four Articles that were adopted in 1681 by the Assembly of the Clergy under the theological leadership of Bossuet (1627–1704). Similar points were structured into the Civic Constitution of the Clergy that was voted on 12 July 1790 by the Constituent Assembly of the French Revolution and into the Organic Articles adopted by Napoleon as First Consul in 1802. Conciliarist opinions among the Clergy of France petered out only in the wake of Vatican Council I (1870). But in Germany and Switzerland, similar opinions were responsible for the rejection of papal infallibility by the Old Catholic Church.

The history of the matter, however, is itself of ecclesiological significance. One cannot deny that the unified papacy as it was restored in 1417 was grounded in the principles of conciliarism, the eventual rejection of the doctrine and the later predominance of papalism notwithstanding. Pope Martin V's legitimacy depended precisely on the legitimacy of the council of Constance and its decrees. The later condemnation of conciliarism that was implicit in the definition of papal infallibility in 1870 was itself made possible, historically, by conciliarism. The Roman Catholic Church is therefore in the paradoxical situation that its most specific doctrine, the definition of papal infallibility, presupposes—not doctrinally but historically—its opposite, the superiority of the council over the bishop of Rome. Papalism presupposes conciliarism.

In this situation, the following doctrinal options are logically possible:

1) Whatever happened in the fifteenth century, the doctrine of Vatican Council I is today the only valid one. As proclaimed by an undoubted general council, supported by another one (Vatican II), and as being in any case the received doctrine in the Catholic Church of today, it is embodied in contemporary canon law: *Contra sententiam vel decretum Romani Pontificis non datur appellatio neque recursus* (can. 333 §3)—"Against the Roman Pontiff's decision or decree there is no appeal or recourse." This rules out the superiority of a council over a pope.

2) Or opting for the other extreme, one can reject the doctrine of Vatican I as being in contradiction to that of Constance, perhaps thinking, as Calvin presumably would have said, "*On abuse le pauvre peuple!*" In this case, one has to hold either that Vatican I was not a true council or, as Luther concluded at the Disputation of Leipzig in 1519, that councils are not protected from major error.

3) Or being unwilling to pit one council against another, one can hold that since both doctrines were proclaimed by general councils, conciliarism and papalism must be true in some sense, even if this sense is not yet manifest: further theological reflection should discover their mutual compatibility. This, I take it, is Hans Küng's understanding of the matter in his major study of the problem.

4) Or one can hold that conflicts and disagreements in the government of the Church should be serenely assessed and not seen as causes for dissent. Since the Church's structure is not, strictly speaking, an object of faith, these tensions do not affect the essence of the Church or the heart of the faith. As the whole of human life is lived in situations of tension between opposite pulls, there is no obvious reason why the life of the Church on earth should be exempt from similar tensions. The quarrels of the past over the relative authority of the council and of the pope illustrate a tension that is intrinsic to the community that professes the Christian faith. The exact point of tension lies in the polarity between the universal and the particular, between catholicity and apostolicity. It is intrinsic to the twofold belief that the Church is universal and that its apostolicity resides particularly, though not exclusively, in the episcopal see of Rome. This fourth interpretation corresponds to my own view of the question.

The Church is Apostolic

We are thus brought to consider the last of the four credal marks of the Church, apostolicity. This mark reflects the belief that the Church at every moment lives off a tradition received from the apostles. Like oneness, holiness, and catholicity, apostolicity affects the entire Church. It applies to all that the Church is. And it would apply to all the Church's decisions and actions if these were always made in imitation of the apostles and according to their mind. Apostolicity is therefore turned to the past that has been inherited. It is the reason why the writings of the New Testament were chosen and were assigned the status of Holy Scripture. Being the primary locus where the witness of the apostles is formulated, they are the apostolic Scriptures. The Church of the first centuries selected its books because it recognized the apostolic witness in them, leaving out apocryphal writings that may be more colorful but which abound in non-apostolic material. It is also on account of the retroactive aspect of apostolicity that the council of Trent at its fourth session referred to "apostolic traditions," that is, traditions received from the apostles as binding on the Church at least when they refer to the essence or content of the Christian faith, matters of discipline being bound to vary according to circumstances of time and place.

But apostolicity is also turned to the future. For the witness of the apostles, valid as it was for the beginnings of the Church, remains valid for later ages. For this reason, the older exegesis spoke not only of the historical meaning of Scripture but also of its spiritual meaning. While history may be past, the spiritual value of it perdures. And this spiritual meaning was thought to include not only analogy—or doctrinal teaching—and tropology—or moral teaching—but also anagogy, that is, teaching regarding the eschatological orientation of the faith and the present participation in the eschatological fulfillment. In this perspective, apostolicity designates the faith and the Church in their aspect of permanence. From the beginning to the end, the Church is one Church only. Time and history alter many of its superficial aspects and its ways of doing things. But they do not affect what lies at their heart, the witness of the apostles and of all those who, with and like the apostles, share their experience of being the Church of Jesus Christ.

Apostolicity therefore implies the perduration of the Church to the ends of the world. By the same token, it qualifies the preparation of the future and the future itself by the Church's members. It points to the task of continuing the mission of preaching the gospel and baptizing the nations. The apostles received this mission in the name of the Church of all ages, and it belongs to this Church to fulfill it in their name.

Undoubtedly, there have been complementary nuances in the perception and the experience of the Church's apostolicity. For Hincmar (c. 806-882), archbishop of Reims, apostolicity was the Church's continuous fidelity to the pastoral virtues of the apostles, and especially of Peter; it was turned to past models of government. At the time of the Reformation, Martin Luther saw it as radically turned to the present: it is the capacity to distinguish the gospel from the law. As such, it implies the commitment to preach the gospel and thereby the discernment of it from all fashionable or esoteric pseudo-gospels that speak to the contemporary mind. The Church is apostolic when it searches for "the heart of the gospel," when it places the purity of the gospel above all law—not only above the Torah of the Old Testament, but also above its own internal regulations and its canon law and even above the requirements of the natural law as these are elicited by its theologians and bishops. In the nineteenth century, John Henry Newman (1801-1890), when still an Anglican, related apostolicity more to the past than to the future when he described apostolicity as faithfulness to the apostles' doctrine. He found this faithfulness in the Church of England.[6]

Apostolicity is in fact all of this, and more. For if it makes sense to speak of the Church today as being apostolic, then it makes equal sense to say that the apostles are present and active in the Church of today.

Apostolic Succession

This manner of speaking corresponds well to the doctrine of apostolic succession. The Church of today succeeds the Church of apostolic times that received the first witness of those who had seen the risen Christ with their own eyes and that passed on this good news to the new and younger members who were destined to be the Church of the next generation. In this successive

[6]John Henry Newman, *Lectures on the Prophetical Office of the Church*, 1837 (*The Via Media of the Anglican Church*, vol. I, [London: Longmans, Green and Co., 1897]), p. 1-355.

transmission of apostolic witness, however, a special place has been traditionally given to the bishops of the Church: they are said to stand in apostolic succession, to be the successors of the apostles. Whether these are primarily identified with the Twelve or with the missionaries on the Pauline model is of little consequence at this point: all of them were called to witness to the gospel.

Even though the Creed of Nicaea-Constantinople was used in Spain in the sixth century and in the empire of Charlemagne toward the end of the eighth century, the stress on apostolicity comes somewhat later. In the ninth century in some areas of Western Europe, a special feast celebrates the *Divisio Apostolorum*, the departure of the twelve apostles on their mission. But the adjective "apostolic" was often used in the Carolingian age to designate the position of bishops "in apostolic succession" and the special position of the bishop of Rome who sits in the "apostolic see" of Peter and who was at times simply called *Apostolicus*, the adjective functioning as a noun.

It is in relation to the Church's apostolicity that the function of the Church in Rome and of its bishop has traditionally been seen in the Roman Catholic tradition. As Ignatius of Antioch wrote to the Christians of Rome around 115, their Church "presides in charity [in *agapè*]," which may well mean, in the Communion. Before the end of the second century, pilgrims travelled to Rome out of devotion to the great apostles. Because of its foundation on the tombs of Peter and Paul, "those from everywhere (*ab undique*)," as was recorded by Irenaeus of Lyon, had recourse to it when they enquired about the apostles' doctrine.[7]

The presidency in charity has taken many forms in history. From being a center of pilgrimage to the memory of St. Peter and St. Paul, the Church in Rome became a final court of appeals for disputes among Christians. As appeals multiplied and the bishop of Rome took more initiatives for the sake of the universal communion, St Peter was said to rule the Church "mystically" in his successors. But the apostolicity of the Church and bishop of Rome does not stand by itself. The bishop of Rome has called regional synods and general councils of the West. He has shared authority with metropolitans (archbishops) and with regional primates. More recently he has ruled corporately with his assistants, the cardinals, themselves forming a college. Over many centuries, the growth of ecclesiastical bureaucracy has given its present form to what amounts to a central system of administration in Rome. But none of these practical and political arrangements belongs to the essence of the Petrine primacy.

This essence lies in apostolicity. As was taught by Vatican II in chapter 3 of *Lumen Gentium*, the college of bishops succeeds the apostolic college, and the bishop of Rome personally succeeds Peter at the head of the college.

---

[7] *St. Irénée, Contre les Hérésies,* bk III, ch. 3, n. 2 (SC, n. 211, Cerf, 1974, p. 32).

Thus the primacy of the bishop of Rome is tied to his succession. It is then said to have a scriptural and apostolic foundation, even though Peter, the chief among the Twelve, was never a bishop of Rome and though the universal primacy, or Petrine office, cannot be traced back to the first bishops who occupied the Roman see. But apostolic succession is not only a historical fact. It is not just succession in an office, in a see, or in a function. There cannot have been much difference between Peter and the other apostles since Jesus addressed all the apostles through Peter. Therefore all bishops, as successors of the apostles, are also successors of Peter. This was Hincmar's interpretation of Matthew 16:19. And the archbishop of Reims was not reluctant to give a warning to Pope Hadrian II (pope, 867-72): "The privilege of Peter does not persist when judgement is not passed with Peter's equity."[8] Hincmar, who was a distinguished canonist, regarded equity as that special qualification of decision and action that derives from justice being tempered with charity. Equity is the telltale of apostolicity in the Church's decisions. In the long run, the value of the apostolic succession of bishops in general, and of the Roman Petrine succession in particular, will be judged by their effectiveness in safeguarding the gospel and in promoting its proclamation within the whole communion of the Churches of God.

Yet, notwithstanding some tendencies that were rampant among the ultramontane theologians of the nineteenth century, neither apostolicity nor apostolic succession are restricted to the bishop of Rome or to bishops in general. In his *De sacramentis*, Hugh of St. Victor taught that priests succeed the seventy-two disciples just as bishops succeed the Twelve.[9] Remarking that Paul often designates priests and bishops with the one term, *episcopi*, he hinted that, in terms of succession, there is little difference between the two. Whatever the shortcomings of Hugh's biblical exegesis, the point is well taken. What, over the long haul, matters the most in apostolicity and apostolic succession is not who does what, but the apostolic fidelity of what is done.

The Communion

The credal marks of the Church underline four aspects of the Communion of the faithful with Christ and with one another. While these four aspects can be distinguished and can in turn be subdivided, they stand together in mutual implication. The Church is not one apart from or in addition to being holy, catholic, and apostolic. It is not holy without at the same time being one, catholic, and apostolic. It is not apostolic without being one, holy, and cath-

[8]Tavard, "Episcopacy and Apostolic Succession according to Hincmar of Reims," *Theological Studies,* vol. 34/4, Dec. 1973, p. 594-623.

[9]Hugh of St. Victor, l. c., bk II, part II, ch. XII (PL, 176, 429).

olic. Rather, the Church's oneness is itself holy, catholic, and apostolic. Its holiness is one, catholic, and apostolic. Its catholicity is one, holy, and apostolic. Its apostolicity is one, holy, and catholic. Each mark includes all the others.

Yet this is not to say that all the marks of the Church are equally visible at all times and in all places. When he was an Anglican, John Henry Newman thought that the Church of England set a better example of apostolicity, while the Church of Rome set a better example of catholicity. Whether Newman was right or not, it would be a mistake to treat the marks of the Church as tools for apologetics. They should not be used, although they have been, to feed polemics against or amongst the Christians who followed the Reformation in the sixteenth century. They are principles. And they are ideals. As principles, they underlie everything that is truly Christian. All communities in which the word is preached and the sacraments administered share in them. As ideals, they set a goal for the Church's actions and hopes. But they never reach the peak of perfection. The Church is one, yet it always prays for unity. It is holy, yet it is also affected by the sinfulness of its members. It is catholic, yet it needs to be liberated from constantly reemerging cultural and national particularisms. It is apostolic, yet it often lets non-apostolic devotions and rules stifle or hide the truth of the gospel.

Despite this mixture of good and bad in the lived experience of being the Church, the conciliarity of the Christian community opens a window on the perfection to which God calls it. As the dwelling of God with his human creatures, the Church holds the promise of eschatological fullness for all the faithful. Age after age, the Church's members have come to know the indwelling of the divine Persons in their hearts. In their communion with one another, they also recognize their community as the tabernacle of the divine presence on earth, if not also in the whole cosmos.

For Further Reading

E. I. Watkin. *The Church in Council.* New York: Sheed and Ward, 1960.

Paul Tillich. *Systematic Theology,* vol. 3. Chicago: The University of Chicago Press, 1963.

Hans Küng. *Structures of the Church.* New York: T. Nelson, 1964.

Jerome Hamer. *The Church is a Communion.* New York: Sheed and Ward, 1964.

Archbishop Methodios Fouyas. *Orthodoxy, Roman Catholicism and Anglicanism.* London: Oxford University Press, 1972.

Juan Luis Segundo. *The Community called Church.* New York: Orbis, 1973.

Avery Dulles. *The Catholicity of the Church.* Oxford: Clarendon Press, 1985.

7

Monasticity

Vatican Council II devoted chapter 6 of its constitution *De Ecclesia* to "the religious," taking this term in a broad sense that covers all forms of officially consecrated life. In doing this, the council followed the Catholic tradition which has always closely associated the monastic or religious life both with the "call to holiness" that is addressed to all the faithful and with the "eschatological nature of the Church." These are precisely the titles of chapters 5 and 7 of the same document. That is to say, three chapters out of eight deal with the particular calling of religious within the broader vocation of all Christians. This calling is grounded in the universal call to holiness, and it is oriented toward the eschatological expectation of the whole Church. The historical place of religious orders in the Churches of both East and West and the theological self-understanding of monastic foundations and religious orders denote more than the idiosyncrasies of a peculiar way of life. They express a fundamental dimension of the entire community of the disciples. This dimension I will name, in the present chapter, monasticity.

Is Monasticism Christian?

Monasticity is not usually regarded as a basic dimension of the Christian Church. Historically, it does not originate in apostolic times. Its scriptural basis is slim or non-existent. It is often said or suggested, in defense of the monastic life, that Jesus called the generality of his followers to obey a minimal law of salvation and invited a select few to adhere to some more specific counsels of perfection. But such a duality in the teachings of the New Testament does not bear close scrutiny: Jesus called everyone to perfection, not a few only. Further, one can now argue, after the discovery of the Qumran monastic writings, that monasticism as such was purposely ignored by the authors of the New Testament. That a strict form of monasticism did exist in Palestinian Judaism at the time of Jesus is certain. But the monks of Qumran, who were known to the Jewish historian Josephus (born 37/38) under the name of Essenes, are not even mentioned in the New Testament. This, however, does not imply that they were without influence. Yet monasticism did not exist in the older, normative tradition of Israel, unless one assimilates to monastic communities the "schools of prophets" that flourished here and there before the Exile and the disciples of the prophet Elijah at Mount Carmel. Nor did the monastic tradition exist in the Greek and Roman religions except in the very particular though central case of the Vestal Virgins in Rome itself.

Christians have from time to time explicitly rejected the validity of religious vows. The Protestant Reformers did so in the name of the gospel and in the light of justification by faith as they understood it. But this is not a convincing objection to monasticism being Christian though it is a vivid reminder that a fundamental dimension of the Church can be, as it were, so distorted that it betrays and destroys what it ought to signify and support. Whenever this happens to monasticism, it becomes normal for sincere believers to reject it as alien to the gospel.

In these conditions, the title of the present chapter is meant to underline a basic contention: as it has historically developed out of its Jewish cradle, the Christian Church has acquired and preserved a dimension that is closely connected with a central institution of most of the great religions of the world, the monastic life. At some periods and in some places, this dimension has been more latent than patent. Yet it has been present among Christians since the third and fourth centuries. When, with the end of the persecutions, the highest Christian ideal ceased to be martyrdom, witnessing to Christ in the face of death, the faithful found a substitute for it in the monastic devotion to seeking the one thing necessary, the kingdom of God that is within. After trying the anachoretic life in isolation, most of those who were so engaged entered the cenobitic life, seeking for the kingdom in community.

The history of Latin Christianity after the patristic period has naturally been marked by the understanding of conciliarity that had been inherited from the Latin Fathers whose works were the most constantly read and the best known through the many centuries of what is usually, though hardly accurately, referred to as the Middle Ages. These were St Augustine, the most influential of the Latin Fathers, though not a monk in the strict sense, and St. Gregory the Great (c. 540-604), a monk who became bishop of Rome. Undoubtedly, the patristic heritage that was passed on to the Middle Ages was one-sided. The Greek Fathers were generally little known. Translations from their original texts were few. A reading knowledge of the Greek language all but disappeared from continental Western Europe during the Germanic invasions so that few Latin theologians could read the Greek writings. Between the restoration of learning under Emperor Charlemagne (768–814) and the Renaissance of the fifteenth century, the Latin author who was the most knowledgeable in Greek was the Irish monk John Scotus Erigena who was active at the court of Charles the Bald before 847. And the Greek theologian who was the most familiar to the West was the anonymous Syriac monk designated as Pseudo-Dionysius whose works, known through several Latin translations including one by John Scotus, expounded a mystical approach to the knowledge of God, to angelology, and to ecclesiology. Pseudo-Dionysius was read in the light of Augustine. Indeed, the works of Augustine and of Gregory along with those of a few others such as Isidore of Seville (c. 570–635) presented enough data for solid reflection on the Christian community. But these data were evidently sifted through the general approaches to Christian life and teaching that shaped the Carolingian mind and later dominated the monastic and the scholastic approaches to theology. As it was transmitted to the Carolingian age and thence to the medieval period, the conciliarity of the Church took the form of monasticity. The specific conditions of this transformation of conciliarity were bound to affect deeply the self-understanding of the Western Church.

There is, however, a backdrop to the question. A slight detour through the history of religions will be useful at this point.

The Example of Sakyamuni the Buddha

If one compares the religions of the world, Christianity and Buddhism appear to have one thing in common that is absent from the other major religions. Sakyamuni the Buddha (born, c. 550 b.c.e.) did not start a new religion. He started a monastic movement within Hinduism. As this movement, however, could not be identified with any of the six *darçanas* (systems) of orthodox Hinduism, it eventually became not only distinct from but also opposed to the religion of its origins. Buddhist Scriptures came to replace the Hindu Scriptures for the followers of Sakyamuni. Hindu representations of the divine were abandoned. As it is still evident today in Theravada Buddhism, the true Buddhist is not just the one who generally follows the teaching of the Thatagata concerning the eightfold path of suffering and of liberation. He is the monk who, taking shelter in the Buddha, the dharma, and the sangha, devotes his life entirely to the process of liberation through a meditative search for enlightenment. Thus there are two levels of Buddhist discipleship—the monastic one, which, at the start, was closed to women, and the lay one.

One finds something similar at the origin of Christianity. Jesus of Nazareth never intended to inaugurate another religion other than the one in which he was born. He started a movement within Judaism. This movement was centered on a reinterpretation of Torah. But it eventually became distinct from and even opposed to the Judaism that had nurtured it in its cradle. There were of course many reasons for the uprooting of the Christian community from its Jewish ground: the rejection and crucifixion of Jesus by the leaders of Palestinian Judaism; the focusing of Jesus' teaching on the expectation of a universal kingdom of God in which Gentiles would have their place along with Jews, and of which Jesus himself was the forerunner and the instrument; the teaching of the Pauline and Johannine authors concerning the role of the Christ as the only Mediator between God and humanity and their conclusions concerning his preexistence in God; the expulsion of Judeo-Christians from the synagogues toward the end of the first century (by decisions that are often attributed to a hypothetical synod of Jamnia, c. 100); and also the peculiar structure that the community of the disciples gave itself from the start. This was not, admittedly, a monastic structure. But as Jesus made an indefinite number of disciples and called twelve of them to a special function, he implicitly established two levels of discipleship among his followers.

This was precisely one of the problems of the patristic Church: how to identify these levels and to delineate their proper relationships. The Twelve died without successors in what lay at the heart of their apostleship: no one was henceforth alive who had been called visibly and audibly by the Lord and who also had witnessed his resurrection. But thanks to the missionary apostles who carried the gospel to the diaspora and to the Gentiles, the Church soon acquired a quasi-permanent ministerial structure. And this structure preserved two levels. There were ministers—bishops, presbyters— ordained by laying on of hands, who were all male, along with deacons, who in the East at least could be male or female. And there was the generality of believers.

At the end of the patristic age, however, when the Christian movement and the Christian Church had found their quasi-permanent shape, the level of ordained ministry borrowed notable features from monasticism.

The Monastic Movement

The monastic movement in Christianity originated in the deserts of Egypt and Syria and soon spread to the forests and mountains of Dalmatia and of Western Europe. It began among men who left what seemed to be a decaying civilization in order to find in solitude and serenity an approximation to the kingdom of God. The basic model presented in the *Life of St. Antony* by St. Athanasius of Alexandria (295-373, bishop in 328) was that of anchorites who lived alone. Soon, solitude gave place to ascetic life in common or "cenobitism." The cenobite model was propagated, among others, by St. Basil (c. 330-379), bishop of Caesarea in Cappadocia, and his family, notably his sister Macrina the Younger (d. 379). In the West, St. Ambrose, bishop of Milan from 374 to 397, was the main advocate of a quasi-monastic life for women who did not marry, lived in their parents' home, and gathered for prayer and edification in the cathedral under the bishop's guidance. Once the age of persecutions and martyrdoms seemed to be over, the monastic model became, in one form or another, the ideal of the holy life, and the monastery the ideal of the holy community.

This is immediately relevant to ecclesiology. For the conception of the Church that was outlined by Augustine and developed in the Western Middle Ages was profoundly influenced by the monastic ideal. After his ordination to the episcopate in 396, Augustine built his theology of the Church as a mixed body of saints and sinners, in opposition to the Donatists and their conception of a Church of the pure. His ecclesiology was in keeping with the theology of grace that Augustine opposed to the Pelagians: it is not human efforts, but rather Christ and his Spirit who act in the sacraments, as also in the process of conversion and in the interior ascent of the soul to God. In its interiority as the realm of God's grace, the *Ecclesia* is God's creation and gift. It is placed on this earth as a *communio sanctorum*, the communion of the saints who, from the beginning of humanity—"from Abel the just to the last of the elect"—witness to the holy City of God. It is also the *catholica*, the universal community, which as *communio sacramentorum* (communion in the sacraments) is the refuge of sinners no less than the paradise of the saints. This Augustinian perspective is of course grounded in Christ. Only by virtue of their union with the risen Lord do the *ecclesia* and its members constitute *Christus totus*, the "total Christ." As the total Christ, the Church functions through universal consensus over against the particularisms of sectarian movements and conventicles. Such a consensus is to be reached through the persuasive guidance and authority of bishops who arrive at and express their own consensus through regional and universal councils.

Augustine's ecclesial outlook includes, however, another pervasive component. Throughout his career as a bishop, Augustine tried to safeguard the ideal of the monastic life that he had projected for himself at the time of his conversion. In a garden that was provided for that purpose by Bishop Valerius of Hippo who ordained him, Augustine, the reluctant presbyter as he insisted he was, established a monastery. In it, Augustine the bishop lived with his priests, forming with them a quasi-monastic community. This was a Christian version of the community of wisdom-seekers of which Augustine had dreamt at the time of his conversion. Fired by the Neo-Platonist ideal of a community of friends who would search for true wisdom in common, Augustine had then learned of the existence of Christian monasteries in Egypt and near the city of Trèves. He had himself visited such monasteries on the outskirts of Milan and of Rome. As he journeyed from Manichaeanism by way of Neo-Platonism to Christianity, Augustine was converted not only to Christ and not only to the Christian community, but also to a monastic conception of the Christian life.[1]

---

[1]George H. Tavard, *Les Jardins de Saint Augustin* (Montreal: Bellarmin, 1989).

It is no wonder, then, that the City of God—to which the Church testifies in the midst of the earthly city—is said by Augustine to be built on "love of God even to contempt of self," whereas the earthly city is built on "love of self even to contempt of God."[2] Precisely, "love of God" and "contempt of self" distinguish a Christian monastery from a philosophical community of wisdom in which there may be love of wisdom and desire for "the blessed life" but there are no contempt of self and no knowledge of the Word of God and of the divine Persons. Like the two cities, the two communities pursue glory, the one in self-renunciation before the glory of God, the other in self-glorifying complacency. Reflecting on his conversion in the *Confessions*, the younger Augustine, recently made a bishop, described the cosmos, God's creation, on the model of a garden in which both space and time are organized in view of the nurture of seeds and plants. Likewise, the older Augustine saw the Church on the model of his own "monastery in the garden." It is the place where the Heavenly City, the City of God, is experienced on earth, where communion in the sacraments becomes the communion of the saints.

The Benedictine Input

Augustine gave a monastic form to the life of his clergy. Yet he did not found a monastic order as such. Furthermore, the instructions he left, chiefly in his Letter 211 that was addressed to a community of women, as to the mode of monastic organization and living, were too vague and unsystematic to have had, by themselves, a great impact on the monastic institution and on the Church's self-understanding. Yet Augustine's insistence that priests must renounce marriage was clearly inspired by the monastic ideal and, beyond that, by a Neo-Platonic conception of wisdom. It eventually passed into the mentality of the Western Church. But the lasting impact of Augustine's monastic ideal upon the whole Church was due to the powerful support it received from what was to be the typically Western monastic tradition, the conception and the practice of community that are generally associated with the name of St. Benedict of Nursia (5th c.).

This ideal had its model in the Institutes (*De Institutis monachorum*) and the Conferences (*Collationes*) of John Cassian (c. 360–435), a widely traveled monk who finally settled in Marseilles where he founded a monastery and a nunnery. In his writings, Cassian adapted to the Western mind principles and customs he had admired in Eastern Europe, in Palestine, and in Egypt. Cassian's descriptions inspired most of the monastic rules of the West, notably the *Rule of the Master* and the Rule that is traditionally attributed to St. Benedict. This ideal was appropriated by St. Gregory the Great who wrote

---

[2] *De Civitate Dei*, bk XIV, 28.

his *Dialogues* in its light. And it is to Gregory that St. Benedict, who is otherwise unknown, owes his fame.

The Benedictine ideal constitutes a remarkable instance of the application of the principle of conciliarity to a relatively small gathering. The monastery is a permanent council. Where Augustine had hoped for unanimity of hearts and minds on the model of the early community of Acts 2:42-47, the Rule of St. Benedict devised ways to reach such unanimity: all the members are at one in their desire to seek and to serve God (*opus Dei*) since that is the chief motive for joining the community (*Rule,* ch. 58, 7). The father abbot who acts, one would say today, as the "guru" of his monks is not imposed on them but elected by them (ch. 64, 3), the diocesan bishop, abbots of other monasteries, and even the lay "Christians of the area" having the duty to intervene if "depraved monks" have elected one who is lenient toward their vices (ch. 64, 4-5). The mutual relationship between the abbot and the monks is one of fatherhood (ch. 2, 24) and obedience, but this should be the obedience of love, not of fear (ch. 64, 15). Furthermore, the abbot's leadership is molded by the needs of the monks (ch. 2, 24-25). There are times for common liturgical prayer (ch. 8-20) and common work (ch. 48), times for common reading of the Scriptures, Cassian's *Conferences*, and the Lives of the Fathers (ch. 42). The Rule must be read frequently to all the community (ch. 66, 8). The sacramental distinction between those who are ordained and those who are not does not affect their monastic status (ch. 62, 5; 63, 7). As a shortcut to unanimity of heart and soul, all monks should practice mutual obedience (ch. 71). The Rule, however, is for those who begin their conversion; those who "hasten to perfection" should further be cognizant of "the teachings of the Fathers," the "page" *(pagina)* or "word" *(sermo)* of the Old and the New Testament, the *Conferences* and *Institutes* of Cassian, the Lives of the Fathers, and "the Rule of our holy Father St. Basil" (ch. 73, 2-5).

The Monastic Church

In the absence of other striking examples of holiness, once the times of persecutions were over, monastic institutions were pervasive enough at the start of the Carolingian period to set the ideal of holiness for the whole Church. Whatever examples of Christian devotion may have been provided to lay believers by emperors and other politically prominent persons, they could not compete with the more universal and more total devotion of monks and consecrated virgins. Thus the Church became, in fact if not in theory, monastic.

The monasticity of the Church is manifested in a multitude of ways. A few examples will suffice. The monasteries, Benedictine or Irish (following the more ascetic Rule, or Rules, of St. Columban [d. 615]) and, later, Carthusian (founded in 1084 as a synthesis of community and eremitical life) and

Cistercian (founded in 1098 as a stricter form of Benedictinism), acted throughout Europe as the vanguard of civilisation. Around them, forests were cleared for agriculture, schools were opened and instruction given in the seven liberal arts and in theology. As their churches became centers of pilgrimage, some neighboring villages grew into towns where market days brought people from far away lands. Meanwhile, the meditative reading of Scripture led to discussion of theological themes and inspired the more talented monks to write down their thoughts and meditations. In the Celtic Church of Ireland, diocesan organization was introduced only in 1111 by the synod of Rath Breasail. Until that date, the Irish Church was strictly monastic: monasteries provided episcopal services by having one of their members ordained to the episcopate.

Where secular society preserved castes and classes inherited from Roman law or Germanic customs, monasteries were socially leveling entities where serfs were freed by monastic vows. Presbyters have always been taken from the common people of the Church. But when dioceses were properly organized in northern Europe on the model of the previous organization of Italy and the Mediterranean lands, bishops were most frequently provided by monasteries. This continued until the relatively late time in the fifteenth century when the nobility began to orient its younger sons toward ecclesiastical careers with the expectation of a lucrative bishopric. In the twelfth century, the orders of canons extended the monastic ideal to the pastoral service of the people. When bishops opened their cathedral schools, they emulated the older monastic schools. And when the schools developed into universities, the new orders of friars provided a sizable proportion of the professors, including of course the greatest pre-Reformation theologians, Albert the Great (Dominican, c. 1200-1280), Bonaventure (Franciscan, 1221-1274), Thomas Aquinas (Dominican, 1224/25-1274), and John Duns Scotus (Franciscan, d. 1308).

Sunday vespers which were faithfully attended by the people for centuries were simply borrowed from the monastic office. In fact, the temporal cycle of the liturgy derives from the monasteries. And every reform of the Church before the sixteenth century was spearheaded either by a reform of existing monasteries or by the emergence of new forms of religious life. It is to the monastic ideal that the Catholic clergy owe the obligation of celibacy that was progressively included in canon law during the Middle Ages. And when the council of Trent reorganized the diocesan clergy and its training, it merely adapted monastic forms, the seminary acting as a temporary monastery and the breviary being borrowed from the monastic office of the hours.

The transformation of conciliarity under the impact of monasticity took different forms in the East and in the West. While the Western Church gradually imposed celibacy on all clergy, the Eastern Church ordained men to the diaconate and the priesthood whether they were married or not. But celibacy or widowhood was a precondition for the ordination of bishops. It is not marriage that is an impediment to diaconal and priestly ordination; rather, ordination is an impediment to marriage. But since most priests are married, Oriental bishops are usually taken from monasteries. This monastic model for episcopacy fits the Orthodox or Pravoslav practice of episcopal authority that has remained close to the patristic model of conciliarity: Eastern patriarchs and bishops wield their full measure of authority only in the context of their synod and not outside of it. Their authority is that of their see. Being communal, it is properly effective in a synodal context. The authority of Western bishops, on the contrary, is understood to accrue to them simply by virtue of their ordination and of the responsibility that has been vested in them, the reference to a wider spread of authority, as in a synod or a council, remaining occasional and exceptional.

Tensions and Conflicts

With the hindsight of history, one can well see that the monasticity of the Church, especially as it has been experienced in the West, can easily turn into a breeding ground for conflicts. Tensions between personalities and between theologies are normally absorbed in the give-and-take of community life. But they are infinitely more difficult to resolve once the Church at large is their theater. The monastic polarity between authority and obedience, between abbot and monks, abbess and nuns, between common calling and individual talents, between general ideals and particular interests requires mutual listening and concern. For without mutual acceptance, the sharp edges of diversities cannot be blunted. Monastic life is supportive. Life outside the monastery, "in the world," is competitive, easily dominated by rivalries that are not conducive to mutual listening and concern. Mutual support is all the more necessary an ingredient of the monastic life as, from the start, Christian monasteries have required celibacy. Unanimity of purpose at the heart of the monastic community makes celibacy a commonly bearable burden, if not a spiritual asset for everyone. The requirement of celibacy was itself a relic of the ancient philosophical ideal of the Stoics and Neo-Platonists who generally regarded marriage as a superfluous nuisance rarely compatible with a life of wisdom. St. Augustine himself had transferred this philosophical conception to his understanding of the monastic life as a search for Christian wisdom.

But mutual support cannot be experienced at the same level in an isolated parsonage as in a monastery. The celibacy that the Western Catholic Church has required of priests in imitation of the monastic model became unlivable at several points of time and in certain countries when it gave birth to unbearable loneliness or where it ran afoul of accepted norms of adulthood. And in any case, the married state being that of most of the Christian laity, the monastic ideal introduced a division of castes in the oneness of the

Church: that of the married and that of the unmarried, the second caste being considered more perfect in itself, whatever the shortcomings of individuals.

Once such a distinction is in effect, it is difficult not to remark that, in the context of the Church, the unmarried are of two kinds. There are those who pursue a life of wisdom or of a search for wisdom in monasteries and those who adopt the celibate state in order to be free for pastoral service. Clergy and monks are not celibate for the same reason, even if the ultimate justification of their life is their interior devotion to the expected kingdom of God. Hence, the distinction that was entertained in Counter-Reformation theology, with its mania for logic: monks and nuns are in a state of seeking perfection *(perfectionis acquirendae)*, and bishops are in a state of acquired perfection *(perfectionis acquisitae)*. This is clearly a purely formal distinction without connection to real life. And it suffers from two blatant gaps. Secular priests, who are neither monks nor bishops, are left high and dry, in total uncertainty as to where they stand in relation to perfection; and the married laity are implicitly excluded from any claim to perfection, even *acquirendae*.

This aspect of the Church's monasticity sets the stage for many of the conflicts that have in fact taken place. Beginning in the Carolingian age, a succession of political and theological quarrels agitated the Church. Clergy and laity fought each other over the investiture question when the lay nobility acquired rights of nomination and appointment to certain ecclesiastical positions. There were conflicts between pope and emperor, each vying for supremacy over the people of God; between kings and bishops, kings trying to lay their hands on ecclesiastical incomes; between bishops and monks, as in the protracted struggle over the doctrine of predestination between Archbishop Hincmar of Reims (c. 808-882) and the monk Godescalc (c. 803-867). Eventually, there were conflicts between the higher clergy, when bishops were mostly taken from the nobility and frequently had huge resources at their disposal, and the lower clergy, who belonged to the lower classes, were poorly educated, and often abjectly poor. Such conflicts came to a head on the eve of the French Revolution when people and clergy presented their *cahiers de doléances*, or lists of complaints, at the meeting of the General Estates of the kingdom.

Anti-Feminism

It was chiefly, though not exclusively, in monasteries that medieval civilization partially erased the differences of social status between men and women that had been inherited from the ancient world. Not only were the rules identical for monasteries of men and for those of women, but there were also "twin monasteries" comprising a house for women and one for men, both being under one head who was usually a woman, the abbess. At Fontevrault established in 1100, the founder, Robert d'Arbrissel (d. 1116/17), even required the abbess to have been married and to swear that she was not a virgin, though this was an unusual feature. In other foundations, as in the order of St. Bridget of Sweden (d. 1373), men were admitted only for the sacramental service of women: St. Bridget wanted them to be in the proportion of twelve to seventy-two! Men and women, whose tasks in society were in a relation of complementarity, stood, monastically, in a relation of identity. For monasticism implies, for both women and men, the transcendence of sexuality in a bridal relationship of the creature with God and with Christ in the Holy Spirit.

Furthermore, the medieval mind was not loath to apply to human reality the allegorical method that was commonly used in popular explanations of the Bible. Thus, the Cistercians developed the doctrine of the abbot's spiritual motherhood: the abbot is mother to the monks; in other words, he is really an abbess. And Hildegard of Bingen pushes allegory further. She sees the world as a cosmic egg in the bosom of God: God becomes the universal Mother. And this gives women a natural affinity with everything religious.

From the point of view of the religious status of women, the medieval Church was very open. And yet the monasticity of the Church was not able to balance the forces of anti-feminism that triumphed at the Renaissance when pagan antiquity and Roman law were idealized as models of civilization. In fact, the monastic institution itself was not exempt from some degree of anti-feminism. Women and men were not equal in the beginnings of monasticism. In the first place, the anachoretic life was not suitable for women, protection being needed from the banditry that was endemic in the remoter sections of the land. Unless women hermits lived close together, as they presumably did in the Egyptian desert where they counted in the thousands, the cenobitic life was safer. In the second place, women obtained their legal identity through men. When they began to form communities, these needed to be directly under the aegis of the bishop, for that was the only way the consecrated virgins could be saved from being forcefully married off by their male kin. In the third place, as soon as the religious life in Western Europe began to shift to non-monastic forms as in the friaries of the thirteenth century, women formed the "second order" in imitation of, and often in subordination to, the "first order," that of men. Soon afterwards, the Premonstratensian Canons and the Cistercians decided not to open any more monasteries for women, though such decrees were not universally applied. The powerful Benedictine order of Cluny, with hundreds of monasteries all over Europe, was never interested in nunneries. A movement for the curtailment of twin monasteries under an abbess began also in the thirteenth century. Yet abbesses with quasi-episcopal jurisdiction over priests lasted in Spain until 1873 when Pope Pius IX did away with the institution in the bull *Quae diversa*. The medieval episode was closed. Though the monastic model perdured, the actual monasticism of the Church had shrunk within the straitjacket of male domination.

Reformation

Whatever their immediate causes and their eventual solution, these various conflicts and tensions reveal the insufficiency of the monastic model for the Church as a whole. It was not by accident that one of the first major targets of the Reformation was the validity of monastic vows and of the clerical obligation of celibacy (*Augsburg Confession*, art. XXIII). But the abolition of mandatory celibacy for the clergy in the Churches that issued from the Reformation should not mislead us: the monastic ideal was not thereby made obsolete. What was in question in the sixteenth century was not the existence of authentic calls to consecrated virginity and to the single life for the sake of the gospel. It was not even the value of monastic forms and institutions for those who are led by the Spirit freely to choose them. It was the universal relevance of monasticity for the Church.

Yet elements of monasticity have remained in the Churches of the Reformation. Except in places where local history and situation account for another polity, bishops are elected, ministers are chosen just like the abbots and abbesses of monasteries. Daily liturgical prayer, where it is kept, is still modeled on the monastic office. In the sixteenth century itself, the monastic ideal found a refuge of sorts in the Spiritual Reformation when small groups of people who believed themselves especially chosen by God hoped to experience holiness and to find heaven in their very life on earth through the close fellowship of their communities. Subsequent movements of reform and renewal were still led by a search for a quasi-monastic ideal as is notable in Lutheran pietism, in the *Unitas fratrum* under the guidance of Count Zinzendorf (1700-1760), and in the Methodist movement under the impetus of John Wesley (1702-1791). In the late nineteenth century, the Holiness Churches, which are at the origin of the more recent charismatic movement, issued from a search that was not unlike the motivation for the foundation of religious orders. Instead of the monastery being, as in the Cistercian tradition, the school of perfection and the school of the love of God, the gathering of the faithful was to fulfill that role for its members. It was in the Holiness Churches that the movement for the equality of women and men in ministry found its most fruitful ground. In this, the Holiness Churches—free from the weight of clerical tradition—were simply carrying out a logic that is inscribed in the monastic ideal of equality by liberation from, and transcendence of, the divisive aspects of sexuality.

Monastic forms of Protestant life mushroomed in America in the eighteenth and nineteenth centuries, often no doubt tied with unorthodox doctrines, as with the Shakers of Ann Lee (1736-84) and in the Oneida Community (1848) and sometimes with no explicit connection with the Church, as in the literary and philosophical colony of Brook Farm (1841-47) that was related to Transcendentalism and to the birth of the Unitarian reform. In the nineteenth century, the Church of England experienced a remarkable revival of the monastic vocation with the recovery of the Benedictine life and the foundation of new religious communities, especially among women. And in the twentieth century, the Community of Taizé and several others came to life in Churches of Lutheran and of Calvinist traditions.

Monastic institutions have not always flourished. There are times when calls to the consecrated life seem to diminish both in numbers and in intensity. Indeed, our own period is apparently such a time. In the Orthodox Church, the monasteries, including those of the monastic republic of Mount Athos, have had few candidates for a long time. In the Catholic Church, the religious or consecrated life has been adapted to modern conditions, first through the emergence of "religious congregations with simple vows" that multiplied in the nineteenth century, then, under Pope Pius XII, with the creation of "secular institutes" whose members, united in spirituality and purpose, practice a looser form of community. Yet most religious orders have had a dearth of postulants since the end of Vatican Council II despite the importance that was recognized to them in chapter 6 of the constitution *Lumen gentium*. It may be that the time is ripe for new forms of the monastic tradition to emerge. Indeed, many "new communities" have arisen in recent years in Western Europe. Most of them are inspired by the charismatic movement. And in the freedom of the Spirit, they often are new kinds of communities, as most of them do not require vows and several make provision for the participation of married couples and their families.[3]

The Spiritual Hierarchy

There is nonetheless an aspect of the Church's monasticity that is now as alive as it ever was. Monasticity is not primarily a matter of escaping the world to retire in the closed garden of a sheltered community. It lives first of all in the hearts of the faithful when, in their love for Christ and their grateful reception of his gifts, they constitute, as it were, an "invisible monastery," a cloister "without walls." Monasticity, in this sense, is closely related to the Church's holiness.

In Vatican II's constitution, *Lumen gentium*, the chapter on the laity is followed by chapter 5, "On the universal call to holiness in the Church," and then by chapter 6, "On the Religious," and chapter 7, "On the eschatological character of the Pilgrim Church and its union with the Heavenly Church." Monasticity begins, not with the foundation of monasteries, but with the call of all to holiness. It is embodied in the many diverse forms taken through the centuries by the monastic institution and its sequels: the communities of canons of the eleventh century, the friaries of the thirteenth, the English recluses and the beguines of the Netherlands in the fourteenth century, the

[3]Pascal Pingault, *Renouveau de l'Eglise, Les Communautés Nouvelles* (Paris: Fayard, 1989).

Society of Jesus and other foundations in the sixteenth, the congregations with simple vows of the eighteenth and nineteenth centuries, the secular institutes of the twentieth, along with new communities that have grown out of the charismatic movement. But the multiplication of these forms of Christian life is no more than a flowering of the union between Christ and the trustful soul in which the eschatological unity of the Pilgrim Church and the Heavenly Church is already experienced on earth.

From Origen (185-255) and St. Gregory of Nyssa (bishop in 371) to contemporary authors, through the *Theologia germanica* edited by Martin Luther in 1516 and 1518 and the poems of St. John of the Cross, a steady stream of writings illustrate the existence in the Church of a "spiritual hierarchy." This is not tied to ordination and official functions, but only to God's call and the response to it that God's grace itself enables. Thus saints have been recognized. This has been done in many ways, from canonizations by popular acclaim to the formal procedures that have been used in the Roman Catholic Church since Pope Benedict XIV (pope, 1740-1758). Unofficially, saints have been recognized also in Protestantism, in which the memory of certain holy persons is cherished even in the absence of a formal cult of the saints.

Thus, a mystical tradition runs parallel to the doctrinal tradition. It relates to the way doctrine is experienced as life in the hearts of the faithful. One may see it as a hierarchy of holiness. It is not limited by the bounds of sex, by the conventions of society, or by the privileges of official functions. Many are the mystical tractates and "diaries of a soul" composed by women. Indeed, certain periods have seen a harvest of female spiritual authors. Such were the twelfth and thirteenth centuries with the mystical writings of Elizabeth of Schönau (1129-64), Hildegard of Bingen (1098-1179), Gertrude of Helfta (1256-1302), Mechtild of Magdeburg (1210-1295), Mechtild of Hackeborn (1241-99), Hadewijch of Antwerp (who wrote between 1230 and 1250). Hildegard, Catherine of Siena (d. 1380), Bridget of Sweden (c. 1303-1373), and, later, Teresa of Avila (1515-1582) corresponded with princes, kings, bishops, and popes, to tell them prophetically what they considered to be the will of God. Jeanne d'Arc (1412-1431), boldly speaking in the name of the king of Heaven, persuaded King Charles VII of France and his episcopal and lay advisers to let her guide an army of liberation in the name of what she held to be feudal and social justice. Pope Paul VI, in 1970, had the wisdom and courage to draw the proper conclusion when he proclaimed Teresa of Avila and Catherine of Siena "doctors of the Church."

Undoubtedly, there are other shadows to the picture of the Church's mosticity than the previously mentioned tensions and conflicts. In the Church, holiness can never be far from sinfulness. The spiritual hierarchy has been commonly ignored, often misunderstood, occasionally silenced, and even at times condemned by the magisterial hierarchy. It is by no means certain that Bossuet (1627-1704) was right in his attacks on Fénelon (1651-1715). Yet

Fénelon's book, *The Maxims of the Saints*, was condemned by Pope Innocent XII in 1699.[4] And Pope Clement XIV (pope, 1769-1774) disgraced himself and the whole Church when, bowing to political pressure and to Jansenist intrigues, he disbanded the Society of Jesus in 1773. (It was restored in 1814 by Pius VII). Worse, the monastic institution has itself been blind to the spiritual hierarchy in its midst. Such was the case in 1577-78 when, in application of decisions made at the General Chapter of the Carmelite Order in Piacenza (Italy) in May 1575, John of the Cross was incarcerated and maltreated by his confrères of the unreformed Carmel until he was able to escape after nine months of unmitigated hardships.

Yet signs of the continued assistance of the Spirit have never been missing, and the Church has been experienced as the locus where the holiness of Christ is extended to the members of his Mystical Body. As was commonly held in the Middle Ages, there is a strict correspondence between the Church, community of salvation, and the soul, depository of Christ's grace and holiness. Indeed, the Cistercian abbot, Isaac Stella (d. c. 1169), proclaimed in a sermon,

> One and the same thing is said universally of the Church, especially of Mary, singularly of the faithful soul . . . Christ remained nine months in the tabernacle of Mary's womb. He remains until the end of the world in the tabernacle of the Church's faith. He will remain for ever and ever in the knowledge and love of the faithful soul.[5]

In final analysis, monasticity is born of this correspondence in the community of the Church between collective and personal holiness. Its persistence through newly emerging forms bears continuing witness to this dimension of the holiness of the Church.

Esse *and* Bene esse

It is proper to ask at this point what theological note attaches to the monasticity of the Church. That conflicts have arisen precisely from the extension of the monastic ideal to the whole Church underlies one of the fundamental questions that were raised by Martin Luther: is monasticity essential to the Church of Christ, or is it only a historical, if also providential, accident?

The historical overview of the previous pages leads me to agree with Luther and the Confession of Augsburg (art. XXVII) that monasticism as institution is not essential to the Church. The gospel can, as a matter of

---

[4]George H. Tavard, *La Tradition au XVIIe siècle en France et en Angleterre* (Paris: Le Cerf, 1969), p. 191-193; 220-222.

[5]Quoted in de Lubac, l. c., p. 258-259.

principle, be preached and the sacraments administered without the monastic model. One may even wonder if the development of the monastic institution was not, in a sense, a mistake. As he reacted against the place taken by the monastic life in the late Middle Ages, against its neo-Pelagian interpretation as a capacity to merit divine rewards, and against the distortion of the gospel that was fostered by overemphasis on the monastic vows, Luther stressed the Christian holiness of all calls of life. He thus restored an often neglected point of the Catholic tradition: the whole of human life is renewed by the incarnation of the Word of God.

Yet something needs to be added. It is theoretically impossible to reshape the history of the Church to our liking. And it is practically impossible to eradicate the monastic element and inspiration from the structure and life of the Church. Even the Reformation was unable to do it. One may appeal here to the Anglican distinction between *esse* and *bene esse*, between the essence and the welfare of the Church. Monasticism is not of the *esse* of the Christian Church if one means by this that there must absolutely be monasteries of some sort for the life and fidelity of the Church to be truly authentic.

Nonetheless, being the most basic form in which the Church's conciliarity has been transmitted, monasticity certainly belongs to the *bene esse* of the Church. The Church does not cease to exist if and when its leadership fails to recognize the call of a few to a consecrated life of service and prayer, to discern the marks of holiness in the life of the faithful and in the experience and writings of the Christian mystics, or if and when the bishops of the Church are so involved in the tasks of this world as to lose the sense of life in the Spirit and to forget the eschatological dimension of the gospel. Whenever this happens, the holiness of the Church lies in kenotic latency until the Spirit enables new prophets to recognize the traces of the Heavenly Church in the Earthly. Meanwhile, the Church exists in a kind of "Babylonian captivity," in a paradoxical state of self-contradiction and self-condemnation.

The credal marks of the Church and the qualities that are characteristic of its life are at the same time principles, realities, and hopes. Yet this is by no means a frozen trilogy. One aspect is often more evident than the others. The principle is not always visibly embodied in the reality, yet thanks to the Spirit, it can never be lost and those in the Church who thirst for holiness and justice are therefore never without hope.

Mary as Icon

This perspective throws light on the place that is occupied by the Virgin Mary in the doctrine and piety of the Orthodox and the Catholic Churches. Following Martin Luther's emphasis on justification by faith alone through Christ alone, the Protestant Churches have in general abstained from focusing the holiness of the Church on any one other than Christ and on anything other than the twofold way of the communication of Christ, the Word and the sacraments. But the Orthodox and the Catholic traditions have celebrated the presence of the holy, not only in the word and in the sacraments, but also in the saints, thus placing the spiritual hierarchy at the summit of the Christian ladder. As divine grace comes down through the word that is read, spoken, preached, and meditated, and through the sacraments that are offered and received, so does it return to its source in the saints' ascent to God. And first among these is the Virgin Mary.[6]

The Mary of the annunciation, Handmaid of the Lord and Theotokos, the Virgin Mother of the Savior, has been seen as the first in the spiritual hierarchy, higher than all angels and than all the saints who, canonized and not, are gathered in God's eternity in the Heavenly Church. From the patristic interpretation of the Scriptures, Orthodox and Catholic theologians have concluded that, by God's grace and gift, Mary kept her virginity throughout her life—not by way of selfish self-centeredness but as God's holy gift for the sake of her Son. They have also concluded that the Virgin was all-holy throughout her life. To these basic doctrines, later meditation about Mary's end and beginning added the belief that her life on earth was immediately crowned by her Dormition or Assumption when she was taken body and soul to heaven and the correlate belief that she was exempt from original sin whether a short time after her conception (Orthodox and medieval Catholics) or in her very conception (more recent Catholics). Mary's Immaculate Conception was defined a first time by the conciliarist council of Basle in 1438 and a second time by Pope Pius IX in 1854. Her Assumption into heaven at the end of her earthly life was defined by Pope Pius XII in 1950.

These doctrines are relevant to ecclesiology and to the awareness of being the Church because of the traditional ties between Mary and the Church in the Catholic imagination. The expectation of the eschaton implies much more than a hope in the promises of God for the end of time. These promises are presented symbolically in the Scriptures as the transformation of the cosmos into a new heaven and a new earth and as the descent of the New Jerusalem from heaven. To this, the tradition has added that the face of the New Jerusalem is already known. It is seen in the icons of Orthodoxy, which image God's gift of holiness and glory, and primarily in the icons of the Theotokos. It is seen in the Virgin Mary as she is venerated in East and West under a multitude of appellations and representations, not least under many symbols and titles that are attached to holy places and shrines where the faithful often believe that the Mother of God has appeared at various times to privileged seers. All such apparitions are historically doubtful, and they may often be explained by reference to natural phenomena such as halluci-

---

[6]George H. Tavard, *The Forthbringer of God: St. Bonaventure on the Virgin Mary* (Chicago: Franciscan Herald Press, 1989).

nations, extra-sensory perceptions, or illusions.[7] But the questionable historicity of such episodes is of little importance to devotion. What matters in the long run is the sensed presence of the eschaton, of the Heavenly Church, in the midst of the faithful who persevere in their earthly pilgrimage to the Holy City of God.

What the members of the more traditional Churches perceive of the eschaton in the pictures of the Theotokos and of the saints, the Protestant faithful tend to experience in the warm singing that has been nurtured among them—especially, following Martin Luther himself, by Lutheran chorals and following John and Charles Wesley, by the hymnody of the early Methodists. As the eschaton is affirmed and desired, the community at prayer knows itself to be anticipating the last days and already participating in Christ's ultimate triumph over sin and death. The Church that the faithful experience is the community of salvation, the holy Assembly of God, the Upper Room of the disciples, the gathering of the saints, the full number of the elect, the herald of Christ's second coming, the mystical garden of the Lord.

The monasticity of the Church has its focal point precisely in the joyful discernment of the eschaton. In the words of Vatican Council II,

> All of us who are children of God and who form one family in Christ (cf. Heb. 3:6), when we are in communion with one another in mutual love and in the one praise of the Holy Trinity, we respond together to the Church's intimate vocation and we participate in a foretaste of the liturgy of consummate glory (LG, n. 51).

For Further Reading

Maurus Wolter. *The Principles of Monasticism*. St. Louis: Herder Book Co., 1962.

Gustave Martelet. *The Church's Holiness and Religious Life*. St. Mary's, Kansas: Review of Religious, 1966.

George H. Tavard. *Woman in Christian Tradition*. Notre Dame: University of Notre Dame Press, 1973.

Avery Dulles. *The Resilient Church. The Necessity and Limits of Adaptation*. New York: Doubleday, 1977.

Basil Pennington. *Called: New Thinking on Christian Vocation*. New York: Seabury, 1983.

Matthew Fox, (ed.). *Illuminations of Hildegard of Bingen*. Santa Fe: Bear & Co., 1985.

---

[7]Michael Carroll, *The Cult of the Virgin Mary: Psychological Origins* (Princeton: Princeton University Press, 1986).

PART THREE

STRUCTURES

In the first two parts of the present study, we have explored what may be called the deep structures of the Church. This linguistic expression is enlightening at this point as it well conveys the dimension of interiority that is hidden under the veil of what is seen of the Church. There are invisible elements within the Church, or in a more hazardous vocabulary, there is an invisible Church. Yet the grouping of Jesus' disciples is patterned on an incarnational analogy grounded in the belief that the Word became flesh (John 1:14). The gathering of the disciples cannot be a quasi-Platonic communion purely interior and largely invisible to the eyes of the world. But the law of incarnation applies to the disciples no less than to the Lord whom they profess to follow. The Christian Community of salvation has surface structures no less than deep structures. These surface structures have grown out of the primal "vision" of the revelation that emerges from the Scriptures. Their shaping has followed the gradual implementation of *diakonia, koinonia,* and *leiturgia* in the disciples' life and relationships. They have evolved slowly through the tradition, and they have been molded by fundamental images into conciliar and monastic forms.

The surface structures of the Christian Church should evidently be such as will promote the preaching of the gospel to all nations. But since the preaching of the gospel and its efficacy depend radically on the Holy Spirit and not on human schemes and planning, human reason cannot arrive at a theoretical conception of what would be the optimal structures for such a task. An *a priori* ecclesiology or a speculative "ideal of the Christian Church" cannot possibly do justice to the freedom of the Spirit of God. This is the basic weakness of the deductive ecclesiologies that draw normative ecclesial structures from what can only be incidental indications in the New Testament. This weakness is endemic in all the attempts that have been made, notably in

Catholic and in Calvinist circles, to elicit a "divine constitution" of the Church from the Scriptures or from the tradition. There is no other way to delineate the Church's surface structures than *a posteriori*, after these structures have emerged from providential guidance of the Christian community.

Since the preaching of the gospel consists in announcing the Word of God to a pagan world, the Church's structures are missionary in intent and ministerial in form. They derive from, and in turn determine, the necessity to minister to—that is, to serve—the members of the people of God. And this in a twofold sense: the structures must nurture the people through the service of the Word and the sacraments, and they must enable the Church to answer the missionary call to carry the gospel to all nations.

It is debatable whether one should start from the broad notion of ministry or from the specific Christian experience of Word and sacraments. Either way has its validity. Ministry is unintelligible without reference to Word and sacraments, and Word and sacraments would not be available without the Church's ministry since Christian believers experience the Word not only in reading the Scriptures but also in hearing the gospel proclaimed and in partaking of the traditional sacraments.

We will begin with the Church's ministerial structures (ch. 8), then continue with the normative aspect that is taken on by these structures when they become magisterial (ch. 9). From the communication of divine grace that enables it to preach the gospel and to administer the sacraments, the Church relates to the whole world according to God's creative purpose. Both as ministerial and as magisterial, the ecclesial structures exist in interconnection with the world. But this relation is not a simple affair since the world has its proper integrity apart from the visible structures of the Church. It is, in addition, infinitely varied and much more so than was taken for granted until the present century. This undoubtedly raises new questions for ecclesiology as it opens up new dimensions in the experience of being the Church in its cosmic setting (ch. 10).

8

Ministerium

The Church is to be found wherever the Word is preached and the sacraments are administered according to the gospel (CA, art. V). On this twofold criterion, the Reformers based their understanding of the Church. The Catholic tradition may well be satisfied with the same principle. Yet the Church is not defined in two competing ways, according to the Word and according to the sacraments. These undoubtedly correspond to the chief pastoral tasks of Christian ministers. The Church's ministerial structure has been focused on activities relating to the Word and to the sacraments. All other areas of concern in the care of soul such as catechetical education, spiritual counselling, initiation into prayer, the direction of consciences, spiritual and physical healing, the service of the poor and afflicted are always directed, in the long or the short run, to a better ministry of Word and sacrament.

It follows that there is not one structure of ministry for the Word and another for the sacraments. The Church is structured around one ministry, but this ministry exists in diverse modes and may be looked at from different angles. In fact, the Churches of divided Christendom have often found their specific characteristic and ethos in the choice of a vantage point from which they have organized ministry, and they have justified this organization theologically.

Common Priesthood and Special Ministries

Several points appear clearly in the New Testament regarding the ministry of the Christian Church and its structure.

In the course of his own ministry in Palestine, Jesus assigns a mission to all those who believe in him. He sends the Twelve to the people of Israel with power to drive away evil spirits and to heal all infirmities (Matt 10:1-15). According to Luke, he also sends seventy (or seventy-two) disciples two by two to all the cities where he intends to go, and they drive evil spirits away in his name (Luke 10:1-17). After the resurrection, he sends all the disciples, represented by the Eleven, Judas being gone, to baptize all nations (Matt 28:19).

After the destruction of the Temple, later reflection led to a sharp distinction between the Christian ministry and the Old Testament priesthood. Under the new covenant in Christ, there are no priests (*iereis*) in the old sense of the term. Rather, the entire people of the Church is priestly (1 Pet 2:9). Jesus Christ is the only "high priest" (Heb 5:5). Indeed, Jesus was never a levitical priest at the service of the Temple. The priesthood that is ascribed to him is of another kind, "according to the order of Melchisedek" (Heb 5:10). It is therefore, in the eyes of Christians, anterior to the Aaronic priesthood of Mosaic times and, still more, to the Zadokite priesthood of the Temple. Jesus became a priest—indeed, *the* High Priest—after his resurrection and ascension when he entered the Holy of Holies in heaven with the blood of his sacrifice (Heb 9:12). His high priesthood is modeled on that of the Temple, but it is implemented only in heaven where it is operative for all times, thus assuring the universality of God's salvific action.

All Christian believers are closely associated to the high priesthood of Christ. In the Epistle to the Hebrews, they are related to it passively in that they are saved by it and they receive the fruits of it in grace. Both the First Epistle of Peter and the Book of Revelation, however, open a further perspective—the faithful being associated actively to the high priesthood of Christ. They now are, in contrast with the people of the old covenant, "the chosen race, the royal palace (*basileion*), the college of priests (*hierateuma*), the holy nation, the people set apart . . ." (1 Pet 2:9). The Book of Revelation adds a clarification that ties together the passive and the active dimensions. It is their redemption by the blood of Christ that has made the faithful "a kingdom, priests before his God and Father" (Rev 1:5-6). The only acceptable sacrifice is Christ's own. And it is offered to God in the Church, not by a select group of Levites but by the entire people.

The association of the faithful to Christ's exclusive high priesthood has been traditionally called the general priesthood, common priesthood, or royal priesthood of all believers. The notion of priesthood is appropriate here since all the faithful take part together in the Eucharistic meal and offering that is at the heart of Christian worship. Given the formulae of the New Testament and the nature of the Eucharistic experience, it is manifest that this priesthood is not individual. Not any one of the faithful has priestly status in isolation from the others. It is the collectivity that is priestly in its doxological worship of God through Christ the High Priest. The priesthood of the people is corporate. It is communicated virtually to all believers through their baptism and is actuated in them by their Eucharistic participation.

There is no opposition at this point between the task of all the disciples and the specific mission of the Twelve. This mission was truly foundational:

the Twelve were eye-witnesses of the resurrection of Christ. It also was symbolic and eschatological: they were "to judge the twelve tribes of Israel" (Matt 19:28). Yet there is a basic oddity in regard to the Twelve. Except for Peter, they did nothing that the authors of the New Testament deemed worth recording! In the Church's memory, it is to the other "apostles" of the New Testament that was due the spread of the gospel. These were missionaries who were commissioned for various tasks. Thus Barnabas and Paul were sent by the Church in Antioch, first to represent it in Jerusalem and then to preach the gospel among the Gentiles. There may well have been such women-apostles as for instance the Junia of Romans 16:7 or the Prisca of Acts 18. The chief task of these missionaries was to establish Christian communities throughout the Roman empire and perhaps—though documentation is lacking on this point—beyond its borders. Paul, however, may have been in a unique position in that he claimed—and apparently was recognized—apostleship not on the basis of the commission he had from the Church in Antioch but on account of a direct divine revelation, including a vision of the risen Christ (Gal 1:16; 2:6; 1 Cor 9:1).

As one gathers from the Epistles and from the Acts of the Apostles, the first communities of Christian believers were organized around presiding officers, approximately on the model of the synagogues. James, one of the "brothers of the Lord," presided in Jerusalem (cf. Acts 12:17). The Beloved Disciple presided over certain communities that recognized his unique relationship to Jesus. Paul, "apostle to the Gentiles" (Gal 2:8), was the chief officer for the communities he established in the Diaspora. As he moved on to other cities, he appointed officers who represented him and were designated by various terms: overseers (*episcopoi*) in Paul's letters, elders (*presbyteroi*) or overseers in the Acts of the Apostles. In addition, the communities used the services of a multitude of other ministers. In Jerusalem, the Twelve called a meeting of the disciples who themselves appointed the seven, ostensibly to serve food to poor widows, thus freeing the apostles for evangelistic preaching (Acts 6:1-6). But some of the seven also preached the gospel (Stephen, in Acts 6:8 ff.; Philip, in Acts 8:5 ff.). There were also prophets and teachers (1 Cor 12:28), deacons (1 Tim 3:8-12), women deacons (Rom 16:1), and many others according to their gifts (1 Cor 12:4-11).

Early Developments

The early history of the Church saw certain developments of this basic pattern. Some lines appear clearly. In whatever form and with whatever title, all ministry has its archetypal model in Jesus himself as he is remembered in the memory of the communities. The central task is to set a good example for Christian life and to provide spiritual leadership. One cannot know who presided over the Eucharistic meals of the earliest communities.

Neither the apostles nor Paul himself are ever mentioned as presiding over such a meal. Yet the task of presiding over the Eucharist was soon reserved to overseers and presbyters, and most probably also to prophets, as appears in the *Didachè*.[1]

As early as the writings of Ignatius of Antioch (c. 115), there is evidence of a streamlining of official ministry. The ministry follows a threefold pattern comprising bishops (one bishop for one community), presbyters (who form a presbyterium or council around the bishop), and deacons. Where the threefold ministry is established, it is the bishop who presides at the Eucharist, presbyters, but not deacons, doing so in his absence. Nonetheless, the threefold pattern was not adopted everywhere at the same time. In Rome itself, neither the *Letter of Clement to the Corinthians* (c. 95) nor the *Shepherd* of Hermas alludes to the presence of a bishop in the community: the *Letter of Clement* is sent in the name of the presbyterium, and the *Shepherd* alludes vaguely to "the shepherds" of the Church. In these conditions, it is impossible to ascertain whether the first bishops were designated as such by the founders of Churches, as Paul selected Titus as his personal delegate (Titus 1:5), or whether they simply were presbyters to whom special responsibilities were entrusted by the community or by their peers.

In the oldest ordination rituals that have been preserved (Hippolytus, *The Apostolic Tradition*, c. 200), it is by the laying on of hands that bishops, presbyters, and deacons are designated on the model of the sending of Paul and Barnabas by the Church in Antioch (Acts 13:3) and of what was believed to be a laying on of hands on Timothy by the elders (1 Tim 4:14) or by Paul (2 Tim 1:6). At least in Greek areas, women as well as men are included among deacons, though not among priests or bishops.

The Christological Center

When the relevant facts regarding the origins of the Christian ministry are interpreted theologically, two dimensions emerge. First, far from diminishing its essential dependence upon Christ and the Spirit, the evolution of the Christian ministry emphasizes this dependence. Second, the actual structure of the ministry derives from its ecclesial context.

The most striking phenomenon in the evolution of the Christian ministry was undoubtedly the eventual return of the faithful to the sacral language that was used in the Old Testament to designate those who served the Temple. By the end of the second century, the ordained ministers that were originally called overseers (bishops) and elders (presbyters) were also named *iereis* (*sacerdotes*, priests). There is no clear documentation for the adoption of this sacral vocabulary. How and when it was done are matters of conjecture.

[1] *Didachè* X, 7 (*The Apostolic Fathers*, vol. I, l. c., p. 325).

As to why, there is a hypothesis that seems fairly certain: it presumably derives from early applications to the Eucharist of the sacrificial language that was used in the Epistle to the Hebrews for the heavenly presence of the risen Christ. Since the risen Christ, who is now in heaven as the high priest of his own sacrifice, is also present in the Eucharistic celebrations of the community, this ecclesial presence may be seen as sacrificial, on the model of Christ's presence in heaven as described in the Epistle to the Hebrews. This passage to a sacral vocabulary for the ministry may have been hastened by the progressive abandonment of the early Christian hope that Christ would soon return and by the ensuing feeling that since his high priesthood in heaven is effective among the faithful in their liturgy, it must be somehow represented in it.

The sacral vocabulary that was used for the heavenly presence of Christ was thus read back into the account of the passion and death of Jesus. The events of the passion, including the Last Supper, were deemed to be themselves sacrificial. As the Eucharist comes from, and reenacts, the Last Supper, so president of the Eucharist was seen to represent the High Priest.

This change of vocabulary highlights the close relationships that unite Christ the high priest and the ministers chosen by the community, who are empowered by Christ himself through the Holy Spirit to act liturgically in his name. It logically entails the assumption that those who preside at the Eucharist participate in a special way in the priesthood of Christ. This is the starting point of the doctrine that was formulated at Vatican Council II: "The common priesthood of the faithful and the ministerial or hierarchic priesthood . . . differ in essence and not only in degree. . . ." (LG, n. 10).

The participation of ordained priests in the high priesthood of Christ led to the doctrine, stressed by St. Augustine against the Donatists, that it is Christ who acts through the priest in the sacraments. The standard Catholic expression reverses this and says that the priest acts *in persona Christi*. Originally a juridical notion, this formula expresses the belief that the priest acts by the power of Christ just as various officials of the empire acted by the power vested in them by the emperor. Yet it soon acquired a more ontological sense: Christ is mystically present in the bishops who "by the Holy Spirit who has been given them have been made true and authentic teachers of the faith, pontiffs and pastors" (CD, n. 2) and in the priests who preside at the Eucharist.

The Ecclesial Context

In the Catholic understanding of ministry, this early history remains normative. The Church is not free to depart from the form of the ministry that was established in the patristic period. The reason for this is to be found in what is considered the normative force of the tradition embodied in ecumenical councils. By the time of the last ecumenical council of East and West

(Nicaea II, 787), the general priesthood of all the faithful was universally recognized, and the Eucharistic or ministerial priesthood was generally responsible for the leadership of the Church. These two priesthoods typified two fundamental aspects of the Church's ministry. The Church offers to God the sacrifice of praise through the faith and actions of a holy life, by which all the faithful witness to God and to Christ before the world. And the Church also continually presents to God the sacrifice of Christ through the service of Thanksgiving (Eucharist) that is led by bishops and priests, with the assistance of deacons, in the local gathering of the whole Church.

In the course of history, there have been variations in peripheral aspects that did not affect the threefold pattern of ministry or the basic relation of the common ministry and the ministry of the ordained. Thus, the Christian emperors exercised a general supervision of the external affairs of the Church, including the convocation of ecumenical councils; and later kings occasionally wielded similar powers over the Church in their land. The ministry of bishops evolved in the details of its exercise. As church order modeled itself on the imperial organization, some bishops acquired authority over other bishops, becoming metropolitans, archbishops, and primates. Finally, special authority was recognized to the bishops of sees that were believed to have been directly founded by apostles. These were the bishops of Rome, Alexandria, Antioch, and Jerusalem. Constantinople was added to the list when importance was given to the legend of St. Andrew who would have founded an episcopal see in Byzantium, the fishing village that Emperor Constantine transformed into the new capital of the Roman Empire, the "Second Rome." Constantinople was even placed second on the list because of the centrality of the new capital and in deference to the emperor. This was the point of canon 28 of the council of Chalcedon, even though the papal legates rejected it.

The powers of bishops have varied according to circumstances of time and place. In some areas the predominance and power of monasteries left the bishop with purely liturgical functions, as was long the case in Celtic lands.

The Pneumatological Principle

The Christological center establishes a norm of worship and teaching that is to be followed and protected in all the acts of ministry and of the Ministry. The ecclesial context gives value to these acts by setting them in the *koinonia* of the faithful with Christ and with one another. But it is only by the continuing action of the Spirit of God and of Christ that the ministerial actions convey divine grace. When the Reformers in the sixteenth century underlined the doctrine that divine grace reaches the faithful through two privileged channels, the teaching of the gospel and the administration of the sacraments, *ministerium docendi evangelium et porrigendi sacramenta* (CA, art. V; see art. XIX in the Thirty-Nine Articles, and art. XIII in the Methodist Articles), they gave a valid formulation of the Catholic tradition, if at least the Scriptures are not believed to reduce the sacraments to the two explicitly mentioned in the New Testament, baptism and Eucharist.

Teaching the gospel and preaching the Word in the liturgy are the special task of ordained ministers. These are guided and supervised by the bishops in their dioceses. Yet all the faithful must also teach the gospel and preach the Word by the witness of a holy life in imitation of Christ for the sake of God and neighbor and, when opportune, by the public testimony of their faith.

The administration of sacraments is also in principle the task of ordained ministers. Their chief administrator is the bishop, who provides for their availability to the faithful through the ordination and appointment of priests and deacons. Yet baptism and, at least in the Middle Ages, the sacrament of reconciliation may, when necessary, be administered by lay persons; and the ministers of matrimony are, in Latin theology, the woman and man who are being married. In contrast, the normal minister of confirmation and of orders is the bishop, even though he may delegate priests to administer confirmation and there were instances in the later Middle Ages when the bishop of Rome authorized a number of Cistercian and Benedictine abbots to ordain their monks.

These variations and exceptions illustrate the principle that there is nothing automatic about the administration of sacraments. The category of magic does not apply. The sacraments are a function of the Church's life in its evolving context as the Church is guided by the Spirit in the service of God and of God's creation. Even when they are said to act *ex opere operato* ("by virtue of the action performed"), the proper reception and the effectiveness of the sacraments in conveying God's grace presuppose faith in the recipient. This axiom expresses the Catholic principle embodied in the decrees of the council of Trent (sess. VII [1547], can. 8: DS, n. 1609) that the value of a sacrament is independent of the holiness of its minister.

In both preaching the word and administering the sacraments, the Church is guided by the Holy Spirit. By the power of the Spirit, the sacraments—elemental gestures to which the Word is added, in St. Augustine's analysis[2]—are channels of God's grace. And it is the Spirit who persuades the faithful of the truths of faith that are expounded in the proclamation of the Word. In this way, there is ensured in the people of God a fundamental harmony between the *sensus fidelium* and the teaching of the ministers to which it assents. Vatican II called this "a singular conspiracy of bishops and faithful" (DV, n. 10). Here again, the experience of being the Church is radically Trinitarian. Not only are ministers aware of acting "in the person of Christ"

---

[2]Augustine's basic definition of a sacrament is: *Accedit verbum ad elementum, et fit sacramentum, etiam ipsum tanquam visibile verbum* ("The word comes to the element, and the sacrament is made, being itself like a visible word" [*In Johannis Evangelium Tractatus 80*, 3, PL, 35, 1840]).

when they administer the sacraments. They also know that they act "in the person of the Holy Spirit" when they preach and explain the Word. And the faithful themselves recognize the voice of Christ and the finger of the Holy Spirit in the guidance of the community. It is for this reason that Martin Luther and the Lutheran tradition have emphasized the point that "the preaching of the gospel is the gospel." In turn, the listening faithful, whether they are themselves ordained or not, become one with the Word of God by faith when they hear the human words of the preaching of the gospel. This results, as John Calvin explained, from the silent testimony of the Spirit in their heart.

Episcopal Stability

In 867 Boris, khan of the Bulgars (852-889), asked Pope Nicholas I (pope, 858-867) to send him Formosus (c. 816-896) as bishop. He met with a flat refusal. Formosus, who had been previously commissioned by the Pope to instruct the Bulgars in the faith, was already bishop of Porto, Italy. The Pope could easily have foreseen that the transfer of Formosus to a see among the Bulgars would attach their nation directly to Rome rather than to the patriarchate of Constantinople. Yet he decided to abide by an old canonical principle: bishops may not be transferred from see to see. The theological reason for this stemmed from the analogy of marriage: a bishop is married to his see and its people, and this bond is unbreakable. For this reason too it would have been abnormal for a bishop to be elected to the see of Rome. For many centuries, the pope was normally chosen from the priests and deacons of the city, and Formosus was a Roman by origin. Yet at the time Pope Nicholas made his response to Khan Boris, the old principle was about to be disregarded: after a checkered career in which he was deposed and excommunicated, restored to lay communion and then to his see, Formosus himself became bishop of Rome in 891. However, the double breach of his marriage with the diocese of Porto (by deposition and by promotion) was easily exploited by his political adversaries. After his death, all his acts including the ordinations he had made were declared invalid by Stephen VI (pope, 896-897). Restored to validity by John IX (pope, 898-900), they were again declared null and void by Sergius VIII (pope, 904-911).

The old rule against the transfer of bishops had a logical counterpart in the requirement that there be only one bishop for one see. The appointment and ordination of "auxiliary bishops" is an untraditional accretion that can be justified only on grounds of expediency. Since the bishop should be for his people the chief institutional sign and instrument of unity, this basic symbolism of the episcopate is lost when several bishops work together in the administration of one diocese. The canonical distinction between "ordinary" and "auxiliary" bishops does not suffice to restore the proper symbolism of the episcopal function. And the appointment of auxiliary bishops to non-existent sees *in partibus infidelium* is only a legal fiction with a remote foundation in history since those sees did formerly exist, but with no correspondence in contemporary reality.

Both rules have now been disregarded for centuries, at least in Roman Catholicism. They probably cannot be restored. Yet when they were understood, they vividly expressed the ministerial principle that a bishop's vocation is to serve the people of a given area. "Bishops," Vatican Council II declared, "should be in the midst of their people as those who serve" (CD, n. 16). But if that is where they are, that is logically where they ought to stay. The only logical alternative to episcopal stability lies in another principle that has been operative among bishops in American Methodism: they are not elected or ordained to a see but to the service of the whole Church, that is, in practice, to the board of bishops, or, in more Catholic language, to the episcopal college as a whole, from which they are then sent to serve the Church in a given territory.

Vatican II in fact achieved an uneasy compromise between the two principles. A bishop, it taught, is ordained into the episcopal college, yet he is also assigned to a local (diocesan) Church where his authority derives directly from Christ through ordination and not through the medium of his appointment (that is normally through the bishop of Rome in the Latin rite), so that a bishop is truly a "vicar of Christ" and not a vicar of the Roman Pontiff (LG, n. 27).

This compromise barely hides a latent conflict between the bishops' ministerial function to serve the people and their magisterial task to teach the people. Because of the multiplicity of needs, ministry necessarily branches out into a multiformity of services. Stability is less important than efficiency. Teaching, however, because it requires continuity and coherence, is generally better served by uniformity than by diversity. It is of course assumed that all bishops teach the same doctrine, and for that reason their transfer from one see to another is not seen as a disservice to continuity of teaching. And the administrative models of business and of public administration encourage the promotion of the more successful to more difficult and more influential positions. This, however, illustrates the unfortunate adoption by the Church of secular rather than theological standards of government.

Structural Tensions

The internal structure of the people of God guarantees and protects a fundamental harmony. Yet it has also been a source of conflicts. Indeed, it cannot avoid being a potential source of conflicts. This is, so to say, the other side of the coin. That there are thus two aspects to the Church's structure is in fact not a modern discovery. Given his concern for "fittingness" in theological argumentation and in the Church's life, St. Bonaventure, in the thirteenth century, was able to envision the Church's structure from two distinct points of view: historical and esthetic. Esthetically, he followed Pseudo-Dionysius and viewed the Church as patterned on the choirs of angels which were themselves patterned on the interrelationships of the three Persons in God. Historically, Bonaventure also understood that the Church's ministerial structure results from temporal causes.[3] After the bitter experience of the Reformation and the Counter-Reformation, modern times have added to such a bi-polar approach the surprising perception that the two aspects of the Church may well be antagonistic. By the same token, when the conflictual nature of these dimensions of the Church's structure emerged in the sixteenth century, it raised a further question: is the Church's structure necessarily permanent?

The Church and its hierarchy have indeed evolved out of their semitic source through a succession of historical circumstances of a more or less accidental character in which national rivalries, political conflicts, social pressure, cultural prejudices, philosophical and theological options, and even economic necessities have had their share. Had these circumstances been other than they were, the Church's structure would presumably have followed a different path. In this perspective, there undoubtedly is something providential, but nothing inherently necessary, in the distinctions between Jews and Gentiles, between lay people and clerics, in the opposition of life in a cloister to life "in the world," in the evolving shape of cooperation within the threefold form of the ordained ministry. Likewise, there is nothing that is intrinsically necessary in the conflictual relationship of male and female. Already, but somewhat prematurely, the very distinction between the sexes was declared abolished by St. Paul for those who have "put on Christ" in baptism (Gal 3:28). It follows that there is nothing absolute in the traditional exclusion of women from ordination to the priesthood. This was in part the result of cultural views of womanhood that were inherited from Judaism, from Greece, from Rome, and from the Germanic tribes of central and western Europe. Its inclusion in medieval canon law reflected immemorial practice as well as the male prejudices of those who held power in society and in the Church. In turn, the practice has been the cause of further "patriarchal" attitudes by which women have generally been, in the Church no less than in society, dominated by men regardless of their capacities, their education, and their achievements.

As has already been mentioned, there were numerous exceptions to this attitude in the medieval Church. In France, the Salic law had been inherited from the Germanic ancestors of the French, the Salic Franks: it made unlawful the transmission of the monarchy to or through a woman so that the

---

[3]Tavard, "Succession et ordre dans la structure de l'Eglise," Guy Bougerol, ed., *S. Bonaventure. 1274-1974*, vol. IV, *Theologica* (Grottaferrata: Collegio S. Bonaventura, 1974), p. 421-446.

crown could only pass from the king to his nearest male relative. Yet in France itself, the Capetian monarchy admitted exceptions to the Salic law when they were convenient. And in any case, the Salic law was exceptional. Other tribes and nations admitted the monarchy of queens. The queens who reigned over England in their own name were even anointed, like the kings, with the same holy chrism that was used for confirmation and ordination. Furthermore, the authoritative intervention of queens in the Church's life was not unusual. It was believed that St. Helena (d. c. 330), the mother of Emperor Constantine, had copresided with him and with Pope Sylvester (pope, 314-335) over a synod of Rome. Pope Adrian I (pope, 772-795) even argued from this to justify Empress Irene's convocation of, and address to, Nicaea Council II in 787. St. Margaret of Scotland (c. 1050-1093), married to King Malcolm, presided over the Scottish synods that changed the liturgy from a Celtic to a Roman model. In a sense, then, kings and queens had a ministry to the Church in their land by virtue of their anointment or enthronement which could be related sacramentally to confirmation or to orders. Undoubtedly, the problem of the ecclesial ministry of kings and queens has been made obsolete by the all but universal adoption of republican forms of government after the example of the American and the French Revolutions. Yet the questions thus raised and the tensions between the ministry of the laity and that of the clergy have remained in other forms and settings.

Whether the emergence of the ministry of the bishop of Rome in the episcopal college was itself necessary is a question that may also be asked. Whether the forms taken by this ministry are themselves permanent may be considered. Seen as a historical phenomenon, this central element of the ecclesial structure of catholicity appears to be in the same category as the institution of the cardinalate. They are the fruits of temporary or local conditions. Yet given the continuing fidelity of most believers to the service of the communion, these institutions have acquired conservative features, as though they necessarily were permanent or quasi-permanent institutions. The question will be examined in the next chapter. Yet it is properly mentioned at this point. For it also illustrates the tensions that are unavoidable and the conflicts that have erupted in the Church.

In the light of the antagonistic aspect of the Church's structure, it is not surprising that at certain periods of turmoil the normativity of this structure has been challenged and various segments of Christian believers have acquired other, more or less different, ministerial structures more patriarchal than papal, more presbyteral than episcopal, or more congregational than presbyteral. Whether the change has been for the better or for the worse is itself debatable. But this is not the point. The point is that the possibility of the challenges that gave birth to such changes was already implicit in the very structure that was challenged.

Ecclesia reformata

It is not only the Churches that issued from the sixteenth-century Reformation that have been reformed. The history of the Church as a whole traces a curve along which sundry elements of the ministerial structure have evolved in their responsibilities, their interrelationships, and their theological underpinning. Any one of the four credal marks of the Church has taken several shapes. The two marks that were emphasized by the Protestant reformers, relating to the preaching of the Word and to the administration of the sacraments, have also been practiced and understood differently in successive ages. The development of the patriarchates out of earlier regional primacies (as the predominance of Churches established by apostles), that of the papacy out of the patriarchates (as the predominance of the Church established in Rome by Peter and Paul), that of the cardinalate out of the papacy (as an extension of powers originally attributed to the deacons of the diocese of Rome) have been sensed by diverse groups of believers as undue human accretions, as the results of providential guidance, as implicitly in harmony with the Scriptures, and even as explicitly taught in them. The parallel development of monasticism in all its forms, from the hermits of Egypt to the "new communities" that have issued from the "charismatic" ferment that followed Vatican Council II, are other examples of the fundamental reformability of the Church. The influence of monastic reforms on the reform of the Church at large is a well documented fact. The doctrinal predominance of certain theological centers at certain periods, and notably of the University of Paris between the twelfth and the late fifteenth century, added a further dimension of variability to the Church's structure.

Thus every Church at any time, even in its most conservative forms, is an *Ecclesia reformata*: what it is, is due to a series of past reforms, some of which were so slow that they were hardly noticed in their time.

semper reformanda

By the same token, there is no reason to think that structural reforms of the Church are likely to stop at any given time, as though miraculously frozen for ever. The Roman liturgy was reformed by Pope Pius V in keeping with the orientations of the council of Trent. But this does not imply, as Archbishop Marcel Lefebvre would have it, that the papal decree of 1570 cancels all future reforms and that, in consequence, the liturgical reforms of Vatican II and Pope Paul VI are invalid. Indeed, the history of structural reform exhibits mistakes, hesitancies, and backward turns, no less than forward-looking advances. It is made of failures no less than successes. And this alone would be sufficient to show that reformability belongs, if not to the basic marks of the Church, at least to its continuing existential experience. Reformability is, by its very nature, never obsolete.

The sense of being the Church implies the awareness of the freedom of the Spirit to guide the Church beyond the conditions of its past. For new urns, new wine! To every moment of its societal context there corresponds a certain shape of the Christian tradition which must be characterized, as John Henry Newman rightly perceived, not only by "preservation of its type," "continuity of its principles," and "conservative action upon its past," but also by "power of assimilation," "anticipation of its future," and "chronic vigor."[4] These are, respectively, the first, second, sixth, and the third, fifth, and seventh notes that Newman identified in genuine developments of doctrine. Three of these refer to, and sum up, the past. The other three prepare and anticipate the future. Whatever weight one assigns to it, the development of doctrine may be seen as a continuing movement of reform within the Christian faith. The marks that have determined its curve, if they can be ascertained, can well be applied to genuine reforms of the Church as a whole.

The fourth of Newman's notes is missing from my list. Newman called it "logical sequence." It is indeed a mark of genuine reform, but only if the logic in question is not the philosophical logic of human reason left to its natural resources: it should be the analogical and anagogical logic of faith. That is, if the ongoing reform of the Church results in part from reflection on Scripture, on the data of the historical tradition, and on the demands of contemporary experience, it is also the fruit of prophetic insights into the revelation given once for all in Christ, of obedience to the promptings of the Spirit, of ineffable perceptions of the glory of God beyond all telling. And should reason and faith appear to be in conflict, it is reason that should bow to faith, not faith to reason.

Newman did not claim that all developments must equally bear those seven notes of genuineness. Some specific developments are more marked by one note than by the others. Thus Newman identified "logical sequence" as the main ingredient in the development of "pardons, penances, satisfactions, purgatory, meritorious works, and the monastic rule." Now, with no exception, these practices and doctrines occasioned the Reformers' objection that the logic of faith, grounded in Scripture and manifested in the earlier tradition, had more recently given way to the logic of Aristotle. Which logic was at work in these relatively late developments? Catholics and Protestants are still divided on the point.

The struggles of the Reformation over these items raise a central question for ecclesiology: does the Church's ministerial structure provide for the resolution of conflicts? I am not thinking of minor differences of culture, custom, education, taste, preference, or personality that can easily be locally overcome through mutual consultation. I have major conflicts in mind, as when a decision that has been made by the Church's highest authority is

---

[4]John Henry Newman, *An Essay on the Development of Christian Doctrine* (New York: Doubleday, 1960), p. 175-207.

received negatively or is just not received by the people at large or when a sizable portion of the Church rejects what another, more or less equal, portion holds to be an authentic development. Thus the Catholic world was rent from 1378 to 1417 by allegiances to different popes. The *post factum* claim that only one of them could have been the true bishop of Rome and successor of Peter, and the more hazardous assumption that the true bishop of Rome must have been the one who happened to reside in the city of Rome, do not resolve the existential conflict of the times. Thus also the Reformation and the Counter-Reformation were at loggerheads over medieval developments relating to the appropriation of salvation by individual believers. Likewise, the contemporary Christian world is still divided over the authority of the teaching magisterium in general and of the papacy in particular, over the Marian dogmas of 1854 (Mary's Immaculate Conception) and 1950 (Mary's Assumption into heaven), over the sacramentality of ordination, and, to a lesser extent, over the eschatological expectation and the doctrine of purgatory. More recently, the statement of Paul VI in the encyclical *Humanae vitae* (1968) that according to "the norms of the natural law . . . each and every use of marriage must remain open to the transmission of life" (HV, n. 11) does not seem to have been received as correct by the generality of Catholic married persons. When they experienced a division of opinion, medieval bishops and theologians who disagreed with the majority frequently appealed to the *sanior pars* over the *major pars*, the "healthier party" over the "majority party." Indeed one may think that the *sanior pars* rarely coincides with the majority. But how is one to decide which is the *sanior pars*?

In a sense, these continuing divisions create a vicious circle. Disagreement over the teaching magisterium cannot be overcome unless there exists a previous agreement on the existence and the normativity of a ministerial structure that has the capacity to resolve conflicts. Disagreement over the modern dogmas on the Virgin Mary cannot be overcome except on the basis of a previous agreement as to the nature of dogmas and as to who is responsible for their proclamation. Divergences over the way to salvation cannot vanish if there is continuing disagreement on the implications of justification by faith.

The Ministry of the Laity

These questions introduce the topic of our next chapter, the "magisterial structure of the Church." But several points can already be made concerning the ministry of those believers who, by definition, do not constitute the magisterium, namely the laity.

The laity's ministry is commensurate with the general priesthood of the Christian people that is given by Christ, the author of salvation, in baptism. The tradition sums it up in such expressions as offering to God the sacrifice of praise through the pursuit of a good life in obedience to God's commandments and the demands of conscience. In normal circumstances, this includes the internal offering of one's life to God in prayer; the outside witness to the Lordship of Christ; solidarity with the Church at large by the observance of its regulations; the practice of love for the neighbor; the fulfillment of duties in regard to family, to profession, and to country, in whatever way country may be defined at the different levels of civilization (tribe, clan, province, or nation).

The Church's missionary saga, however, and the experience of persecution in the twentieth century require some complements and additions to this basic formula. The great effort of preaching the gospel to all nations that started with the discovery of the Americas and the increased possibilities of travel in Asia and Africa, opened up some evidences regarding the ministerial tasks of the laity. In the first place, the missionary task was carried by unordained brothers and sisters no less than by ordained clergy. In the second place, the tasks of catechesis and local responsibility had to be entrusted to unordained laity of both sexes as missionary priests traveled on to announce the gospel further abroad. In the third place, the history of Korea points to another dimension of the ministry of the laity: the Christian faith was introduced not by missionaries from abroad but by Korean mandarins who, in 1783, sought enlightenment from the Jesuits whom they met in Beijing. As they returned home after receiving baptism, they began the work of establishing the Church, and one of them, Yi Sung Hun, even composed a theological writing, the first by an Asian Christian. This illustrates the point that the very preaching of the gospel already pertains to the baptized laity by virtue of their baptism. In the same perspective, the persecutions by the powers that be of the new Christians of Asia and Africa, which began in China in the seventeenth century and continued until the late nineteenth century, showed, no less than those of the early Church, that the witness of martyrdom is equally given by the laity and the clergy. The principle of lay responsibility for spreading the gospel applies to the situation of the Christian laity in the de-Christianized sections of the modern world, notably among the working masses of industrialized countries. This has been recognized in the social encyclicals of the popes from Leo XIII (*Rerum novarum*, 1891) to John Paul II (*Laborem exercens*, 1981).

In addition, the persecutions of the twentieth century, chiefly due to the spread of Marxist ideology and the rise of Marxist dictatorships, have elicited another dimension of the ministry of the laity: they are responsible for spiritual leadership when the magisterium of the bishops is forcefully impeded from functioning. Such was the point made in 1926 when the bishops of Mexico, in response to the expulsion of bishops and priests by President Calles, suspended all religious services by the clergy.

Two points, negative and positive, follow from this aspect of the ministry of the people of God. Firstly, Pope Pius XI (1922-1939) fell short of the full extent of the Catholic doctrine of the laity when, in the encyclical *Ubi arcano* (23 December 1922), he invited lay persons to "catholic action." This he defined as a "participation in the apostolate of the hierarchy." That is, the laity could be entrusted with this apostolate in areas of society where the hierarchy does not normally go, for instance in the world of finance and banking, in the organization and running of workers' trade unions, in the planning and work of secular universities, in the contractual relations between capital and labor, in international and national politics when these do not bring up moral and ethical questions, in partisan politics. The initiatives of Pius XI in this area did much to wake up an apostolic dimension in the Catholic laity that had been largely overlooked in the theology of the Counter-Reformation. Yet the perspective missed the point that such an "apostolate of the laity" belongs to all the baptized by virtue of their baptism and not because of accidental circumstances that hinder the hierarchy's freedom of action.

Secondly, the personal responsibility of all Christians for spreading the gospel and for teaching and witnessing to the faith in all walks of life and all levels of society makes it imperative to uphold the positive value of "public opinion" in the Church. The point was made by Pope Pius XII. In an address given on 18 February 1950 to a congress of Catholic journalists, the pope recognized that public opinion, that is, the opinion of the laity at large, has a positive contribution to make to the life of the Church, "For she too is a living body, and there would be something missing from her life if there were no public opinion within her, a defect for which pastors as well as the faithful would be responsible."[5] The expression of public opinion through the mass media informs the bishops of the state of mind of the Christian laity, draws their attention to the concerns and problems of the mass of the people, and enables them to take account of all parties in the on-going discussion of Church matters.

The most forceful formulation of the task of public opinion is due to Karol Wojtyla when he was a professor of philosophy in Poland. Personhood implies interpersonal relationships. In society itself, and therefore in the Church as a society, the human person is involved with others in relations of "intersubjectivity" or mutual participation through the common project of pursuing the good in the upbuilding of society. But participation in a common project does not imply uniformity of views and opinions. On the contrary,

> the attitude of solidarity does not contradict the attitude of opposition; opposition is not inconsistent with solidarity. The one who voices his opposition to the general or particular rules or regulations of the community does not thereby reject his membership; he does not withdraw his readiness to act and to work for the common good. . . . Far from rejecting the com-

---

[5]Quoted in Karl Rahner, *Free Speech in the Church* (New York: Sheed and Ward, 1959), p. 5.

mon good or the need for participation, [opposition] consists, on the contrary, in their confirmation.[6]

The conclusion is unimpeachable: the common project being the preaching of the gospel, the conversion of the nations, and the progress of the Christian faith and Church, opposition for reasons of conscience to the leaders' conceptions and policies is part and parcel of the authentic life of the community. It contributes to the formation of a healthy public opinion and to the process of strengthening the Church. And this is true regardless of tensions and conflicts, as Wojtyla affirms:

> Undoubtedly, opposition may make the cooperation of men less smooth and more difficult, but it should never damage or prevent it. . . . Dialogue, in fact, without evading the strains, the conflicts, or the strife manifest in the life of various human communities, takes up what is right and true in these differences, what may become a source of good for men. Consequently, it seems that in a constructive communal life the principle of dialogue has to be adopted regardless of the obstacles and difficulties it may bring with it along the way.

The Laity and the Teaching of Doctrine

Cardinal Newman anticipated the modern discussion of these points when, after reviewing the experience of the past, he concluded that, by virtue of baptism and faith, the Catholic laity have a fundamental right to be consulted by the hierarchy in matters of doctrine. This was the point of his opusculum, *On Consulting the Faithful in Matters of Doctrine*, originally published as an article in *The Rambler*, July 1859.[7] As was the case for most of his theological essays, John Henry Newman, cardinal though he later became, was ignored by his contemporaries. His theology, however, has come into its own in the twentieth century, and its prophetic dimension has now been generally acknowledged. In the days after Vatican I, Newman anticipated the spirit of Vatican II. And historian of the patristic period as he was, he did so on the strength of the great Catholic tradition.

The recent dilemmas and the on-going discussion regarding the scope of all these questions illustrate the providential role of tensions and conflicts in the ministerial structure of the Church. Reform, when it is needed, must be made according to the gospel, not according to fashionable theologies or to the imperatives of dominant cultures. As such, reform is never fully achieved. Reformability belongs to the very structure of the Church *semper reformanda* and of its ministry.

[6]Karol Wojtyla, *The Acting Person* (Boston: Reidel Publishing Co., 1979), citations, p. 286 and 287.

[7]John Henry Newman, *On Consulting the Faithful in Matters of Doctrine* (London: Geoffrey Chapman, 1961).

I may at this point refer to some of my previous studies. I have pointed out several times that, if catholicity is the basis of ministry, the Eucharist its horizon, and culture its context, the ministry of the Church as a whole follows in fact a fourfold pattern.[8] Whether it is recognized as episcopal or non-episcopal, as sacramentally ordained or not, the ministry of all the faithful and, by implication, the official ministry of the ordained are focused on the leadership of prayer, on the proclamation of the gospel in word and sacrament, on pastoral care or service, and on education or catechesis. Like the four points of the compass, these tasks are necessary for the ship of the Christian Church to find its way in the dangerous seas of the world. In diverse places and at sundry times, one task may have prevailed over others. In the long run, however, the people of God need all of them to make headway along the pilgrimage of the present life.

One may well wonder how this fourfold pattern relates to the twofold division of lay and ordained and to the threefold hierarchy of bishops, priests, and deacons. This is tantamount to asking at which point of this fourfold pattern ordination becomes necessary. On the basis of the patristic and medieval tradition, the Catholic answer has set this point at the level of the liturgy and the presidency of Eucharistic assemblies. Yet by what many would see as a strange quirk of history, the necessity of ordination has also been extended, *de facto* if not always *de jure*, to the leadership of prayer, to all preaching of the gospel, to the supervision of pastoral care and of catechesis. And this in spite of the fact that the spiritual hierarchy of holiness is obviously competent to lead in prayer, that pastoral care can be adequately performed by trained lay counselors, and that the tasks of catechesis require knowledge and pedagogical efficiency rather than sacramental grace.

There has thus taken place a process of extension: *ministerium* (from *minus*, "less") tends to become *magisterium* (from *magis*, "plus").

For Further Reading

Emile-Joseph de Smedt. *The Priesthood of the Faithful.* New York: Paulist Press, 1962.

Jerome D'Souza. *The Church and Civilization: An Appraisal of the Church's Relations with Secular Cultures.* New York: Doubleday, 1966.

Yves Congar. *Lay People in the Church.* Westminster, Md.: Newman Press, 1966.

Joan Morris. *The Lady Was a Bishop: The Hidden History of Women with Clerical Ordination and the Jurisdiction of Bishops.* New York: Macmillan, 1973.

Hans Schwartz. *The Christian Church: Biblical Origin, Historical Transformation, and Potential for the Future.* Minneapolis: Augsburg Publishing House, 1982.

Avery Dulles. *A Church to Believe In: Discipleship and the Dynamics of Freedom.* New York: Crossroad, 1982.

[8]George H. Tavard, *A Theology for Ministry* (Wilmington: Michael Glazier, 1982), p. 75-92.

9

Magisterium

The starting point for this chapter is provided by the constitution *Dei Verbum* of Vatican Council II:

> Holy Tradition, Holy Scripture, and the Church's magisterium are, according to God's wise design, so interconnected and united that none can stand without the others, and that all together effectively contribute, each in its own way, under the motion of the Holy Spirit, to the salvation of souls (DV, n. 10).[1]

This is a remarkable assertion. The magisterium in question is that of the Roman Catholic Church. The council therefore teaches that Holy Scripture stands together with the tradition and the Roman Catholic magisterium or teaching office. But it is evident that, in the Protestant Churches that have rejected the authority of this magisterium, Holy Scripture still "stands." Likewise, it is not the entirety of the "Holy Tradition" that has vanished from the Churches of the Reformation. Martin Luther firmly believed, and liked to show, that his understanding of Justification by faith was supported by the Fathers of the Church. And John Calvin himself, though more radical than Luther, frequently appealed to the testimony of the past, especially to St. Augustine among the Fathers and St. Bernard in the Middle Ages. Now, this is precisely what "magisterium" fundamentally means: the service of true doctrine. In usual Roman Catholic parlance, the actual teaching of those who have authority in the Church by virtue of their office is a determinative and necessary point of reference for the promulgation and explanation of

---

[1] I quote *Dei Verbum* from my own translation: *Dogmatic Constitution on Divine Revelation of Vatican Council II* (New York: Paulist Press, 1966).

doctrine. Evidently, however, Vatican II was not in this text making a statement about what other Christian Churches might consider essential to their formulation of doctrine. It presented what the Catholic experience has taken to be the ideal situation. In this ideal situation, "the singular conspiracy (*singularis conspiratio*) of bishops and faithful comes into being in the preservation, the practice, and the confession of the traditional faith" (DV, n. 10). In its etymological sense, of course, conspiracy ("breathing together") implies harmony and unanimity.

Vatican II's Triptych

It is not self-evident, yet I consider it to be certain, that Vatican II's three-fold reference—Scripture, tradition, magisterium—should not be opposed to the self-understanding of Christian authority in the Churches of the Reformation. The testimony of the Fathers of the Church functions as magisterium in all the Christian communities that are faithful to the Trinitarian teachings of the first councils and to the Christology of Chalcedon. This fidelity is abundantly documented in the works of Luther and Calvin as well as in those of the Anglican Reformers. It can be illustrated from the Book of Common Prayer of Anglicanism, the Confessional Books of Lutheranism, and the classical Confessions of faith of Calvinism, such as the Second Helvetic Confession (1566: see ch. 2) and the Westminster Confession (1647: see ch. 31).

Yet the threefold reference of Vatican II would actually be misleading if it were assumed to be complete. For one thing, the three factors mentioned are not of the same order. Scripture is a series of books that embody the witness of the Old Testament (in the Law, the Prophets, and the Writings) followed by that of the apostles and their immediate followers. Tradition is the memory by which the Christian community, today and at any time, is reminded of what Christians believed and taught in the past; as such, it involves both the present knowledge of the past and the contribution of the "great cloud of witnesses" (Heb 12:1) who lived in former ages. In the usual Roman Catholic meaning of the word, magisterium is the voice of those who lead the Church in its daily life, being ultimately responsible for the communication of the gospel in word and sacrament. Yet in actual fact, as *Dei Verbum* clearly states, the magisterium is not above, but under, the Word of God.

The magisterium does not decide where the Scriptures begin and end: the canon of Scripture cannot be traced back to a specific decision made in the first centuries of the Church. If one alludes to such a decision, it is by way of inference from later canonical statements that the canon of Scripture is complete. But a retroactive hypothetical conclusion such as this is not tantamount to factual documentation. Likewise, the magisterium does not decide what is the actual meaning of specific scriptural passages. This is a matter of biblical scholarship. Nor does it determine what is the testimony of the historical tradition: these are questions for historians and theologians.

Rather, the value of official teaching depends on its fidelity to Scripture and to tradition. Being already given, Scripture and tradition form a deposit that cannot be tampered with, even though, by its very nature, the tradition keeps growing with the passage of time as it adds new testimonies to those that have already been received. St. Irenaeus called it a *depositum juvenescens*, a deposit that constantly renovates itself and is a permanent fountain of youth.[2] And since it is the harmony between Scripture, tradition, and their service by living pastors that functions as leader and teacher in the Church, the actual magisterium is always broader and older than the individual persons who sit for the time being in the chairs of authority.

Another element that is at work in the magisterial process is not mentioned at this point in Vatican II. The very notion that three factors "conspire" together requires an implicit process of mutual acceptance. Scripture and the tradition stand in a relationship of mutual acceptance whenever the tradition is faithful to Scripture and Scripture can be shown to support the tradition. Likewise, Scripture and the tradition need to be received and recognized by the living magisterium if they are to function in the living Church. This is implied in a related passage of *Dei Verbum*:

> The Tradition that issues from the apostles progresses in the Church under the assistance of the Holy Spirit. Insight into the realities and the words transmitted grows: this results from contemplation and study by the faithful who ponder over them in their heart, from their experience of a profound understanding of spiritual realities, from the preaching of those who, with the episcopal succession, received the unfailing charism of the truth (DV, n. 8).

At first sight, this text describes the development of tradition. But as it does so, it draws attention to an underlying element in the process: before being able to contemplate and study the formulations of faith that have been transmitted and the realities that are covered by them, the faithful need to receive these formulations and realities. Likewise, before they can experience a profound understanding of spiritual realities, they must have received both the self-revelation of God in Jesus Christ and the gift of gratuitous justification by grace through faith. And this they cannot do unless their hearts are open to the Spirit of God. Reception of divine grace is essential to the process of belief and thereby to that of receiving, believing, and handing on the evangelical doctrine about Jesus Christ.

Reception, in fact, functions in each panel of the Catholic triptych. Unless they have been received in faith by the people of God, the Scriptures convey nothing to any one. Unless they have been received in the Church's memory

---

[2] [*Fides nostra*] . . . *quasi in vaso bono eximium quoddam depositum juvenescens et juvenescere faciens ipsum vasa in quo est* (*Adversus Haereses*, III, 24, 16 [SC, n. 211, 1974, p. 472]); the vase that contains this deposit is the Church.

and are reactivated from time to time by those who are aware of them, the doctrines and experiences of the past do not contribute to the on-going communication of the gospel. And unless the decisions and formulations of the magisterium are received and assented to by the people of God, they become dysfunctional, for they then testify not to a "singular conspiracy" or harmony but to a split within the community. Thus Vatican II's triptych includes a fourth element, reception. It is in fact a tetraptych.

The Quadrilaterals

To the magisterial tetraptych of the Catholic tradition, one may compare the quadrilaterals that some Churches have deemed to be at work in the formative process of teaching and protecting the faith in their midst.[3] The Chicago-Lambeth Quadrilateral of 1886 and 1888, which is generally accepted in the Anglican Communion of Churches, did not use the term *magisterium*. Yet it was designed precisely as a statement of what points of reference for the determination of Christian doctrine are necessary to the eventual reunion of the separated Christian Churches. The Quadrilateral comprises (1) the Holy Scriptures of the Old and New Testament "as the revealed Word of God" (Chicago) or "as containing all things necessary to salvation and as being the rule and ultimate standard of faith" (Lambeth), (2) the "Nicene Creed as the sufficient statement of the Christian faith" (Chicago) or "the Apostles' Creed as the Baptismal Symbol and the Nicene Creed as the sufficient statement of the Christian faith" (Lambeth), (3) "the two Sacraments ordained by Christ himself—Baptism and the Supper of the Lord—ministered with unfailing use of Christ's words of Institution and of the elements ordained by Him," (4) "the Historic Episcopate, locally adapted in the methods of its administration to the varying needs of the nations and peoples called of God into the Unity of the Church."

Point (1) is evidently identical with the Catholic principle of Scripture. Points (2) and (3) itemize the central elements of the tradition in its doctrinal and its liturgical forms. Point (4) touches directly on what is intended by magisterium in the Catholic tetraptych: the bishops' responsibility for the welfare of all in the Church.

The *Book of Discipline* of the United Methodist Church in the United States puts forward another Quadrilateral in keeping with the belief of John Wesley and his early disciples that a "marrow" of Christian truth "strikes at the root of Christianity" and must therefore be preserved and taught: "This living core, as they believed, stands revealed in Scripture, illumined by tradition, vivified in personal experience, and confirmed by reason."[4] In this con-

---

[3]J. Robert Wright, *Quadrilateral at One Hundred: Essays on the Centenary of the Chicago-Lambeth Quadrilateral, 1886/88-1986/88* (Cincinnati: Forward Movement Publications, 1988).

[4]See *The Book of Discipline* of the United Methodist Church, 1980, p. 78-83.

text, "personal experience" and "reason" are factors in the reception of doctrine by the faithful. If this Methodist Quadrilateral is compared with the Lambeth Quadrilateral and with the Catholic tetraptych, the main difference relates to the place and role of bishops or leaders of the Church. The *Book of Discipline* envisages a special form of the "conciliar principle." Conciliarity gathers the "collective wisdom of living Christian pastors, teachers and people" that is manifested in the "collegial process." This is expected to take place in "the annual conference," the gathering in which lay and clerical delegates of the Churches within a given area gather for information, decision making, and mutual edification. The Catholic and the Anglican systems maintain a personal authority of bishops in the areas of liturgy and doctrine within the context of collegial consultations and consensus. In the episcopal system of American Methodism, the bishop is the one who is to elicit a consensus in the collegial process of the annual conference under the wider authority of the quinquennial general conference of the whole Church.

The Lutheran and Calvinist magisterial systems are more difficult to pin down. For they are not clearly focused on a teaching office. They tend to relinquish doctrinal magisterium to scholarship, on the academic rather than on the conciliar model, or, especially in Calvinism, to a consensus of ministers gathered in a presbytery or synod. Yet the Augsburg Confession sets up a core doctrine—namely, justification by faith—as the standard by which all doctrines and doctrinal statements, whatever their source, are to be assessed. And the Second Helvetic Confession denies that the Scriptures are open to "private interpretation." In both cases, a magisterial standard is implied. For the Augsburg Confession and for Lutheranism in general, it is the consensus of the Catholic tradition on the matter of justification, grace, and salvation (CA, art. 4–5) to which the authority of ministers and bishops is itself subject. For the Second Helvetic Confession and for Calvinism in general, it is that interpretation of Scripture which, gathered from Scripture itself, is in agreement "with the rule of faith and love, and contributes much to the glory of God and man's salvation" (ch. 2). In both cases, responsibility for right teaching lies with the community of Christian scholars no less than with the ministers who have been entrusted with pastoral care.

Indeed, that the exercise of Christian authority is collegial would seem to be a common principle in all Churches. Even the autonomy of Baptist congregations is self-limited by a "covenant" that has been agreed upon by the members. Nonetheless, the contrasts between the systems of governance in the diverse Christian Churches point to a central problem of ecclesiology, a problem that relates to the principle of authority.

Magisterium and Management

The agreed statement on authority between Anglican and Roman Catholics, included in the *Final Report* of ARCIC-I (September 1981), declares:

"This is Christian authority: when Christians so act and speak, men perceive the authoritative word of God."[5] In context, "so" refers to the preceding sentence: "The common life in the body of Christ equips the community and each of its members with what they need to fulfill this responsibility: they are enabled so to live that the authority of Christ will be mediated through them." In a sense, then, ministerium, the service of the community and of the world that is performed in faith, by the power of faith, and for the sake of faith, spontaneously tends to become magisterium, the transparency of Christian life and actions to the authority of Christ as the sole Mediator and as the Revealer of the true reality of God.

Two questions ensue. Firstly, the societal structure of the Christian community is such that the exercise of magisterium or authority requires a growing amount of management. It was not by mistake that the Chicago-Lambeth Quadrilateral associated "the Historic Episcopate" with "methods of administration." The historic episcopate is common to the Orthodox, the Catholic, and the Anglican Communions. "Administration," the methods of which were expected to "be adapted to the varying needs of nations and peoples," was what, by the second half of the nineteenth century, bishops were primarily doing. After turning into magisterial authority, the ministerial call has merged with managerial skill. But in this case, it is difficult to see how the Christian community differs from the secular society to which it adapts. If the earliest bishops were primarily mystagogues who initiated the faithful into the paschal mystery as in the *Mystagogical Catecheses* of St. Cyril of Jerusalem (c. 348-386), later bishops largely developed into managers of the Church's assets. But one may ask if this is what was intended in the Scriptures by the call to discipleship and to apostleship.

Secondly, whether magisterial or managerial, the exercise of authority tends to polarize around key persons and offices. This polarization has been the more effective in Christian history as, until recent centuries, secular authority in Europe followed imperial and royal models, supreme authority being concentrated in one person. The older (Catholic) Churches have in fact preserved certain forms of the imperial or royal models while the more recent (Protestant) Churches have taken over large slices of both political-democratic and business-managerial systems. Yet all systems of Christian authority are in fact mixed and complex. And the process of polarization and centralization has been somewhat tempered by the lingering influence of the conciliaristic-monastic forces that have been at work in the Christian community since the early centuries of the Church. Still, one may ask, what is the proper balance between centralization and collegiality?

---

[5]See J. Robert Wright, l. c., p. viii. The text of the *Final Report* of ARCIC-I is included in Joseph W. Witmer and J. Robert Wright, eds., *Called to Full Unity. Documents on Anglican-Roman Catholic Relations, 1966-1983* (Washington: BCEIA, 1986).

A Documentary Magisterium

In the logic of the triptych of Vatican II as in that of the Quadrilaterals, Christian catechesis resides chiefly in communicating the data that are to be found in Scripture and in the tradition. This does not place Scripture and tradition on the same level, nor does it make them independent sources of, or witnesses to, authentic Christian doctrine. When the fourth session of the Council of Trent (April 1546) determined that "the Scriptures and the apostolic traditions" are to be held "in equal esteem and reverence" (DS, n. 1501), it did not endorse the notion that Christian doctrine is somehow divided up between them, complementary doctrines being found in each of them. In fact, the council explicitly rejected such a formula. The Tridentine meaning is quite other. Trusting in the divine guidance over the Church, the council teaches that the doctrine contained in the Scriptures has also been faithfully transmitted by the apostolic traditions that have come down to us.

In this perspective, magisterium is first of all a process: it is the transmission of Christian doctrine by teaching. In consequence, one may properly ask where the memory of this doctrine is located and ask further when, to whom, and by whom it is taught. The questions when, to whom, and by whom are easy: all the faithful communicate their beliefs when they live by them, when they worship according to them, when they teach them to their children, when they explain to others "the reason for the hope" that is in them (1 Pet 3:15). Likewise, ordained ministers transmit the faith in preaching the gospel, in administering and explaining the sacraments, in guiding and counseling the faithful, in catechizing neophytes. The question of location— where has the Christian community stored the memory of the doctrine?—is also, in principle, easy to answer, though the demonstration and discussion of the answer would take longer: the memory of the gospel is located primarily in the hearts of believers and secondarily in the documentation that has been left by and about believers of all generations.

These two loci are, in fact, one since there is no access to the hearts of the believers who lived in ages past except through the available documentation. One may therefore truly speak of a documentary magisterium. The Scriptures, the writings of the Fathers of the Church, the tractates of theologians, the sermons of preachers are documents in the public domain. It is up to scholars, using the tools of scientific investigation, to tell us what these documents said in their time. In this sense, the texts have primacy. Their very letter has a coherence that imposes its law on all interpretations. The transmission of the Christian gospel is therefore neither a string of successive divine revelations nor a continuing revelation. It is a faithful remembrance of what was taught once for all at the beginning.

Remembering is not repeating or duplicating. The original event of the communication of the gospel and its reception by successive generations of believers are not to be copied. In fact, repetition became impossible when the original languages of the Bible—Hebrew, Aramaic, Greek—were replaced by other vernaculars. Those who would wish merely to repeat the original teaching have no recourse but to translation. And translation is itself already interpretation. With the help of hermeneutical theories about the meaning and the reading of texts, speculative or systematic theologians have to tell the people how the magisterial documents can or should be interpreted today. Next, the authorities of the Church should tell the faithful what the documents and their interpretations say to the community and how what these teachings say ought to be received and applied. It is then up to the educated faithful to decide in conscience what these interpretations can or should mean for them and how the proper conclusions are to be incorporated into their life. This makes it obvious that a documentary magisterium cannot function without a living magisterium. It takes living persons to read documents and to imagine their application in the on-going life of the people of God.

The Magisterium of Theologians

The necessity and the difficulty of reading documents—in order to know what they say and to determine the limits of their authority—establish a magisterium of theologians in the Church. For those who have the talents and the capacity also have the duty to serve the community through them. Teaching, then, is not optional. It is not merely a side-effect or a by-product of learning and scholarship. It is a duty that pertains to the very structure of the Christian Church as a community of belief. Like all members of a community that is tied together by mutual service, the theologians are at the service of the community to which they must bring the fruits of their labors. And when theologians reach conclusions that they consider to be intrinsically normative, their ministerium becomes magisterium.

Yet theirs is a magisterium *sui generis*. It implies no obligation in others but to listen when they are able to, and it carries no power, not even of moral coercion. Its value is no other than the intrinsic coherence and evidence of what it says, a coherence and an evidence that are always open to challenge in the light of better documentation or better reading of the texts. Whether they are conservative or progressive in content or intent, the statements of theologians necessarily elicit agreement or disagreement. But the expression of agreement or disagreement should be such as to contribute to building up the community. In other words, the magisterium of theologians has its proper locus in the discussions of *academe*. It was precisely in the medieval schools and universities that scholastic theology developed. Theology nonetheless truly implies a magisterium that speaks with the authority of scholarship when the time is ripe. This was evident at Vatican II, as at all previous councils, when bishops consulted theologians before making up their minds, when theologians wrote the decrees and constitutions that the bishops eventually adopted, and when the speeches made by bishops were often composed by theological advisers. For this reason, Pope John XXIII, after inviting the bishops of the world to a council, appointed a selected number of *periti* or theological experts to work in the conciliar commissions. These experts formed the theological backbone of Vatican Council II.

The Magisterium of Bishops

Let us now look again at the passage of Vatican II that was quoted in the opening lines of this chapter. The meaning of this text emerges better in the light of a previous assertion made in the same chapter of *Dei Verbum*: "The task of providing an authentic interpretation of God's Word in Scripture or Tradition has been entrusted only to the Church's living magisterium whose authority is wielded in the name of Jesus Christ." Nonetheless, "this magisterium is not above God's Word; it rather serves the Word, teaching only what has been transmitted, as, by divine mandate and with the Holy Spirit's assistance, it listens to God's Word with piety, keeps it in awe, and expounds it with fidelity" (DV, n. 10).

Now, the Reformation largely turned around the question: did the Catholic magisterium in the late Middle Ages teach "only what had been transmitted?" Did it not at times lord it over the Scriptures? Luther found evidence that bishops and popes, no less than university professors, had been unfaithful to the Word of God while the Catholic controversialists generally denied any such infidelity. Yet no one could claim that infidelity to the gospel is totally impossible among prelates and bishops. Indeed, denunciations of certain popes as being the expected "Antichrist" were not unknown to the Middle Ages and had been hurled at Pope Alexander VI (pope, 1492-1503) by the Dominican, Jerome Savonarola (1452-1498), within Luther's own lifetime. That Savonarola had been burned by the Inquisition hardly helped the cause of the pope: the existence and nature of his heresy were highly dubious! And the very case of Pope Alexander VI raised a nagging doubt about the papacy: should not the bishop of Rome, if he is to be the chief guardian of doctrinal orthodoxy, also be a model of moral striving for holiness? And should he clearly fail the moral test, can he be trusted when he puts others to the doctrinal test?

Undoubtedly a distinction needs to be made. A bishop has authority in his own diocese in which he should function as an instrument of unity for the whole people of God and as the local people's symbolic and effective link with the universal Church. In the diocese, the bishop consults and decides in a collegial manner. But neither is he himself above mistakes nor is he infallibly protected from errors of judgment or from hesitancies in deciding what has been in question and in implementing what has been decided. In the universal Church, a bishop has responsibility for the whole, in common with the entire college of bishops, which represents the universal Church. Convergence of thought and intention with the whole college preserves each bishop from unilateral decisions and idiosyncratic interpretations of doctrine. Yet the Catholic conception of the magisterium is also tied with the special ministry that is assigned to the bishop of Rome.

The Petrine Magisterium

When Pope Paul VI paid a visit to the headquarters of the World Council of Churches in Geneva on June 10, 1969, he declared to the astonished officials of the World Council: "Our name is Peter. And Scripture tells us what meaning Christ wanted to attribute to this name, what duties it imposes on us: the responsibilities of the apostle and of his successors. . . ." At least Pope Paul had the courage to pose the problem of the papacy at the administrative center of an organization of Churches which do not recognize the pope's traditional claim to govern with Peter's authority. In so doing, he squarely raised the question of the Church's magisterial structure.

When the doctrine of the papacy reached its high point is debatable. Some would find it in the claim of Pope Leo the Great (pope, 440–461), anticipated by some of his predecessors, that St. Peter himself mystically acts and speaks in the bishop of Rome. Others would find it only in the formal definition of papal infallibility at Vatican Council I (1870). And one could imagine many intermediate positions. In Catholic doctrine at any rate, the development of the papacy is closely related to that of the episcopate, for papal jurisdiction was said at Vatican Council I to be "truly episcopal" (DS, n. 3060). That is, as a bishop is the instrument and should be the living symbol of unity and charity in a diocese, so the bishop of Rome is a similar instrument and should be a similar symbol in the universal Church.

More exactly, however, papal authority shares the higher degree of episcopal authority that was recognized to the bishops of apostolic sees or patriarchates in the fourth and fifth centuries. But it shares this higher authority with a difference. For little by little, a primacy among the five patriarchs came to be recognized to the bishop of Rome, though this recognition was never identical in the East and in the West. As the college of bishops together succeeds the college of the apostles, so one bishop succeeds Peter, the first among the Twelve. This is the bishop of the Church that was established by Peter and Paul in the old imperial capital. Yet the kind, manner, and degree of authority of the see and bishop of Rome have varied. From the chief witness to authentic apostolic teaching, which it was in the second century (as St. Irenaeus testified), it became, in the third and fourth centuries, a supreme court of appeals in disagreements regarding true doctrine and in problems of conflicting authorities or jurisdictions. Hence the see of Rome came to be seen as "the chair of the truth," when bishops and others queried its bishop as to the bearing of the Roman tradition on various points of doctrine and discipline. In the course of time, the bishop of the Church in Rome was identified in the West as the prime bishop in whom Peter mystically rules the Church. The successor of Peter was "vicar of Peter," later also called "vicar of Christ." He was the spiritual model for all bishops and the teacher of true doctrine.

The relationships between the primate and the other bishops within the episcopal college have also varied considerably. In the time of the Fathers of the Church, ecumenical councils were called by the emperor and presided over by the emperor's representatives. After the breakdown of the Roman empire, the primate of the universal Church called, presided in person or through his legates, and confirmed the "general councils of the West" (so called in Pope Paul VI's letter to Cardinal Willebrands for the anniversary of the Council of Lyon of 1274, although they had been commonly regarded in Catholicism as ecumenical).

The evolution of councils and of their presidency clearly underlines the dynamic character of magisterium as understood and practiced in the Catholic tradition. Teaching responsibility and authority do not reside in merely repeating or restating the doctrines that are in Scripture. Rather, they live and evolve. They presuppose that all in the Church are eager to listen to the Word and to the Spirit of God. The Word, sitting "at the right hand of God" as the risen Christ, intercedes for his followers, and the Spirit, sent by the Father, leads them "into all the truth" (John 16:13). Christian authority is radically Trinitarian.

As the Word and the Spirit are believed to be divine Persons, Christian authority is never anonymous: it is always personal. It is not the dead weight of legislation whose initiators could well be forgotten by those who are expected to follow their decisions. Being personal, it is embodied in particular persons. It is functional in that it extends as far as the responsibility that is necessary for, and adequate to, a function. It is called *ordinary* when it is assumed by virtue of a function and *delegated* when it is obtained from higher authority by special designation. It is also collegial, for all ministerial functions are shared. Christian authority is not dictatorship. Priests constitute a college or presbyterium around their bishop. All bishops form the episcopal college with the bishop of Rome as its head. By virtue of their ordination into the episcopal college, all bishops also share coresponsibility for the universal Church. Each one receives from Christ in ordination the responsibility of the local Church of which he becomes the visible center.

Over the centuries, however, the structure of episcopal and papal authority has become a bone of contention. In the practice of the Counter-Reformation, and already to a large extent in the Middle Ages, the magisterium of bishops acted as a third force in the Church's doctrinal equipment: along with Scripture and the general tradition, there is the magisterium of the episcopal college and the bishops which is itself capped by the magisterium of the bishop of Rome. In principle, *magis*terium is no more than a special kind of *minis*terium: it is the service of teaching. In the course of time, however, it was often placed on a par with Scripture and tradition. It is against this background that the doctrinal quarrels of the Reformation were soon focused on the authority of the bishop of Rome, that Vatican Council I formulated its doctrine of papal primacy and infallibility as a universal service of the truth, and that Vatican Council II reformulated the doctrine of Vatican I with a more pronounced concern for collegiality and subsidiarity in the exercise of authority. Yet careful and attentive to the current concerns as these formulations were, they could not reverse a situation that was made evident by the Reformation of the sixteenth century. Both the principle and the mode of exercise of the Roman magisterium did, and still do, antagonize sizable portions of the people of God in the Orthodox, Anglican, and Protestant Churches. One can even wonder, in the contemporary ecumenical context, if the modern assertions of the Roman primacy, themselves fruits of the Counter-Reformation, have not made the reconciliation of Christians and their reunion into one Church, if not totally impossible, at least extremely unlikely.

Is the Church's Structure Divine?

Christians, especially Catholics, have often said that since the Church of Christ is of divine origin, then it exists *divino jure*, by divine law. Following the ecclesiology of Robert Bellarmine (1542-1621), authors of the Counter-Reformation commonly referred to "the divine constitution" of the Church, thus designating its ministerial and magisterial structures.[6] The sacramental system was believed to have been instituted directly by Christ. And the ministry of deacons, priests, and bishops, including the Petrine primacy, was thought to derive from the apostles and to have a clear foundation in the New Testament, notably in the gospel of Matthew.

Admittedly, in its heyday the Counter-Reformation was unnecessarily aggressive. Yet the formulae that it favored were not all due to some sort of religious imperialism. On the one hand, before the scientific exegesis that has developed since the nineteenth century, Christians read into Scripture aspects of Christian belief and practice that were the fruits of later developments and that the tools of modern scholarship can no longer find in it. On

[6]The first major presentation of ecclesiology in the nineteenth century was based on the principle that the Church has a "divine constitution:" Adrien Gréa, *L'Eglise et sa divine constitution* (Paris: Casterman, 1965 [original edition, 1884]); the same notion is basic to Jacques Maritain's ecclesiology: *De l'Eglise du Christ. La personne de l'Eglise et son personnel* (Paris: Desclée de Brouwer, 1970). See my paper, "Is the Papacy an Object of Faith?" *One in Christ* (1977/3, p. 220–228).

the other hand, canonical language does not always use terms in their popular meaning. In traditional canon law, the adjective, "divine" (*divinus*) is often the equivalent of "religious," as distinct from "profane," "secular," "civil," or "civic." Likewise, in theology, those authors who, writing Latin, called Thomas Aquinas *divus Thomas*, never suggested that St. Thomas was God or even divine. They only meant that, in his field of theological expertise, he was excellent. In the same vein, ARCIC-I agreed in its *Final Report* that to ascribe a *jus divinum* (divine law) to the origin of the papacy, or to assert that the papacy exists *divino jure* (by divine law), does not imply the belief that the papacy was established directly by God or "by Jesus during his life on earth." It need be no more than "the acknowledgment of its emergence by divine providence (*divina providentia*)."

In its legal structure or constitution as a society, the Church can only be human. Yet human efforts are often the fruit of divine grace. They may be guided by the Spirit. And the conviction of being the Spirit's instrument has often inspired exuberant utterances. Those who have experienced salvation in Christ may well apply to the Church, which they know as the community of salvation, the emphatic language that often goes with the expression of love.

Infallible and Indefectible

Two qualifications that have been applied to the Church's magisterium, and by implication to the Church as a whole, now need to be investigated.

The first is borrowed from the category of indefectibility. It is commonly said and believed that the Church and its teaching are indefectible: they will not fail. This corresponds to the insight of the gospel of Matthew when Jesus says to Peter: "You are Rock; and on this rock I will build my Church, and the gates of hell shall not prevail against it" (Matt 16:18). Various interpretations of "rock" have been proposed since at least the time of Augustine: Is it Peter himself? Is it Peter's faith? Is it the apostles' faith that has just been formulated by Peter? Is it, which is more unlikely, Jesus himself? But the ensuing discussions have not dimmed the clarity of the rest of the statement: the powers of evil shall not prevail against the Church. This doctrine is universally accepted by Christians even though there are divergences as to the implications of this biblical saying. Does it mean that the Church can never lapse from the true faith? Does it mean that, although in theory it could lapse, it will never in practice so be let down by divine Providence that it will actually lapse? Does it mean that, in the long run, at the end of time, the Church will be found to have been generally faithful in spite of occasional temporary lapses? Does it imply that there are fundamentals of the faith concerning which no compromise is possible and secondary or "adiaphoral" pious beliefs that should remain optional? And if there are central points of faith that are not expendable, do they include a normative ecclesial structure? Is such a structure revealed? These questions and others were raised in the controversy over papal authority that broke out in the aftermath of Vatican II when Hans Küng suggested that only the indefectibility of the Church is taught in the Scriptures, the later language of infallibility being no more than an emphatic assertion of indefectibility.[7]

The second category is that of infallibility. Vatican Council I summed up a long tradition that had been explicitly formulated since the thirteenth century when it endorsed the doctrine that Jesus, "the divine Redeemer, intended his Church to be taught (*instructam*), in defining doctrine in matters of faith or morals, infallibly" (DS, n. 3074). This infallibility is a "divine assistance that was promised the Church in St. Peter." According to Vatican I and II, it presupposes the conjunction of an "unfailing charism of the truth" (*charisma veritatis certum*: DV, n. 8) with episcopal succession. It is by virtue of this charism that the bishop of Rome acts when, as "pastor and doctor of all Christians, by virtue of his supreme apostolic authority" (DS, n. 3074), he defines a doctrine concerning faith or morals that is to be held by the whole Church.

Ecumenical discussions have distinguished between the principle—that the Church is divinely protected by an infallibility which is God's gift—and the application—that this infallibility is at work in doctrinal definitions made, in certain circumstances, by ecumenical councils or, in others, by the bishop of Rome. There has been much animus in the debate, largely occasioned by interventions of the bishop of Rome in the life of the Church that were perceived to be abuses of authority. Yet possible abuses of authority are irrelevant to the question of irreformable discourse that is envisaged by the notion of infallibility. Whatever their guilt or simply their lack of judgment when and if they abuse their authority, the bishops of Rome may still be qualified to speak for and to the Church when the conditions are ripe for the charism of infallibility to be at work. Moreover, much of the animus of the debate would vanish were it realized by all that irreformability is necessarily involved in all true proclamation of the gospel and in all right administration of the sacraments: what is then done is done irreformably since it is in conformity with the truth of the gospel.

The charism of the Holy Spirit under which the gospel is effectively preached corresponds exactly to what Vatican Councils I and II have meant by infallibility. There is only one difference between sacramental infallibility (*ex opere operato*) and doctrinal infallibility (*ex cathedra*): the first refers to the transmission of divine grace, the second to the transmission of doctrine. But doctrine is no less important to the truth of the gospel than the transmission of grace is to the truth of the sacraments. Therefore, one may well

---

[7]Hans Küng, *Infallible? An Inquiry* (New York: Doubleday, 1971).

ask: why should the transmission of doctrine be less protected by the Spirit than the transmission of grace? This is the Catholic question to Protestants.

One may also hold, with Peter Chirico, that something like infallibility is already involved in a fundamental human experience: "Basically, infallibility has to do with the mind's grasp of a universal meaning." That people find meanings in life is "a datum of consciousness."[8] The experience of mutual understanding across differing cultures shows that there are universal meanings or meanings that are universally understandable among humans. In this perspective, the qualification of infallibility may properly be applied to universal Christian meanings: it is infallibly true, for instance, that Christ is the only Mediator, that Christ is Lord, that sinners are justified by grace through faith, that divine grace is conveyed in the preaching of the gospel and the administration of the sacraments.

Ex sese

According to Vatican Council I, the definitions of doctrine that are proclaimed *ex cathedra* by the bishop of Rome are "irreformable by themselves, and not by virtue of the Church's consent" (*ex sese, non autem ex consensu ecclesiae*). This last statement was aimed at the conciliarist or gallican opinion that definitions of doctrine, whether made by an ecumenical council or by the bishop of Rome, are not binding until they have been endorsed by national and local Churches. In other words, the truth of a doctrine is not dependent on its acceptance.

Yet two remarks may smooth the sharp edges of this idea. On the one hand, a doctrine is not believed if it is not accepted. There is no belief without acceptance of what is believed, no faith without acknowledgment of its truth. Teaching does not take place in a vacuum but in a dialectic of proposition and response. A doctrine that is not received is, by definition, not taught. Vatican I was correct: the consent of the Church is not necessary to the truth of a doctrinal definition. But this self-evident point needs a complement: the reception of doctrine is intrinsic to the nature of doctrine. It is essential to the authenticity of a doctrinal definition. For this reason, Vatican II added: "To such definitions [as meet the four conditions of Vatican I for papal infallibility] the assent of the Church can never be lacking, thanks to the action of the Holy Spirit through which the universal flock of Christ is preserved and makes progress in unity of faith" (LG, n. 25).

On the other hand, if the consent of the Church is not a condition for the truth of an authentic definition of doctrine, there is indeed one aspect of the papal magisterium that originates in the consent of the Church. Vatican Council I specified that the papal primacy includes a "power of immediate

[8]Peter Chirico, *Infallibility: The Crossroads of Doctrine* (Wilmington: Michael Glazier, 1983).

jurisdiction that is truly episcopal" (DS, n. 3060). The power of the Roman primate is episcopal since it accrues to him as bishop of Rome. And episcopal jurisdiction is immediate, for without it no bishop would be able to function as a bishop. But the notion of jurisdiction is itself a legal category that derives from the development of canon law out of Roman law. And the extent of jurisdiction can only be determined by disciplinary decisions of the magisterium. A bishop may well have immediate jurisdiction outside his diocese as in the case of the archbishops of the Carolingian age in their metropolitan province, or in that of the bishop of Rome in the universal Church. But this results from disciplinary options and decisions that may indeed be justified by the requirements of *episcope* in certain circumstances. The effective application of such a decision, however, is conditioned precisely by the consent of the Church.

The Ecumenical Difficulty

One point remains ecumenically difficult. This is the Roman Catholic attribution to one person in one office (the bishop in the see of Rome) of the task of making doctrinal definitions that effectively convey universal Christian meanings. At this point, the evidence of the New Testament is not convincing. For on the one hand, the Fathers of the Church proposed divergent interpretations of the texts that were later used to support papal infallibility. On the other hand, the use that was made of these texts in Roman Catholic polemics (notably of Matthew 16:18-19 and John 21:15-19) is not supported by modern scientific exegesis. In order to find them persuasive, one has to use a concept of the "fuller" sense of the Bible (*sensus plenior*) that is itself a recent and highly dubious invention.

The evidence of historical development is more convincing. The history of the Church is guided and protected by the Holy Spirit. If there is one Christian believer who by virtue of office and responsibility is in a position generally to speak for the whole Church, it can only be the bishop of Rome. But however impressive it may be to the historian, the evidence of historical development is not fully persuasive to the believer without the category of trust. To recognize the infallibility of the Church in doctrinal pronouncements by the bishop of Rome, trust is necessary: one needs to trust that this is the way of the Holy Spirit. But trust is not blind. If the see and the bishop of Rome do not appear to be trustworthy, they will not inspire trust; and if they are not trusted to speak the truth, their teaching will not be received by the people of God. In the context of Roman Catholic history and theology, the necessary condition of trust does not give a merely human status to the definitions of doctrine to which the note of infallibility is assigned. But it takes account of the fact that the Spirit of God works in the Church through human agents.

In the context of the whole Christian world, however, this is not yet a reality. Yet the remaining differences do not seem to be insuperable. Several ecumenical dialogues have already reflected on them and have made recommendations toward finding ways of escape from the present dilemma of the Christian magisterium. Some of these dialogues deserve careful attention and study, notably *Lutherans and Catholics in Dialogue* (USA) in their volumes IV (1970), V (1974), and VI (1980), and ARCIC-I in the second statement on Authority in the Church (1981) included in the *Final Report*.

The Ecumenical Opportunity

Seen in the long run, the contemporary magisterial structure of the Church results from a slow evolution of its ministerial structure. The magisterium is no other than ministerium or service of doctrine. There is only one alternative to a doctrinal magisterium. This is the obsolete proclamation of the believers' right to private interpretation. Such a proclamation, however, although it is frequently ascribed in the popular mind to the Reformers, has never been a serious Protestant doctrine. It has been no more than a polemical and hardly accurate formulation of Calvin's insight that the believers who read Scripture with faith experience in themselves the interior testimony of the Holy Spirit. The assumption of some Churches that they function on a non-credal basis, having "no creed but the Scriptures," is not a proper alternative: it merely shows that one may live the Christian life without formulating its demands. In this case, however, a magisterium is still at work, namely, the magisterium of example by the whole people of God that is often conveyed story-wise in preaching, in Bible-reading, and in personal sharing.

Yet the existence and the necessity of Christian magisterium are not without dangers for the Christian faith and Church. Given the complexities of the capitalist society in which the Church now lives, magisterium tends to function according to a managerial model that has a great deal to do with the management of property and of financial assets but very little, if anything, with the proclamation of the gospel and the administration of the sacraments. Given the spread of political democracy and the corresponding popularity of liberal or permissive standards of public order, one may expect the magisterial structure of the Church to be challenged more and more by the claims of the majority to rule or by those of personal exemption in keeping with the dictates of conscience. But as anyone can tell who has observed the functioning of modern democracies, majority does not amount to unanimity of hearts. It is never a substitute for logical coherence and fidelity to tradition. As to the personal conscience, it needs to be informed by correct principles if it is to reach correct conclusions.

Furthermore, new questions concerning the magisterium and its structure have arisen from the emancipation of women in modern society. A parallel emancipation of women in the Church has become inescapable. Given the number of women in the Church and their active role in the transmission of the faith in family circles, the option is now to open to women, as fully responsible Christians, the access to ministerial and magisterial authority and therefore, where this is socially desirable and sacramentally acceptable, the access to ordination. What stands in the way is not simply, as critics of the traditional system of ordination often contend, a paternalism of the ordained that would be tainted by heavy doses of patriarchal prejudice or even the spontaneous conservatism of religious institutions. It is rather the feeling that the better part of wisdom, for a society that is as large as the Church, is not to engage in untried ways and untrodden paths. This is the basic reason behind the lingering doubt, formulated in some authoritative statements of the Roman Catholic magisterium, that the Church of today has authority to change courses of action that were set by the early Church and have been honored ever since. The question of the ordination of women is a case in point.[9]

One can react to these challenges with pessimism. Then one will hanker after the good old time before the challenges arose and project impossible reactionary moves like returning to a literal understanding of the Scriptures or abolishing the decisions of Vatican Council II or returning to the liturgy of Pius V. One can also react with uncritical condemnations of the traditional magisterium. In either case, the reaction is wrong. For the Christian hope is inseparable from the Christian faith. To doubt the continuing fidelity of the Church to the gospel is to sin against the Word who is present in his Church according to his promise and against the Holy Spirit who guides it.

For Further Reading

Charles Journet. *The Church of the Word Incarnate. Part I: The Apostolic Hierarchy.* New York: Sheed and Ward, 1954.

Paul Empie and Austin Murphy, eds. *Lutherans and Catholics in Dialogue, V: Papal Primacy and the Universal Church.* Minneapolis: Augsburg Publishing House, 1974.

Paul Empie, Austin Murphy, and Joseph Burgess, eds. *Lutherans and Catholics in Dialogue, VI: Teaching Authority and Infallibility in the Church.* Minneapolis: Augsburg Publishing House, 1980.

Jean-Marie Tillard. *The Bishop of Rome.* Wilmington: Michael Glazier, 1983.

Roman Catholic/Lutheran Joint Commission. *Facing Unity: Models, Forms and Phases of Catholic-Lutheran Church Fellowship.* Geneva: Lutheran World Federation, 1985.

Kenan B. Osborne. *Priesthood: A History of the Ordained Ministry in the Roman Catholic Church.* New York: Paulist Press, 1988.

[9]Text of the Statement on Ordination of Women issued by the Congregation for the Doctrine of the Faith, in Leonard and Arlene Swidler, eds., *Women Priests: A Catholic Commentary on the Vatican Declaration* (New York: Paulist Press, 1977), p. 37–49; see Tavard, "The Ordination of Women" *One in Christ* (1987/3), p. 200–211.

10

Church and World

The community of salvation has a social structure. This is a sociological necessity. All groups and societies are structured both internally, in themselves, and externally, in relation to others. Without a structure, they would only be haphazard collections of individuals. The Church's interior structure is primarily ministerial, or made for service: tasks and responsibilities are spread out among the members according to certain patterns. It became magisterial as soon as the Church was too large for decision making by unanimous consent. Soon, distinctions of functions in the membership brought about sharper distinctions of responsibilities: a minority of the members were entrusted with tasks of leadership.

The structural question, however, does not end here. The passage from ministerium to magisterium is decisive for internal relationships but not for the relations of the Church with the pluralistic context of human society or with the natural environment of the world. As long as there remain people—in fact, the majority of humankind—who see the Church from outside or who do not see it at all, the investigation of ecclesial structure needs to be pushed further: there must be structural relations between the Church and the world.

According to the gospel of Matthew, the Church was commissioned to preach the gospel to all nations and to baptize them "in the Name of the Father, the Son, and the Holy Spirit" (Matt 28:19). From the start, therefore, ecclesiology has had a missionary dimension which is relative to those to whom the Church is sent, "the nations." Whether this term was originally intended in the strict sense, meaning the Gentiles as contradistinguished from the Jews, or in a broader meaning that includes the Jewish people, is a moot question to which we will turn our attention later. It will suffice for the time being to regard the world in general as partner-in-dialogue with the Church.

Two Meanings of "World"

Like everyone else on earth, the Christian faithful are born into the world by natural process before being born into the Church by faith and baptism. This self-evident fact sufficiently shows how important it is for Christians to have clear ideas concerning the relations of the Church with the world. Yet this expression may be misleading. For it suggests that the Church is other than, or outside, the world and, if so, that it needs to go out of itself to engage in conversation with those who are not of it. In reality, for the Church and its members, the world is not another country. When Tertullian designated Christians as "the third race," he contrasted their religion with the pagan cults that were still popular in the Roman empire and with the Judaism that had survived the destruction of Jerusalem: within the Church there are no more Jews and Gentiles since "all are one in Christ Jesus" (Gal 3:28). Tertullian did not locate the "third race" alongside the world any more than Paul placed Christianity alongside Judaism and Hellenism. Rather, the Christian faith was a new phenomenon, and it was the vocation of the believers to renovate both Judaism and Hellenism.[1] Yet as is manifest in the gospel of John, the concept of world has, from the beginning, been ambiguous in Christian thought. And so it remains if we are to judge from the Christians' customary manner of speech concerning the world.

On the one hand, Christian theology has not generally seen the world as alien to the Church. Rather, it has presented the Christian vocation as a service to the world. The faithful pray for the conversion of the world and for the coming of the kingdom of God so that the world may be saved. The third race is a leaven in the dough. As this clearly implies, the dough is basically good and is ultimately destined to excellence. There is harmony between God's design in creating the world and God's persistence in sending the eternal Word to save it and to reveal the divine purpose. For this reason, Christian artists contemplating the beauty of the world have discovered in it a sacramental dimension. This is in keeping with the Scriptures. Already in the gospels, the kingdom of God bears the features of worldly events: it is symbolized by a banquet (Matt 22:1-14), by a wedding (25:1-13), by the payment of salaries to workers (20:1-16); its coming is compared with the building of a tower (21:33) and even with the preparations of a king who goes to war against another (Luke 14:31-33).

On the other hand, Christian writers have commonly denounced the world as a place from which one should escape in order to ascend to God. The world is, or has become, evil. It is the realm of Satan. Its inhabitants form, in the hard words of St. Augustine, a *massa perditionis*, a mass of perdition.[2] In the gospel of John, Jesus does not pray that God take the disciples "out of

[1] The Christians are "a race that covers the world" (*Apologeticum*, 37, 4).

[2] Humanity is a *massa damnata* (*Enchiridion*, n. 27: PL, 41, 245), *massa perditionis* (*De Peccato Originali* 29, n. 34; PL, 44, 402).

the world" (John 17:15). Yet in the first Johannine epistle, the disciples are told not "to love the world or the things that are in the world" (1 John 2:15). The monastic or religious life has often been depicted as an escape from the world and its temptations, the way of meditation and contemplation as a path leading away from entanglements with the world.

At first reading, therefore, Christian language and literature appear to be caught in a web of self-contradictions. The questions themselves are simple: Is the world good or is it evil? Should the believers feel a positive responsibility toward the welfare of the world or only a negative responsibility to condemn it and to abandon it? The answers are not so simple.

Since the first century of the Christian era, the Church has in fact functioned with two conflicting perspectives. In the first place, the world is God's creation, and as such, it cannot be other than good. In the second place, the world labors under the weight of sin, and as such, it needs redemption. But since redemption can neither be bought nor be effected by human effort, those who pursue wisdom, and Christians in the first rank of them, should stay as far from the world and its pomp as is possible in this life. Along the first line, Christians agree with the thrust of ancient paganism as a religion of enhancement and enjoyment: since it is good, the world is to be both used and enjoyed. Along the second line, Christianity agrees with the religions and philosophies of escape from dispersion (like Neo-Platonism), from illusion (like Hinduism in most of its *darçanas*), or from unreality (like Buddhism in its two main branches).

These conflicting perspectives turn around the term "world" (*mundus*, in Latin). This word in fact translates two different Greek concepts: *cosmos* and *oecumene*. The cosmos is the material world—nature with its plants and animals, its lands and seas, its stars and planets. The *oecumene* is the inhabited space, that portion of the cosmos that has been humanized through a progressive mastery of nature—from primitive hunting and digging to agriculture, animal husbandry and shelter-building, to urban habitat, transformation of raw materials, planned technical production, and sophisticated architecture. In the Christian as in the biblical perspective, the cosmos is good since it is directly the work of God and not, as was held among the Greeks, that of a demiurge, a transcendent technician of creation who would be more or less morally good in himself. Like all religions, however, Christianity has reflected on the universal experience of physical and moral evil. It has taught that the *oecumene* has been damaged by sin at least from the beginning of humanity and possibly by an antecedent sin of spiritual creatures, the angels; that the sin of the first humans has been transmitted to their descendants (original sin); and that, in addition, all humans have contributed to the evil of the world through their personal sins. Humanity has been at least wounded—some among the Reformers said, corrupted—by sin. Created in a state of friendship with God, the first humans lost divine grace and were left to shift for themselves on an estranged earth.

This general version of the origins of humanity was nurtured among theologians by the ancient cosmology of Ptolemy (who worked around 139 A.D. and was still alive in 161). The Ptolemaic cosmology seemed to support the biblical view of the cosmos and therefore the biblical vision of the creation of the world. It was taken for granted in Europe until the end of the Middle Ages when Copernicus (1473-1543) theorized and Galileo (1564-1642) demonstrated that the earth is not located at the physical center of the universe. But even Galileo's view differed considerably from the contemporary scientific data about an expanding universe that emerged by explosion in an original "big bang." One may then ask: how much of the fundamental pessimism that the Christian tradition has exhibited toward the world is compatible with the modern scientific view of the cosmos?

Church and Creation

Whatever scientific investigation can discover about the material ingredients and the origin of the universe, the universe is God's work. From the point of view of God's creative power, it makes no difference whether the cosmos was made and organized gradually as in chapter 1 of Genesis or was made as a cosmic garden planted with seeds and "seminal reasons" (as St. Augustine and medieval authors believed) or originally appeared as a cosmic egg that exploded into innumerable galaxies of stars or was made, as it were, ready to wear with all its details and variations already set, as is popularly believed by a number of less educated religious persons. The universe was created *ex nihilo*, out of nothing. But it remains debatable whether this implies a temporal beginning of creation or is compatible with a sequence of successive configurations of matter in a process of expansion that may eventually be reversed, as in an everlasting succession of cosmic heartbeats. In any case, the metaphysics of creation are one thing; scientific hypotheses are something else. And the impact that is made on the popular mind by theories on the origins is still another.

Unquestionably, ecclesiology has always been marked by a cosmological framework. And the reason for this is simply that the Church has always interacted with the world both as the natural cosmos and as the inhabited, humanized, *oecumene*. For the Hebrews, the cosmos was made for the *oecumene,* that is, for humanity and humanity for the kingdom of God. And it was in part because they experienced God's guidance over their tribal and national life and because the tribes or nations that they met were hostile to them that the Hebrews and their successors, the Jews, believed themselves to be God's chosen people. After the destruction of the Temple and, later, of Jerusalem, the followers of Jesus severed their ties to the synagogue largely because their missionary efforts in the Roman empire had more success among Gentiles than among Jews. As later generations of Christians read the history of Jesus and of their community as though written by the hand of God, they began to see the cosmos and creation in a new light. They understood their Church, identified with the community of the followers of Jesus, to stand at the junction of humanity and the kingdom of God. The creative process leads to the Church. And the Church is destined to crown the creative process by initiating all humans into the kingdom of God and its justice. This broad perspective was common to the Fathers of the Church and to medieval theologians.

Theologically, creation is not an empirical, observable fact. It is an internal and invisible relation of total dependence of the universe upon God. In all that it is, the universe rests entirely on God's creative presence. There is a divine action that continuously gives the creatures being. Were this action to cease, the universe would be annihilated. But while the divine action is necessarily interior to God, it posits the cosmos as a being of its own, as it were, outside of God (*ad extra*). In the Trinitarian perspective of Christian theology, the three divine Persons are involved in the creative process. It is as Father that the First Person creates, as the Father's eternal Word that the Second Person mediates the creative act, and as the Spirit of the Father that the Third Person guides the life that is elicited from matter in the creative process. It follows that the created universe bears the Trinitarian mark, even though this may be visible only to the eyes of faith.

Along this line of thought, the ultimate purpose of creation cannot be other than doxological. Creation is theophanous. It is the epiphany of the glory of God. As Vatican Council I stated it, the universe was created by God "to manifest his goodness through the goods he has given the creatures" (DS, n. 3002). But this does not make the cosmos a mere theater on the scene of which "creatures" and "goods" enter and meet. The cosmos itself is already creaturely and good. It comes from God by total creation, and it is engaged in a long pilgrimage through time, sustained at every moment by the creative power. If one posits a theoretical point in the future when God's purpose will be fulfilled, then this point will see the ingathering of all creatures for the glory to God; and at that ultimate moment the universe will become Church.

Christian theology has drawn the logical consequence of this cosmic vision. In its yet partially latent doxological dimension, the cosmos is already the Church. Conversely, the Church on earth is the doxological dimension of the cosmos. The religious philosophy of Teilhard de Chardin (1881-1955) attempted to express this insight in terms of modern science: through a process of humanization that is itself grafted on a broader process of evolution, the universe is on the way to "Point Omega."[3] At that eschatological point, the universe unites with its goal. This goal is personalized as

---

[3] Christopher Mooney, *Teilhard de Chardin and the Mystery of Christ* (New York: Harper and Row, 1966); Augustine, *Sermo* 341, I, 1 (PL, 39, 1493).

the risen Christ of the gospels, the cosmic Christ of the epistle to the Colossians 1:15-20, the *totus Christus* of St. Augustine.

Church and Humankind

The cosmic vision of Christianity is broad and bold. It is also consistent. It assigns to the *ecclesia* of the disciples of Jesus an entirely unique place in the cosmos. But that is not all. For if in its essential reality the Church is the doxological dimension of the cosmos, then it must also be the doxological dimension of humanity. The glory that rises up to God from creation can be defined by analogy with human glory, in abstraction; it cannot be defined directly and concretely since it cannot be subsumed under any higher known category. The cosmos is the highest category of creation. Glory is that aspect of it that God designates as the fulfillment of his work. Humanity is the voice which explicitly sings glory to God in the cosmos. The Christian Church is the chorus in which this voice is heard on earth. Yet the glory itself cannot be comprehended by the human mind, even when the mystics of many religions are given some inkling of its radiance.

This doxological reality of the Church lies at the heart of its worship. It is particularly evident in the liturgy of St. John Chrysostom, which is standard in the Byzantine Churches: the Church gathers in one all that on earth gives glory to God and presents it to the Father, through the mediation of the Word, in the power and inspiration of the Holy Spirit. The Latin liturgy of the Mass follows the same principle, although without stressing it so much: the celebrant collects into one supplication—the "collect"—the intentions of all those who are present and all those who are distant. This is admittedly seldom apparent in the text of the collect, given the trivial translations that are commonly used in the English versions of the Mass. Liturgical commissions do not always cope successfully with problems of language and of literary taste. But this does not invalidate the principle: the liturgy is the chief moment when the Christian community fulfills its task of giving voice to the cosmic singing of the glory of God.

In keeping with the doxological principle, the Fathers of the Church frequently affirmed that angels of God are present at, and commune with, the Christian liturgy. Angels rejoice at baptism. They adore at the Eucharist. They watch over the gatherings of the Christian community. They follow the pilgrimage of the Church and of its members through life. Christian art depicts them weighing the soul in the scales of the particular judgment. It was indeed taken for granted in Scripture and in Christian writings before the Enlightenment that God has created a spiritual world beyond this universe. After the Enlightenment gave respectability to a broad skepticism regarding all that is not empirically verifiable, Christian literature began to treat the angelic world as mythological. The faithful in the past were therefore more aware than they are today of their relations to angels and other spiritual creatures. This awareness considerably broadened their view of the works of God, of the universe, and of the Church. But even today, the traditional symbols which still pervade the older liturgical rites have not lost their value. All of God's creation is destined to sing the divine glory. And if there are spiritual creatures that are unimpeded by conditions of time and space, they are welcome to join the glorification of God wherever and whenever it takes place.

The cosmic task of the Church in relation to humankind has a further dimension. If indeed God's revelation in Christ, as it is expressed in the Scriptures and understood in the Christian tradition, identifies the Church as the doxological voice of the cosmos, then the Church is not just a voice that would be occasionally available for doxological purposes. Rather, it embodies no less than the doxological vocation of humankind. The Church is constituted by God as the totality of humankind in its response to its doxological vocation. It is humanity in prayer. The Church is God's free gift of spiritual unity to humankind as the adorer and glorifier of God. It is the bearer of humanity, not as an accidental conglomeration of individuals but as the corporate offering of the universe to God.

As such, the Church does not come from below. It is not made by the disciples when they gather for worship and for mutual support. Rather, it is essentially a grace, the offer of a new beginning to humanity. It is a unity given by God, something like a new creation.

Christian Anthropology

The cosmic perspective on the divine glory entails a specific conception of humanity and the human person itself. This has been obscured in recent centuries by the breakdown of the theological anthropology of the Fathers of the Church and of the Scholastics. Their anthropology was tied at first to the philosophy of Plato, then to the metaphysics of Aristotle as this was made available in Europe in the thirteenth century by Latin translations of commentaries composed by Muslims and by Jews. But the Christian reading of Aristotle and the theology that came from it could not survive the questioning of all knowledge by René Descartes and the ensuing emergence of the philosophies of the Enlightenment. For classical anthropology, the human person is composed of body and soul (matter and form). The soul functions through the three faculties of memory, intellect, and will. Human action occasions the growth of practical, moral, and intellectual powers or virtues. To this, the theologians add that the theological virtues, hope, faith, and charity, inform the faculties, thus enabling the soul to develop Christian virtues and habits. The image of God that is imparted by creation resides in the threeness of the faculties within the oneness of the soul. And this image is transformed by grace into a closer likeness through the theological virtues.

The scholastic anthropological synthesis, however, rests on a faculty-psychology that does not correspond to modern theories. Moreover, the theology of the image of God that it implies does not tally with the modern exegeses of Genesis 1:26: "Let us make Adam in our image and likeness." Nor is it identical with the conception of the image of God that developed among the Greek Fathers and has remained embodied in the art of the icons. The old Christian anthropology has become obsolete. Yet it has not yet been replaced. There is now no generally accepted understanding, even in the Church, of what it means to be human. While the official language of the Roman Catholic magisterium frequently uses the categories of Scholastic anthropology in a somewhat modified form, this language is now too out-moded for the people or the theologians to be comfortable with it. This is why magisterial instructions regarding human sexuality are widely mis-understood, ignored, and disregarded. On the one hand, the popular mind has been affected by the philosophies of the Enlightenment, by varying and often conflicting psychological and psychoanalytical theories, and by grow-ing reliance on the advance of modern medicine, all of which have grown with no reference to a theological conception of the human.

On the other hand, theologians cannot be satisfied with primitive con-ceptions that divide the human into two complementary halves, the male and the female. The physiological complementarity of the sexes, related as it may be to psychological orientations, has no bearing on intellectual and spiritual capacities. At the broader level of human relationships, women and men bring each other, not a complement of capacities but a supplement of humanity. Each being already fully human, no complement is needed, and their relationship cannot be based on complementarity. A complemen-tarity of capacities results in stereotyped social roles.[4] A supplement of humanity flourishes in the sharing of roles for the mutual enrichment of all. From human sexuality one can therefore draw no theological conclusions about the existence of divinely assigned exclusive roles in society and in the Church.

There is, however, in the Christian tradition itself, the seed of another kind of theological anthropology than that of the Scholastics. If the human person is placed in its cosmic setting and the cosmos is the physical theater of God's glory, then the human person is radically doxological, not only in action but already in being. The human person may then be defined, in the words of St. John of the Cross, as "God by participation."[5] In other words, there is a dimension of the human person that is bound to escape the human sciences, ancient or modern. This dimension may be discerned in its main

---

[4]George H. Tavard, "Theology and Sexuality," in Ursula King, ed., *Women in the World's Religions: Past and Present* (New York: Paragon House, 1987), p. 68-80.

[5]George H. Tavard, *Poetry and Contemplation in St. John of the Cross* (Athens, OH: Ohio University Press, 1988), p. 215-216.

delineaments by those who study history as the record of human attempts to know and praise God, with its successes and its failures. It may also be discovered more philosophically by those who, with Maurice Blondel,[6] perceive in human action a nisus that aspires beyond the human horizon: in spite of its unavoidable limitations, action entails an orientation of the human to the absolute, which reaches its acme in the liturgical action of singing the glory of God. One may surmise that all religions and mythologies have their origin in this transcendental dimension of the human: in their wish to give concrete shape to the most fundamental desire of the human heart, women and men have imagined worlds of glory where they have hoped to live after the present life. From time to time, the mystics of all religions have caught glimpses of the reality intended by such images. Yet the religions fail if they are merely human products.

Because they are entirely gratuitous, neither the new creation nor the Church of God can be demonstrated by science. They do not materialize at the end of a philosophical deduction. The Church is a harbor that may be discovered after a voyage of exploration, but only if the exploration has been led by the Spirit of God. When the Church is offered by God, one must enter it through faith alone. As John of the Cross also wrote, "Faith is the proximate and proportional means of union with God."[7] The gate through which one enters this divine revealing is no other than Jesus Christ, the Word made flesh, who "suffered outside the gate" (Heb 11:12) for the salvation of humankind.

In this case, freedom is a fundamental human category. Freedom of choice for oneself, basic to modern civilization, is a debased form of a higher freedom, the freedom of the children of God, that is God's gift to women and men alike. This higher freedom, the freedom of grace, can be experienced anywhere by anyone who lives by faith. But it also has a corporate dimension since it is given to the common humanity of women and men. This corporate dimension is visible in the divine gift that is the Church.

But if the Church is entirely a gift from God, then it cannot be limited to any one of the empirical entities that are called religions or Churches. For it is given to humanity and for humanity as such, and not only in the Hebraic, Greek, Latin, European, or American embodiments of humanity that have shaped the Christian Church. It cannot be equated with a local or a national or even a universal Church. It can be no less than the universe. At this point, one is caught in a paradox. For the universe is, in principle, visible even though it cannot possibly be seen as a whole from within. That which is visible of the universe is its materiality. That which can be known of it beyond the visible is its measurability in mathematical formulae. But the glory of

[6]Maurice Blondel, *L'Action (1893). Essai d'une critique de la vie et d'une science de la pratique* (Paris: Presses Universitaires de France), 1950.

[7]Tavard, l. c., p. 111.

God that pervades the universe cannot be condensed in equations and apprehended mathematically. Nonetheless, the Church, which is the manifestation of the glory of God, is not invisible. It is not a hidden dimension of the universe. It is indeed known by faith alone. Yet if the Church is doxological, it must be visible, for liturgy—as the chorus of the voices that give glory to God—has to be visible and audible for participants to join in it.

This is the reason why the Church of Christ on earth takes the form of a society. As a society it has its rules, its canon law, its members and officers, its buildings, its meetings and conventions, its commissions and committees, its libraries, its newspapers and radio or television stations, its dinners and parties, its symbols and even its slogans. It has its public opinion, its debates, its conflicts. It is liable to misunderstanding and can be the object of distrust and persecution. But the paraphernalia of a world-wide society, that are undoubtedly present and alive in the Church, find their meaning in those aspects that reflect the glory of God and in those moments when the community in prayer gives glory to God in the name of all creation.

Extra Ecclesiam Nulla Salus

Some aspects of the doxological conception of the Church raise questions that are undoubtedly difficult from an apologetical point of view. If, because of the Lordship of Christ over all, the Christian Church is ultimately identical with the doxological dimension of the universe, then all the human race is called to be part of it. The "third race" of Tertullian should eventually absorb the previous "races" of Jews and Gentiles. But this notion is perceived today as intolerable imperialism. Misunderstood by the Christians themselves, it has inspired the persecution of Jews through the centuries. The nations of advanced religious civilization have taken offense at the missionary impulse of Christianity, which they have experienced as a threat to their identity. Muslims and Hindus have therefore frowned upon the Christian missionary witness, so that in some Islamic nations today the public expression of the Christian faith is no more tolerated than it has been in hard-line Communist regimes that, following the October Revolution, made atheism a political dogma.

In addition, the liberalism of democratic countries sees mutual tolerance as a condition of public order. Then, all opinions being equally respected, the claim of one opinion to absolute truth tends to be resented as undemocratic and therefore as dangerous to the very fabric of society.

In these conditions, the traditional axiom of Catholicism, "Outside the Church, no salvation" (*Extra ecclesiam nulla salus*), and its popular rendering among Roman Catholics, "Only one true Church," are often committed to oblivion, if not contradicted, by the believers themselves. But if the Protestant mind has generally no problem with disregarding a traditional principle that appears to be obsolete, the Catholic mentality is then bewildered: if the tradition transmits the truth of faith, then should a traditional axiom be discarded simply because it has become uncomfortable? The answer to this question touches directly on ecclesiology. The Church's missionary task hangs in the balance.

In its historical origins, the formula, *Extra ecclesiam nulla salus*, derives from St. Cyprian of Carthage (d. 258). It was originally a polemical expression that opposed sectarian groupings of heretics—gnostics and others—to the Church. Cyprian's chief concern was about baptism. Baptism is necessary to salvation, and in his theology, there is no true baptism except in the Church that goes back to the apostles and no baptismal grace outside the visible Church. Cyprian's conception of baptism, however, was opposed to that of Stephen, bishop of Rome (pope, 254–258), for whom baptism is perfectly valid outside the visible Church as long as it is properly administered with the intention "to do what the Church does." For then it is not the minister, but Christ himself, who baptizes. Yet the principle, *Extra ecclesiam nulla salus*, was not thereby rejected.

In the Middle Ages, the axiom acted as a weapon against all schisms and heresies, the distinction between the two remaining largely undefined. At Lateran Council IV in 1215, it was opposed to the doctrines of the Albigensians: "There is one universal Church of the faithful, outside of which no one is saved. . . ." (DS, n. 802). The council's concern was sacramental: in this universal Church "Jesus Christ the priest is the sacrifice. . . ." His body and blood are truly present in the sacrament of the altar. . . ." The council further affirmed the necessity of ordination to "confect this sacrament," baptism in the name of the Three Persons, the sacrament of penance, and the access of the married as well as the single to salvation "by right faith and good action."

Extra ecclesiam nulla salus was also appealed to in the medieval struggles of the Church with the secular powers. But when Pope Gregory VII (pope, 1073–85) in the unofficial *Dictatus papae* that are found in his Register and Pope Boniface VIII (pope, 1294–1308) in the bull *Unam sanctam* (1300) identified the Church with the jurisdiction of the bishop of Rome, the axiom became a tool in support of the papacy against emperor and kings whenever the secular powers claimed to have authority over the Church.

With the breakdown of Christendom and the division of Christian believers in competing Churches, the axiom raised new questions: which is the Church outside of which there is no salvation? Is it the visible Church of Rome? Is it the collection of Christian Churches? Is it an invisible Church underlying the empirical Churches? In the polemics of the Counter-Reformation, the traditional axiom was often taken to mean that no one can be saved outside of explicit membership in the Roman Catholic Church. But this narrow interpretation which was already rejected by most theologians was officially denied when the question was raised in Boston in 1949.

The Letter of the Holy Office to the Archbishop of Boston, Cardinal Cushing (August 1949), on the doctrines taught by the chaplain at Harvard University, Leonard Feeney, stated: "This dogma"—*Extra ecclesiam nullam esse salutem*—"is to be understood in the sense in which it is understood by the Church itself" (DS, n. 3866). It flows from the commission to preach the gospel to all nations: those who receive the gospel and believe must then act according to their faith. "Therefore no one will be saved, who, knowing the Church to have been instituted by Christ, nonetheless refuses to submit to the Church or to obey the Roman Pontiff, who is Christ's vicar on earth" (DS, n. 3867).

In other words, salvation requires good faith. Those who know the Church's or the pope's place in the Divine Plan must act accordingly, obeying the Church or the pope. As to those who do not know such things, they must naturally follow the dictates of their conscience since conscience always provides the proximate rule of action.

Membership in the Church

The question of membership in the Church is nonetheless important. If the Church is indeed the community of salvation, then one cannot be saved outside of it. But there may be more or less flexibility in defining membership in the Church. The answer to that question is bound to determine the believers' understanding of the Church's stance in an unbelieving world. The various theories that have been put forward regarding the "salvation of infidels," the "theology of paganism," and the nature of the Church's missionary calling have their origin precisely in the underlying problem of membership in the community of salvation. Contemporary questions about announcing the gospel, about disturbing the good faith of Hindus or Muslims, about relations with the adherents of other religions, about the nature of interreligious dialogue, about the task of missionaries and the proper training in view of this task also originate in the previous question of membership in the Church.

The claim that the Christian faith is necessary to salvation is of course grounded in the dogmatic belief that Jesus Christ is the only mediator between the Creator and creation. But the sharp edge of this claim is blunted by several qualifications.

1) First, many persons in the world are in a position of invincible ignorance of the Lordship of Christ; and this takes away their responsibility to acknowledge Christ and join his Church.

2) Second, the Church, membership in which is necessary to salvation, is not an empirical institution. It is the Church "of God" or "of Christ" in an absolute sense. In the words of Vatican Council II, this absolute Church is believed by Catholics to "subsist" in the Roman Catholic Church (LG, n. 8).

But it is not limited to the visible boundaries of this Church. And it presumably also "subsists" in other institutions of salvation.

3) Third, membership is itself not a clear concept. It may be explicit or implicit. Implicit membership, which is often called membership in desire or by desire (*in voto*), is explained in the letter to the Archbishop of Boston: in the case of invincible ignorance, "God accepts an implicit desire, so called because it is contained in the soul's good disposition by which a human person wants its own will to conform to God's will" (DS, n. 3870). Such a will implies an "orientation toward the Church," provided it be "informed by perfect love" (DS, n. 3872). Yet given the shortcomings of the human condition and the natural self-centeredness of the human heart, perfect love is rare, so that the theory of membership *in voto*, if qualified by the requirement of perfect love, remains quite restrictive.

The problematic of *Extra salus*, however, may be reversed. Rather than trying to identify that community, membership in which is necessary to salvation, one can believe that God's grace is active everywhere and in all human persons. And wherever someone experiences God's gifts, bestowed in view of eternal salvation, there is the holy community, the Church, in its inner spiritual reality of communion with God. In this case, *Extra ecclesiam nulla salus* reflects no restrictive doctrine on membership. It is a negative form of the positive statement, *ubi salus, ibi ecclesia:* where there is, by God's grace, salvation, there the Church of God is. What this implies for the relations between the Christian Church and the followers of other religions will be examined in Part Four of the present volume.

The "Person" of the Church

The expression is in Thomas Aquinas: "The Lord's prayer is said by the common person of the whole Church."[8] The Catholic philosopher Jacques Maritain argued from this that the Church "itself—in that as it is the one and universal totality of the multitude [of its members]—has, supernaturally, . . . truly, and ontologically, a personality, . . . it is a person in the first and proper sense of the word, a person who worships God, presents to us the truths revealed by God, sanctifies us through the sacraments, speaks, teaches, and acts." With all its sophistication, Maritain's philosophy tallies with a popular manner of speaking that is not unusual among ordinary believers, and not only among Catholics. Thus the Church is endowed with personality. It—or, she—preaches the gospel; she prays and suffers; she is persecuted. Maritain specifies that the personality of the Church is not to be taken in a juridical or moral sense: the Church is more than a legal entity. In fact,

[8]*Summa theologica* II II, q.83, a.16, ad 3; see Jacques Maritain, *De l'Eglise du Christ. La personne de l'Eglise et son personnel* (Paris: Desclée de Brouwer, 1970). See above, ch. 5, p. 85 and note 4.

the ecclesiology of the Mystical Body has often followed this line of thought: as the Mystical Body of Christ, the Church would be a created person, associated with and modeled on the Person of the Word of God Incarnate. Maritain argued that he found this doctrine in St. Irenaeus, in the creed of Nicaea-Constantinople, and in the encyclical of Pope Pius XII, *Mystici corporis* (1943).

Now such an ecclesiology, taken too literally, can have lethal consequences that may poison the pluralistic society of today by threatening the common good of the citizens. If indeed the Church has a God-given existence of its own, independent of its members, then one should say not only with the Catholic tradition, that the Church is holy in spite of its members' sinfulness, but also with the standard theology of the Counter-Reformation influenced as it was by Robert Bellarmine, that the Church is a "perfect society." As such it would have rights that must be respected and protected by political legislation and government. The conclusion logically follows: in confrontations between Church and State, basic morality and public legality, the teaching of truth and the tolerance of mistakes and untruths, priority belongs to the Church, to morality, to the teaching of truth. But if Christians pursue this line of thought, there is nothing to stop other religions that also believe in divine revelation to make similar claims and demands. The result can only be the identification of State with Church or of land with religion, the division of the world between Christian and other nations, and, in the countries in which there exists a plurality of religions, the confrontation of opposite claims to truth and the public rivalry of religious pressure groups. This is the shortest cut to oppression of religious minorities by a majority and to social disorder in the name of religion and of God.

The expression of Thomas Aquinas, "the common person of the whole Church," should therefore not be taken in this ontological sense. Person, in the Thomist context, has an older sense related to the original meaning of *persona* in Latin and of *prosopon* in Greek. An actor, in a play, speaks in the name of a more or less fictitious personage. In Greece and in Rome, as in the Nô plays of Japan, the actor put on a mask (*prosopon*) that symbolized the personage in question and the actor's role. Likewise, in the Lord's prayer, each believer speaks in the name of the Church, thus representing and identifying with a role that is immeasurably beyond the believer's personal limitations. Just as the celebrant acts at the Eucharist *in persona Christi*, "in the person of Christ," so all the faithful pray "in the person of the Church." The term, "person," in this case, directly denotes not a metaphysical status but an intention of praying with the Church, and it ultimately connotes the consensus of believers.

This discussion throws light on the disputed question of relations between Church and State. As a publicly organized society, the Christian Church, in the singular or in the plural, has no more and no less rights than all religious organizations. It has the right to be given legal existence and to be protected by law in the pursuit of its goals. Hence the decree of Vatican II on religious liberty, *Dignitatis humanae.*[9]

In this decree, religious freedom is grounded in the inherent dignity of the human person. When they get together as a society, human persons lose none of the basic rights that are theirs as individuals. Except when their goal is subversive of the common good, as in the Mafia in which crime is organized for profit or in terrorist groups that conspire to destroy the fabric of civilized society, associations have the same rights as their members. And they in turn have correlative duties, notably the duty to abide by just laws, to regulate their life in pursuit of their legitimate aim and purpose, to protect their members' liberty to join or to leave the society, and to respect the rights and duties of other associations and persons.

On the Sea of the World

Ever since the time when the artists who decorated the sarcophagi of the Christian catacombs represented the boat of the apostles in the sea of Galilee, the Church has been compared to a ship sailing the seas of the world. This allegory expresses the fact that the relations between Church and World, Church and Humankind, Church and State are, of necessity, in constant flux. By their very nature, they cannot be regulated once and for all. The world that is the habitat of the human race, the humanity that Christians constitute together with all other human persons, the states in which men and women have organized political societies, are not static entities. They are living realities, most of whose aspects are constantly evolving. The Christian Church in the midst of them needs to adjust and readjust to the many facets of its environment. In traditional terms, the Church is constantly to be reformed, *semper reformanda.* In the more recent language of Pope John XXIII and Vatican Council II, it must undergo an *aggiornamento*, an updating.

When it comes to reform or updating, however, all human groups tend to be divided. Some people spontaneously welcome reform and updating. Being future-oriented in their personal goals, they have no difficulty riding the flow of future-oriented reforms in society and in the Church. But others react negatively to the very notion of reform and updating. They are anxious lest some of the riches that have been inherited from the past be lost. The history of the Church is witness to this dichotomy. All major councils were taken up by tasks of adjustment to new circumstances. And most of them have in fact been followed by periods of turmoil when two sides—that may be called, by analogy with political orientations, conservative and progressive—struggled, more or less peacefully, for balance.

[9]John Courtnay Murray, *Religious Liberty: an End and a Beginning* (New York: Macmillan, 1966).

The way to deal with the ensuing situation is not confrontation. It is dialogue. As Pope Paul VI clearly saw it in the encyclical *Ecclesiam suam*, the awareness of being the Church is closely related to the experience of dialogue within the Church. If the Church's worship may be described as a dialogue with God, both the preparation of worship and the subsequent drawing of consequences for the Church's missionary preaching of the gospel require dialogue and the sharing of experience among all members of the Church.

The Church's structure starts with ministry. As ministry includes the teaching of the faith, the structure then becomes magisterial. But magisterium is not the last word. For magisterial teaching is not effective unless it is truly communicated. And the structure of communication is dialogical. In dialogue, ministry and magisterium coinhere.

For Further Reading

Pierre Teilhard de Chardin. *The Future of Man.* New York: Harper and Row, 1964.

Francis J. Klauder. *Aspects of the Thought of Teilhard de Chardin.* North Quincy, MA: Christopher Publishing House, 1971.

Hans Schwartz. *Our Cosmic Journey: Christian Anthropology in the Light of Current Trends in the Sciences, Philosophy, and Theology.* Minneapolis: Augsburg, 1977.

Avery Dulles. *The Catholicity of the Church.* Oxford: Clarendon Press, 1985.

Stephen W. Hawking. *A Brief History of Time: From the Big Bang to Black Holes.* New York: Bantam Books, 1988.

PART FOUR

DIALOGUE

"Awareness, renewal, dialogue:" under these three headings Pope Paul VI reflected on the Church in the encyclical *Ecclesiam siam*. Awareness corresponds to the relationship of the Church to itself, and to that of Christians to themselves and to one another in knowledge and love. Renewal was the perspective that, in the spirit of Vatican II, the Pope wished to open before the community and all its members. Dialogue was the central structure that Paul VI identified as a major object of awareness and the chief instrument of renewal for the Church of our times. Dialogue is first of all internal: it takes place in the Church among its members. It is also external: it consciously relates the Church as institution and its members to the cosmos and to that part of humanity which does not share Christian discipleship.

At no time has the Christian community been, or been regarded as, an unmoving entity. Even before the awakening of historical consciousness during the eighteenth century, the Church and its scholars had never entertained a purely static view of themselves. History and historiography are of course not understood and practiced in the same way at all times. The sense of history in fact has evolved considerably in the two thousand years of the Church's existence as the recognizable community of the disciples of Jesus. The Church itself lives, and as it lives it evolves. For this reason the Church's life should not be described in its theological principles only. It should also be studied in its unfolding. Theologians learn from the past. They are thus brought to compare successive stages of the community, to trace the formative processes of its doctrine and its structure, to understand the growth of its teaching and the geographic and cultural spread of its institutions.

In these conditions one may wonder if it is also, under certain circumstances, possible and legitimate to proceed in the opposite direction, to think, not backward into the past but forward into the future. Can the Church's future be anticipated? Whether it is a science or not in the full sense of the term, futurology is now commonly practiced in social and business studies, in urban planning, in economics and in politics. If it has been seriously drawn, the outline of a five-year plan, in whatever field, relies on projections that cover several decades of the future.

In the context of the Christian Church, some sort of futurology would at first sight be quite appropriate. For if it is impossible to know the future for certain and if the attempt to know it is tied, in Genesis 3,4-6, with the sin of Eve, trust in the future as God's coming creation is consistent with the theological virtue of hope and with the traditional teaching about the end of the world, the eschaton. These doctrines imply a radically forward-looking orientation. The nisus toward the future is experienced by Christians at the two levels of hope for the present life and of hope for the next life. Hope, in this perspective, is not a vague expectation from the human future (as would be called, in French, *l'espoir*). It is a certainty grounded in theological faith (*l'espérance*). In regard to the present life, the Christian faith trusts that the near or distant future will bring about the fulfillment of all the promises of God that were confirmed or made in Jesus Christ. Implied in this expectation is the belief that, being now justified by faith, the disciples, taken separately, will be sustained by divine grace in all the temptations and tests of human life and, collectively, will present to the world a better image of the kingdom of God. In regard to the eschaton and to eschatological hope, the Christian faith projects into the indefinite future of the end of the world a vision of the total victory of Christ over sin and death and of the sharing of all the saints in his triumph.

At these two levels, some sort of futurology would seem to be implicit in the Christian faith. But projections into the near or distant future of the community and of oneself need to take into account the past as it is remembered and the present as it is lived. Projection requires extrapolation. Much of our investigation so far has chiefly taken account of the past and of the present. Yet in the Christian community today the experience of salvation is not a matter only of sensing the meaning of the present moment. It also includes a concern for the future as the coming time of the Church's continuing fidelity.

This fourth part of our reflection on the Church is therefore turned to the future. It is of course not ours to discern "the days and the hours" (Mark 13:32) that are known to the Father alone. We may neither read the future nor commune with God's contemporaneous sight of all times. But with Vatican II, we may discern the signs of the times and tentatively imagine what these signs portend for the future of the Christian Church. After several centuries of division, the Christian community now lives, and has been living since the beginning of this century, in an ecumenical horizon. Surely, this cannot be without relevance to the future: the divided Christian Churches are not destined to remain separate (ch. 11).

As an extension of its ecumenical outreach, the Christian Church is also beginning to experience a new sense of commonality and solidarity with the great religions of the world that are all equally threatened by the secular imperialism of modern society, by the shrinking spiritual horizon of contemporary culture, and by the spread of agnosticism and of practical and political atheism. These threats to religious experience thrive on the fascination exercised on people's minds by the material advances of modern technologies. A "wider" ecumenism, concerned with religion as such, is inseparable from the challenge of inculturation that confronts the Church in societies that have been shaped by the great religions of the world (ch. 12).

Moreover, the last years of the twentieth century are not yet excessively distant from the experience of Vatican II, the memory and the rumor of which are still much alive. Now, the council was called because Pope John XXIII, in a spiritual intuition, expected it to open a privileged period of grace, a kind of "new Pentecost." This charismatic orientation is not without similarity with the eschatological concerns of some among the more conservative Protestant Churches. It has influenced the Catholic mentality in the aftermath of Vatican II (ch. 13).

11

The Ecumenical Horizon

A critical question has undoubtedly come to many readers' minds in the course of the previous chapters. I have never yet ventured to determine the identity of the Church clearly. I have referred to the Church, the Christian Church, the Catholic Church, the Churches, the Christian Churches. I have spoken of the gathering, the assembly, the community, the communion. But one may well ask: which and where is this Church that is constantly mentioned, and never identified, in the present book? Does it coincide with any of the numerous organizations that call themselves Churches?

The term itself, "church," has many interconnected meanings. At its most empirical, it denotes a building where Christian believers gather for worship. It is larger than a chapel and is more or less comparable to what a synagogue, a mosque or a temple is in other religions. It may also designate the administrative unit corresponding to that building or the totality of the people who usually frequent it. But church may also mean a larger association of Christian believers on a regional level, as in a diocese or an ecclesiastical province (archdiocese), or at the still wider level of a nation, a continent, and even the whole world. Moreover, Christian theology speaks of the invisible Church which may be understood as the spiritual association of those who belong to visible Churches. It also speaks of the Church "militant" on earth, "triumphant" in heaven, and even, in Roman Catholic theology, "patient" or "suffering" (that is, undergoing purification) in purgatory.

Clarifications are obviously needed. Yet the diversity of language, which I have deliberately adopted, truly reflects the situation of the Christian world. There is only one Christian religion. One may even say that there is only one Christian faith. But there are many ways of being Christian and of expressing the one faith. The common use of the term, "church," assumes the coexistence of many Churches, each of which considers itself faithful to Christ and the gospel even though it may differ from others on important points of doctrine and discipline. All Christians of the twentieth century are, in certain circumstances, aware of being the Church. Yet they personally identify with visible Churches that do not wish to be mistaken for one another. Being the Church is the object of a conviction that pertains to the spiritual order. The Church is a spiritual entity. As such it always is virtually universal, for what is spirit is not bound by limitations of space and time. Yet the ecclesial context of the awareness of being the Church is always identifiable with an organization, and it is in fact, whatever its size, particular. The word, "denomination," precisely designates the particularity that corresponds to the "name" of a Church: Oriental Orthodox (Coptic, Armenian, Syrian), Eastern Orthodox, usually distinguished along national lines, Catholic (itself subdivided in the majority Latin rite and a number of oriental rites), Anglican, Lutheran, Reformed, Methodist, Baptist, etc. In the pluralism of the Christian Churches, the term, "church," and the empirical reality and history of each identifiable Church, are sufficiently ambiguous to justify the doubt of many sincere believers that any particular Church can be recognized as truly that which Jesus Christ intended to build.

Separate Identities

For many centuries now, the experience of being the Church has been lived in relative isolation from other Christians. Until the middle of the twentieth century, Catholics at least were officially discouraged from establishing religious ties with other Christians for fear of doctrinal contamination and indifferentism. This was the point of canon 1258 in the code of 1917: there must be no sharing in liturgical prayer (*communicatio in sacris*)[1] with other Christians. Protestants meanwhile also experienced their own ecclesial identity in isolation from Catholics and often from other Protestants, and even in opposition to them. For the most knowledgeable or the more sensitive, membership in the Church has therefore included an awareness of being separated not only from what pious Christians have conventionally called the world but also from other believers. United at first in their common allegiance to the Lordship of Christ manifested in the resurrection of Jesus, the Christians found themselves, as early as the second century, divided over diverging interpretations of the apostolic doctrines concerning the Christ and over mutually exclusive identifications of the Church. Orthodox and Gnostics of all kinds could no longer worship together.

In the fifth century, the Orthodox recognized the council of Ephesus (431), and those who did not were known as Nestorians, followers of Patriarch

---

[1]George H. Tavard, "Praying Together: 'Communicatio in Sacris' in the Decree on Ecumenism," Alberic Stacpoole (ed.), *Vatican II by Those Who Were There* (London: Geoffrey Chapman, 1986), p. 202-19.

Nestorius, bishop of Constantinople from 428 to 431. Shortly after the council of Chalcedon (451), Chalcedonian and non-Chalcedonian Churches split over the doctrine of the incarnation as it was formulated at that council. Then came the schism between Constantinople and Rome, or Orthodox and Catholics, that was consummated in 1054 with the excommunication of the ecumenical patriarch, Michael Cerullarius (patriarch, 1043-1058), by the papal legate, Cardinal Humbert de Moyenmoutier (d. 1056). The Great Schism divided Latin Catholics in 1378 when there were two and even three claimants to the bishopric of Rome and the papacy, until Catholic unity was restored in 1417 by the council of Constance.

Catholics were later divided by the Reformation after Martin Luther in 1518 protested against the sale of indulgences and the underlying doctrines. The ensuing disagreement over justification and grace and its implications regarding the nature of the Christian tradition gave rise to the Protestant and Anglican Churches which no longer accepted the authority of the bishop of Rome. Other contemporary Churches have inherited the stance of the "spiritual Reformers" of the sixteenth century who were equally opposed, for a variety of reasons, to Rome, to Canterbury, to Wittenberg (Luther), and to Geneva (Calvin). Later emanations from these Churches are responsible for the emergence of other communities that have more or less modified the positions of the original Reformers: thus Methodism came out of the Church of England and the Salvation Army out of Methodism.

Some more recent divisions were occasioned by hostile reactions to some attempts to modernize the Church. Among the Orthodox of Russia, the "Old Believers" protested against the reforms of 1653 devised by Patriarch Nikon (1605-81) and imposed by Czar Alexis (1645-76); yet while the Old Believers continue to hold their own worship meetings, most of them are not separated from the Orthodox Church in doctrine. Among Catholics, the "Old Catholics" of the Netherlands disagreed with the rejection of Jansenism by the popes, which started with the condemnation of the "five propositions" of Jansenius in 1643. They were joined in 1871 by those Catholics of Germany and Switzerland who considered false the definition of papal infallibility by Vatican Council I. Finally, Archbishop Lefebvre initiated a minor schism in 1989, when, in a belated protest against the liturgical and other reforms of Vatican Council II, he ordained several bishops uncanonically. It is now too early to tell whether this will result in a formal and lasting separation.

The twentieth century has also witnessed the emergence of a new type of Churches. These do not trace their pedigree back to the early schisms or to the Reformation; they have been born from the impact of prophetic personalities whom their disciples believed to be inspired by the Holy Spirit. These Churches are known under diverse appellations: "Pentecostal" in America and Europe, "Independent" in Africa. They ultimately relate to the pietism of the eighteenth century and to the "Holiness" Churches that grew out of the Methodist movement in the nineteenth. This outcrop of new Churches, more or less focused on the doctrine of the Holy Spirit, made a quantum leap when prophetism spread to many parts of Africa among populations that had been touched by the Christian gospel while remaining attuned to the inspired and healing dimensions of the older African religions. This phenomenon cannot be ignored by the more traditional Churches. In contrast with the Orthodox and Catholic Churches and the Churches of the Reformation, it constitutes in fact the third side of the contemporary ecumenical triangle.

In any case, the varieties in the concrete forms of Christian fellowship are now such that they affect the sense of belonging to the Church of Jesus Christ. Whatever the original cause or occasion of the separations, children born to Christian parents are introduced by the accident of birth into the domain of one particular Church that is separated from others. Then they receive along with the grace of justification and regeneration, both their general spiritual identity as Christian believers and the particular social identity of one denomination. As to those who enter the Church as adults, they cannot avoid selecting a denomination when they choose the ecclesial locus of their baptism. Their longing for salvation and their acknowledgement of Christ unavoidably connotes an option that is divisive in regard to the very community of salvation.

The Ecumenical Imperative

Whatever the history that stands behind them, these divisions weigh heavily on the claim of any Christian community to be the Church of Jesus Christ as Christ intended it to be, or even as the Holy Spirit has guided it in its being and its becoming. One can indeed understand how and why historical circumstances and doctrinal divergences have occasioned temporary separations. But there is no biblical model and no traditional ideal that can justify continuing divisions and rivalries among those who profess to believe that Christ is the only Lord and Savior for all humanity. It is not normal, yet it is a daily fact of experience, that the profession of the Christian faith today implies separation from other Christians. This abnormal fact is the reason for the urgency of the ecumenical imperative: the Churches and their faithful members have the imperious duty to pray and to hope, with Jesus in the gospel of John, that "all may be one" (John 17:21). This alone makes it necessary to envision the experience of being the Church, and thereby the very nature of the *ecclesia* of God, in the light of the ecumenical imperative.

The problem, however, is by no means simple. The desire for unity is, for all Christian believers, grounded in the insight of the gospel of John: the disciples should relate to one another as Jesus and his *Abba* relate to each other. In other words, the oneness of the disciples does not find its model in the unity of the divine essence but in the Trinity of the divine Persons. The disciples should experience a spiritual compenetration of mind and soul analogous to the "circumincession" or "perichoresis" that is operative between the Father, the Word, and the Spirit.[2] The Three Persons interpenetrate one another. Among Christians, this should imply a universal concern for the communion, mutual support and assistance, the sort of mutual commitment that is called love for the neighbor in the New Testament, and a fundamental devotion to justice and to that delicate perfection of justice that is traditionally known as canonical equity.

Relations among Christians are evidently far from that point. Not even within any one empirical Church or denomination have they reached such a level of mutuality. The very imperfect state of love and justice within and among the Churches is undermined by class struggles, nationalism, sexism, racism, and by the divergences in temperament and outlook that are commonly labeled "conservative" and "liberal." These differences act as obstacles to a common Christian witness and to sisterly relations among the Churches.

Diverging Views of Unity

Besides the impact of sin and imperfection on the behavior of Christians and their Churches, there are also doctrinal divergences in regard to the nature of Christian unity. The ecumenical imperative does not resonate in the same way in all traditions. One may generally distinguish between the Orthodox, the Catholic, and the Protestant understandings.

In the context of Orthodox theology and ecclesiology, the ecumenical imperative is focused on the Holy Spirit. The Spirit, who allowed the divisions to take place, is slowly leading the believers forward to their future unity. Even though the ways of the Spirit are not ours, and one thousand years are for God like one day, one may find a model of this future unity in the actual relationships of the Orthodox Churches that are at the same time many and one. Being many according to their national, linguistic, and cultural identities, they are nonetheless one in the confession of one faith, in the doxological worship of God according to a common liturgical model, and in the cohesiveness of the local Church gathered around one bishop.

This view of the future oneness of the reconciled Churches differs only in part from the generally accepted Catholic conception: unity in faith and liturgy must be tied to unity of the magisterium even though, in the context of a reconciled universal Church, there may be great diversity in the way the magisterium functions; once the oneness of belief is assured, matters of discipline are open to unlimited varieties. Even the Petrine ministry of the

[2]George H. Tavard, *The Vision of the Trinity* (Washington: University Press of America, 1981), p. 126.

bishop of Rome can conceivably relate to several sections of the reconciled Church in different ways. The example of the Uniate Churches is in many ways less than convincing as a model of reconciled diversity because of the way the massive weight of the Latin Church has affected the delicate balance of tradition and universality in the Eastern Churches that are in communion with the bishop of Rome. These Churches do nonetheless witness to an inchoate adaptation of the Petrine ministry to varying ecclesial conditions.

In both instances, however, the critical question regards the minimal unity of doctrine that is desirable in a reunited universal Church. Both the Orthodox and the Catholic Churches see oneness in faith as an ingredient of ecclesial unity. Yet they differ on the qualities of that oneness in faith: should it be equated with the credal unity endorsed by the ecumenical councils of patristic times? Or ought it to include the medieval doctrines that were taught by the general councils of the West (transubstantiation, purgatory) or the more recent ones that were formally defined by Vatican Council I (papal infallibility) and by the bishop of Rome (the Immaculate Conception and the Assumption of the Virgin Mary)?

The Protestant Churches in general do not locate the visible structure of the Church among fundamental or necessary doctrines. Christians are united by faith in the one gospel of Christ. But it is not self-evident that faith must or even can be formulated in the same way in all places and by all Churches. Indeed, it has not been formulated in the same way at all times in any of the classical Churches. The three traditional creeds (of Nicaea-Constantinople, the "Apostles' creed" used in baptism, and the "Athanasian creed") have been translated into numerous languages. But it is quite impossible for the central statement of Nicaea, that the Word of God is *homoousios* with the Father, to be properly conveyed in most of those languages. One may then fittingly ask: Why should differences in doctrinal formulation that are acceptable in time—between two moments of one Church—be unacceptable in space—between two groups in the same Church or between two Churches? In other words, a difference in doctrine need not be identical with a difference in faith.

In the light of this, a universal reconciliation of the separated Churches can be conceived as an agreement to develop sisterly relations on the basis of unity in faith, despite diversity in the beliefs that are formulated in creeds, confessions, covenants, and other doctrinal and theological statements. Such an agreement can go further than a mere tolerance of disagreement. It can include a deeply felt commitment to mutual understanding, to sharing ideas and projects, to opening the Eucharistic table and the other sacraments to one another, to organizing Christian education and Christian missions in common, to responding jointly to secular challenges, and even to cooperating in preaching the gospel and in training ministers. Coresponsibility and collegiality of government can conceivably be practiced wherever doctrinal diversity is respected.

The Ecumenical Problem

The ecumenical problem lies to a large extent in the difficulty of reconciling the three broad points of view—Orthodox or Catholic, Protestant, Pentecostal—that have been outlined. It is also complicated by the lasting conflict in Roman Catholicism between an "integralist" wing and a progressive wing, by the growing impact of fundamentalism in Protestant Churches, and by the peculiar slant that is given to Christian behavior in the charismatic or Pentecostal movements. The experiences that are called "accepting Christ as my personal savior," or "being born again," or "speaking in tongues," or "being slain in the Spirit," may be genuine or illusory. But they are no substitutes, even when they are genuine, for fidelity to the biblical witness concerning Jesus Christ and for its traditional formulation. The Third Person does not replace the Second, any more than the Second can take the place of the First. Differences in doctrine and practice cannot be nullified by sensitivity to interior motions from the Holy Spirit.

The problem is compounded by differences in ecumenical outlook within each Church. Such differences may be due to culture. For instance, Spaniards and South Americans do not share the experience of Lutheranism that Catholics have in Germany or in Scandinavia. And vice versa, Scandinavian and German Lutherans do not see Catholics through the eyes of Portuguese or Spanish Protestants. Differences in ecumenical outlook can also result from diverging senses of history. Members of the "younger Churches" in Asia and Africa cannot feel deeply concerned with, even if they are forcibly affected by, European quarrels of the sixteenth century.

In addition, there are huge differences in theological awareness within all the classical Churches. The mass of the members either are unaware of the depth of the ecumenical question or do not realize its urgency. The attempts that have been made to enlist Christians to pray for reconciliation and to educate them in the theology of ecumenism have nowhere met with great and lasting success. Under these conditions, it is understandable that the leadership of the Churches is largely reluctant to take the bold steps that may be necessary to go forward toward the recovery of unity among divided Christians.

The World Council of Churches

The main attempt to prepare the Churches for their reconciliation was made in the context of the World Council of Churches created in 1948. As defined at New Delhi in 1961, the WCC is "a fellowship of Churches which accept the Lord Jesus as God and Savior according to the Scriptures, and endeavor to respond together to their common calling, to the glory of the one God, Father, Son and Holy Spirit." The very existence of WCC offers all Churches a unique opportunity, whether they have joined it or not. The Council is an agency for cooperation in evangelical and social projects (in several *ad hoc* commissions), a platform for cooperation in mission (in the World Missionary Council), and a forum for exchange and discussion of ideas (in the Faith and Order Commission). Even the Churches that have not formally joined the World Council—among them the Roman Catholic Church—have opportunities for cooperation, as in meetings where they are welcome to send observers, in the Faith and Order Commission which does coopt participants from outside the WCC itself, and, in the case of the Roman Catholic Church, in a special Coordinating Committee with the Pontifical Council for Christian Unity.

The existence of the World Council, however, raises other ecclesiological questions. Should this Council, an association of Churches, be considered a Church? If the universal Church is a Communion of communions, one may wonder if the Council is not potentially the universal Church. Indeed, the WCC has always refused to define itself as a Church, still less as *the* Church. If it is neither a Church nor the Church, then is it, as was feared for some time in a number of Protestant circles, a kind of "super-church," with no basis in the Scriptures? Or is it a potentially rival organization, the existence of which would possibly preempt the reconciliation of the Churches and their integration in a Communion of communions? Many such questions have been asked within and outside the World Council of Churches.

The plenary meetings of the WCC (Amsterdam, 1948; Evanston, 1954; New Delhi, 1961; Uppsala, 1968; Nairobi, 1981; Vancouver, 1988; Canberra, 1991), the meetings of its Faith and Order Commission, and the bi-annual meetings of its Central Committee have defined its self-understanding and have thereby answered some of the critical questions that have been raised concerning its ecclesial status. That the WCC has ecclesial significance can hardly be denied, but the determination of this significance can only be done within the ecclesiologies of the respective Churches. For the doctrines have been handed down by the traditions of the Churches, and it is the Churches that have the actual responsibility of professing and teaching them. Yet if it cannot speak for the Churches without their specific endorsement of what it says and if it can still less impose on them its point of view, the WCC has nonetheless proposed specific ideas that should contribute to the future ecclesiology of a reconciled universal Church.

At Toronto in 1950, the Central Committee formally received a statement on the ecclesial status of the WCC: the WCC "is not a Super-Church. It is not the World Church. It is not the *Una Sancta* of which the Creeds speak."[3] By the same token, the WCC does not endorse, and is not based on, one particular ecclesiology. Nor is a specific ecclesiology implied in membership

---

[3] *The Church, the Churches and the World Council of Churches: The First Six Years, 1948-1954* (Geneva: WCC, 1954), Appendix A-4, p. 114.

in the Council. In 1961, the New Delhi Assembly noted that the experience of working and talking together in the WCC is not without influence on the understanding of the WCC by the Churches: "We are learning what the WCC is by *living* together within it."[4] It also attempted to define the nature of Christian unity:

> We believe that the unity which is both God's will and his gift to his Church is being made visible as all in each place who are baptized into Jesus Christ and confess him as Lord and Savior are brought by the Holy Spirit into ONE fully committed fellowship, holding the one apostolic faith, preaching the one Gospel, breaking the one bread, joining in common prayer, and having a corporate life reaching out in witness and service to all, and who at the same time are united with the whole Christian fellowship in all places and all ages in such wise that ministry and members are accepted by all, and that all can act and speak together as occasion requires for the tasks to which God calls his people.[5]

This description is open to criticism. It seems to imply a strictly local view of the Church: the one Church is where the baptized "in each place" gather into one committed "fellowship." It assumes, or perhaps hopes, that the baptized of each place are "united with the whole Christian fellowship in all places and all ages." As to the nature and the means of this universal unity, the text brings them down to preaching the one gospel and to mutual acceptance of ministry and members, without mentioning doctrine otherwise than as the Churches may be called to "react" jointly to secular challenges.

In 1963, the World Conference of Faith and Order in Montreal endeavored to complete the picture. It interpreted "all in each place" in a dynamic rather than a static way: "It is in each place where people live, work and worship that our partnership in the body of Christ has to be made manifest and lived out."[6] This is to be done through sharing worship and sacraments, faith and doctrine, witness and service. Even where this is not yet possible, all the faithful have "a strong obligation to pray and work constantly for the day when all Christians in each place can come together freely in common worship and at the Lord's Table."

Unitatis redintegratio

The proper response to the challenge of the WCC is for each Church to identify as clearly as possible its own principles of ecumenism. Some Churches had done it before the creation of the WCC, notably the Anglican Com-

---

[4]*New Delhi Speaks* (New York: Association Press, 1962), p. 121.

[5]l.c., p. 92-93.

[6]P. C. Rodger and Lukas Vischer (eds.), *The Fourth World Conference on Faith and Order*. (New York: Association Press, 1964), p. 81; next quotation, p. 83.

munion with the Chicago-Lambeth Quadrilateral.[7] At Vatican Council II, the Roman Catholic Church explained its principles of ecumenism in the decree *Unitatis redintegratio* (promulgated in 1964). Vatican II does not abandon the Catholic tradition's teaching on the Petrine ministry, the primacy of the bishop of Rome, and what this entails for the structure and the functioning of the episcopal magisterium. Yet it adds to this older stance the confession that the causes of the Reformation and of other separations were not one-sided, that all sides have been guilty of the disunion, and that the bishop of Rome, the bishops, clergy, and faithful should pray and work for the organic reconciliation of Churches. Without anticipating what form such a reconciliation may take in the more or less distant future, Pope John XXIII created a special agency to work for it during the council, the Pontifical Secretariat for Promoting Christian Unity. It was made permanent by Paul VI in 1964, and it was renamed "Council" by John Paul II in 1988.

This is not the place to survey the numerous activities of the Council for Promoting Christian Unity. It will suffice to indicate what contribution it has made directly to an ecumenical ecclesiology. This appears best from Cardinal Jan Willebrands' proposal that the universal Church need not be a communion of communions that are similar in liturgy and in style of ministry and teaching.[8] It may very well include communions that belong to differing ecclesial *typoi*. A *typos*, in this perspective, is best seen as a style. Each Church has inherited from its past a certain way of thought and action, of preaching the gospel, of determining and teaching doctrine, of defining and administering sacraments, of praying and worshiping. There results from this a specific and pervading kind of spiritual sensitivity which in turn gives a unique tone to all the activities of a Church.

It would be superfluous to survey the many dialogues among Churches that have been taking place for several decades. But one ought to face the crucial question: How much time shall it take for the Churches so to understand, appreciate, and accept the ecclesial typology as to agree on the conditions that should be met in order to form one great Communion of communions? Many would say, with Psalm 90:4: in the eyes of God, "a thousand years are like one day." But others would prefer to say: "The time is short" (1 Cor 7:29), or "See, the harvest is abundant" (Matt 9:37), or yet "The Lord is coming; let us go out to meet him" (Matt 25:6). In this, differing mentalities may be at work in support of differing theologies.

The Question of a Fundamental Difference

The differences between Churches are, up to a point, matters of mentality and culture. This corresponds to the experience of the ecumenical dialogues

---

[7]J. Robert Wright (ed.), *Quadrilateral at One Hundred* (Cincinnati: Forward Movement Publications, 1988).

[8]Joseph W. Witmer and J. Robert Wright (ed.), *Called to Full Unity* (Washington: USCC, 1986), p. 45–53.

that have been carried out between Churches on the doctrines that separate them. There are several pointers in this direction. First, it has long been noted that the schism between Rome and Constantinople had its remote origin in the use of different languages among the Greek and the Latin Fathers of the Church. Likewise, the local Churches that kept their allegiance to the bishop of Rome in the sixteenth century were chiefly Mediterranean, while most of the Nordic Churches cut their ties with Rome, Ireland being the major exception. Second, it soon appears in bilateral and multilateral dialogues that, if official differences separate the Churches, the theological orientations that undergird these differences lie between diverse intellectual leanings within each Church. No Church is an intellectual monolith. And one may suspect, although this would be harder to establish and one should wonder to what extent it is truly relevant, that theological preferences have their source in more basic diversities in mentality and sensibility.

Admittedly, credal differences regarding the gospel and the sacraments, the ministerial and magisterial structures of the Church, and the Church's relations with the world, cannot be reduced to psychology. Yet in the absence of a developed theological anthropology that would be grounded in the gospel and the Christian tradition, one cannot simply deny that there may be a psychological and cultural basis for theological and doctrinal differences and for the ensuing ecclesial divisions of the Christian world. In this case, however, the eventual reunion of Christendom into one Communion of communions must be the work of the Holy Spirit rather than the fruit of human efforts, projects, and plans.

For these various reasons, the question of a fundamental difference between Catholics and Protestants comes to the surface from time to time. However, whatever national and cultural influences were at work in fomenting misunderstandings between Eastern and Western religious presuppositions and in creating the divisions of the sixteenth century, the Christian faith has been able, in a multitude of circumstances, to rise above cultural diversities. There is no insuperable reason why it cannot do so again. Yet the following considerations are to the point.

At the disputation of Heidelberg in 1518, Martin Luther contrasted "a theologian of glory" and "a theologian of the cross." The former "beholds what is invisible of God through the perception of what is made (Rom 1:20)," and "is not rightly called a theologian" (Thesis 19). The latter "perceives what is visible of God, God's 'backside' (Exod 33:23) by beholding the sufferings and the cross" (Thesis 20). The former acts as a philosopher who knows nothing of Jesus Christ; the latter as a theologian following the way that was opened by the incarnation of the divine Word and by the redemption of sinful humanity through his death and resurrection.

A similar contrast underlies the ecumenical problem today. The Orthodox and the Catholic traditions generally favor, in diverse ways, ecclesiologies of glory. They see the Church under the image of the New Jerusalem coming down from heaven as in chapters 20 and 21 of the Book of Revelation. The Church is not only given by God. It is also divinely willed in its major features. Orthodox ecclesiology emphasizes its doxological, liturgical, and conciliaristic features, while Catholic ecclesiology stresses its magisterial and primatial structures. Yet in both cases, there is a predominant accent on what God does and therefore on the divine aspect of the credal marks of the Church: its given holiness may be hidden but is not removed by its members' sinfulness; its catholicity is not ruined by the particularisms of the local embodiments of the Church; its historical apostolicity is preserved intact through the cultural innovations of each age; and its oneness survives the historical divisions between Christians.

By contrast, an ecclesiology of the Cross need not deny the givenness of the Church: this is God's undeserved gift to the disciples of Christ. But it constantly reminds the faithful and their leaders that the eschaton, even if it is inchoately "realized," has not fully arrived, that the kingdom of God is still to be prayed for, that the disciples, who are indeed holy in their faith, remain sinful in their self. Like the Christians themselves, the Church as it exists on earth is *simul justa et peccatrix*, at the same time justified and sinful. In this case, it is an illusion to think and to behave as though the Church were already wrapped up in the heavenly glory. On this side of eternity, one should think primarily in terms of the Cross: only through the sufferings and the cross of Jesus is the Christian community, local, regional, and universal, called to share in the resurrection of Christ.

Following the example of Martin Luther, most of the Churches of the Reformation abstain from viewing themselves as already haloed by the glory of the kingdom of God. The preaching of the gospel and the communication of the sacraments are actions along the way that do not yet place ministers or receivers at the goal. The taste of the power of grace and salvation that may well be experienced by those who hear the word and receive the sacraments are no more than partial, temporary, and imperfect anticipations. The norm always remains the Cross, for it is through the Cross that Christ went to the glory of his resurrection. The chief purpose of the Church is to enable its members to fulfill, in faith, their tasks in this world. The glory to come is trustfully left in the hands of God.

As it is raised between Catholics and Protestants, the heart of the ecumenical question lies precisely here: is it possible to live out an ecclesiology of the cross while already sharing the joy of an ecclesiology of glory?

Christians and Jews

It is debatable whether the ecumenical question, taken in the strict sense, extends further than reconciliation among members of different Churches. Does it also encompass the problem or, if one prefers, the mystery of the relations between the followers of Jesus and the followers of what was the religion of Jesus of Nazareth, the Jewish people? The answer will depend on a previous question: is Judaism more closely related to Christianity than is paganism? Clearly, whatever Christians may think of the permanence of the covenant with Moses after the coming of the Messiah Jesus, they cannot deny their origin in the Old Testament and therefore their ties to Judaism.

Christian theology has in fact paid special attention to these ties. Jesus and the first disciples were Jews. The separation between the earliest Christian communities and the synagogues was slow to come. The flow of converts from paganism after the first generations of believers made the separation unavoidable. But when it took place, the parting was traumatic on both sides, for it contained the seeds of later conflicts and of the anti-semitism that became endemic in Christian society. In 386-387, St. John Chrysostom (344-407), a priest in Antioch and future patriarch of Constantinople, violently attacked Jews in a series of eight sermons. This was presumably occasioned by the riots in Antioch between Jews and Christians, for which Chrysostom rightly or wrongly blamed Jews. Whatever his motives, Chrysostom set the tone for the anti-semitism of Christians. Later, at the time of the crusades, Jews were seen in Christian cities as the enemy inside the gates. And the medieval and later mobs did not rest content with anti-semitic diatribes. In central Europe, they passed to action in numberless pogroms. In the West, after the Fourth Council of the Lateran (1215), Jews were also confined to ghettos or they were expelled, as happened in the Spain of the Reconquest after the disputation of Tortosa (1413-1414) failed to convert them.[9] Likewise, Martin Luther wrote vitriolic pamphlets against Jews when they were not converted, as he expected, by the doctrine of Justification by faith alone. But this is not the place to analyze all the reasons for the basic schism between Christians and Jews and all the causes of anti-semitism.

The contemporary dialogue generally started during Vatican II, although in a few places it had been initiated earlier. It mostly collapsed, however, before the thesis that the State of Israel has religious significance. More recently, mutual distrust has increased, at least as regards Catholics and Jews, on the occasion of the establishment of a Carmel at the Auschwitz extermination camp. This unfortunate incident has at least underlined the question whether the *shoah* (incorrectly called the holocaust) has a specific theological meaning. The fundamental question, however, concerns the Messianic status of Jesus and the permanence of the Mosaic covenant after his coming.

This question was carefully examined at Vatican Council II. The decree *Nostra aetate* was originally focused on the relevance and meaning of Romans 11 for Jewish-Christian relations. But Christian theologians were not of one mind in their interpretation of Paul. And the bishops of many countries in which there are few Jews were not eager to deal with the ques-

---

[9] Antonio Pacios Lopez, *La Disputa de Tortosa*, 2 vol. (Madrid: Instituto Arias Montano, 1957).

tion, their own pastoral concerns being turned toward coexistence with Muslims, Hindus, or Buddhists. In fact, it was largely to make the text acceptable to the majority of the bishops that the consideration of Judaism was preceded by reflections on religion in general and on some of the great religions in particular.

In the conciliar text, it is part of "the mystery of the Church" that the people of the New Covenant are spiritually related to the descendants (*stirps*) of Abraham (NA, n. 4). Pius XI had already declared: "Spiritually, we are Semites."[10] This is now explained: "The Church's faith and election began among the patriarchs, Moses and the prophets;" the disciples of Jesus count among "Abraham's children according to faith," for they were included in his call; salvation is "mystically foretold in the exodus of the Elect People from the land of servitude;" the Church receives and is nurtured by the revelation of the Old Testament; in it Gentile twigs have been grafted onto "the good olive tree;" for "Christ, our Peace, has reconciled Jews and Gentiles through the cross, and in himself he has made the two one." Furthermore, the Church remembers the words of St. Paul: to Jews belong "the adoption, the glory, the covenant, the law, the cult, the promises, the patriarchs," and from them Christ comes "according to the flesh." This leads the council to condemn anti-semitism in all its aspects, and notably the contention that contemporary Jews should be punished for the death of Jesus.

In a brief reference to Jews, the constitution *Lumen gentium* had said that the Jewish people, "to which the covenants and the promises were given, . . . is still cherished (by God) according to their election, on account of the patriarchs, for God's gifts and call are without repentance" (LG, n. 16). This is repeated in *Nostra aetate*: "According to the apostle, the Jews remain cherished by God, whose gifts and call are without repentance, on account of the patriarchs" (NA, n. 4). Nowhere, however, does Vatican II explain how this continuing election of Judaism ought to be understood.

Conflict over the Covenant

Catholic and other Christian theologians have reflected on the ecclesial status of contemporary Judaism. The council did not say whether the Jewish community, in its cultural or perhaps only in its religious dimension, should be regarded by Christians as still forming the *ecclesia* of God that it undoubtedly was at the time of the Exodus from Egypt. On the contrary, the council continued to use traditional expressions inspired by St. Paul that Jews consider offensive: the Church of Christ is the "new People of God, . . . the Messianic People, . . . the New Israel" (LG, n. 9). The interpretation of such expressions depends in part on how the teaching of Paul in Romans

[10]Pius XI was addressing the Directors of the Catholic Radio of Belgium, as reported in the Belgian newspapers of 15 September 1936.

10-11 is understood. But there is no agreement among New Testament scholars or theologians. Without going into the details of exegesis and hermeneutics, I would distinguish four different positions.

First, the inauguration of the New Covenant in Christ abolished the Old Covenant with Moses, not only for those who came to believe in Christ, but for all of humanity. For if the Old Covenant was not abolished when it was superseded, it remains valid for Jews; but in this case St. Paul was mistaken when he described the Jewish rejection of Jesus as "blindness, until the totality of the nations would enter and thus the whole Israel would be saved" (Rom 11:25). Acceptance of a covenant offered by God is not blindness; it is obedience, even if another covenant has been offered to others. By the same token, if the Old Covenant has been abolished, Jews have lost their position as the Chosen People. The gospel should be preached to them as to all nations, for there can be no restriction on the Church's proclamation of the gospel. But this should neither encourage anti-semitism nor make dialogue and cooperation impossible. This has been the more common position ever since Justin of Rome (d. c. 165) composed his *Dialogue with Trypho*, although elementary respect for Jews as human persons has often been eclipsed by prejudice, distrust, and even hatred. The modern Church has been, though not universally, more sensitive to the demands of justice and love in regard to Jews.

Second, the Old Covenant was abolished and superseded by the New. Yet it remains provisionally valid for the Jews who have not recognized Jesus as the Messiah. Even if the Church is the New Israel for its members, the Jewish community remains Israel, the Elect People of God, for those who are still waiting for the Messiah. The remarkable resilience of the Jewish community may be seen as a sign that God did not abandon his People: under the guidance of renewed Pharisaic leadership, it survived the destruction of the Temple and of Jerusalem and its own dispersion among the nations, the persecutions and pogroms it suffered through the centuries in Christian lands, and finally the *shoah*. That the Bible is now associated in Jewish religion and scholarship to the Talmuds of Babylon and of Jerusalem is a mark of continued religious vitality. And so are the mystical revival and intellectual movements that have helped shape modern Judaism, notably the Kabbalah of Simeon Bar Yochai (second century) and his followers over many centuries; the medieval Hassidism of the Rhineland, with Judas the Pious (twelfth century); the more recent Central European Hassidism of Israel Baal Shem Tov (seventeenth century); the schools of Orthodox, Conservative, and Reformed Judaism; and finally the Zionist movement itself and the return of the people (or part of it) to the biblical lands. In this case, individual Jews should be welcome in the Church when they come to see Jesus as the Messiah in the Christian sense of the term. But there should be no mission to the Jewish community. There should be dialogue, mutual assistance, and cooperation.

Third, several theologians have enlarged this line of thought and proposed a two-covenant theory: two covenants would be offered by God, and therefore the people of God would have two branches, following two ways of salvation, that of Jews, and that of Christianized Gentiles. The Jewish people would still be as much the Chosen People of God as its ancestors were. Because the gifts of God are without repentance, a covenant once offered by God remains forever valid. But there are obvious difficulties. This opinion is grounded in the image of the Church as the people of God which, as we have seen, is profoundly ambiguous. Above all, however, it undermines the logic of the history of salvation (*Heilsgeschichte*) as this has hitherto been understood. The conversion of the Gentiles requires their acceptance of the Trinitarian revelation. It would be inconsistent with the self-revelation of God in Jesus Christ that the divine plan provide for one part of humanity to ignore the covenant given through Jesus and to continue to worship on the basis of the monopersonal concept of God that is conveyed in the Old Testament and is tied to the Mosaic covenant. In order to overcome this difficulty, one is then led to alter the very heart of the Christian message, making it theocentric and not Christocentric. But once this is done, the logic of monotheism leads directly to Muhammad as the last of the great prophets of monotheism and to the religion of Islam.

Fourth, a small but vocal number of theologians have reached a more radical version of the same basic notion. This calls for revision, not only of traditional understandings of Paul's teaching, but even of the central Christian dogmas about Jesus. The basic idea is that the Covenant with Christ and his disciples is not new in the sense that it replaced the Covenant with Moses, but only in the sense that it extended the Covenant to non-Jews in a form that was more appropriate to their mentality: rather than being new, the Covenant with Jesus is different. Jews continue to be called to God through the old biblical tradition as it has survived and been interpreted in their post-Christian experiences; all others are called to God through faith in Jesus Christ the Jew, thus being incorporated by faith, through Jesus, into the Mosaic Covenant. This, however, necessitates a revision of traditional soteriology: Jesus would be the Way for his followers but not the absolute Way for all humanity. Insofar as classical soteriology is tied to the Christology of the council of Chalcedon, then Christians would have to give up the doctrine that Jesus, the Word made flesh, has two natures, divine and human, united in the Person of the Word of God. An extreme variant of this line of thought proposes that Christians stop worshiping Jesus and worship only the God of Jesus. After being Christocentric, Christianity would then become exclusively theocentric. But this raises the same question: why Moses? why Jesus? why not Muhammad?

The third and fourth interpretations render the Christian way either superfluous or arbitrary. It is superfluous if it is not needed for salvation. But if it is required for one section only of humanity because of a divine decree to that effect, it is arbitrary; and so is the God who decrees it. But arbitrariness is not compatible with the divine attributes of total intelligence, goodness, justice, and love. Such a God would not be worthy of adoration. Thus the proposal is ruinous for theocentric as well as for Christocentric religion. It requires renouncing the specificity of Christ or rejecting the unanimous teaching of the early councils concerning the incarnation. Such a solution to the pending problem between Christians and Jews would destroy the very core of the Christian faith.

It therefore seems to me that the Christian Churches can adopt the first or the second, but not the third or the fourth view. Theologians can hesitate between the first two interpretations of Paul. But I do not believe that the choice between them makes any difference for the mutual relations of Jews and Christians. In both cases, Jews and Christians can relate to one another without proselytizing and without the fear of being proselytized. Thus they should be able to engage in dialogue on such matters as the conditions of the world and their differing interpretations of the biblical revelation. As I see it, the basic conditions to be met by Christians for a dialogue with Judaism were properly stated by Vatican Council II: Christians cannot condone anti-semitism (and, by the same token, they should repent the anti-semitism of their ancestors); and they should blame neither contemporary Jews nor even the majority of Jews at the time of Jesus for the rejection of his preaching and for his condemnation to the Cross.

The Mystery

The previous paragraphs are tentative and inconclusive. This should not be surprising. Before being a visible organization with members and officers, levels of authority, agencies, and buildings, the Church is a mystery. It is the mystery of God's dwelling with humanity through Jesus Christ in the Holy Spirit. Reciprocally, it is the believers' dwelling with God by faith. To be aware of this mutual indwelling is tantamount to perceiving the glory of God in Christ, even under the conditions of the Cross. The existence and the unity of the Church themselves pertain to the mystery.

In the theological sense of the term, a mystery is not a conundrum. It is neither the remaining obscurity of reality after human science and philosophy have thrown their lights upon it, nor the limit of the human capacity to know. It is the unfathomable depth of everything that is, that depth which is precisely the most basic sign of the glory of God in creation. At its deepest and most glorious, the mystery is the depth of the creative act and therefore of the three divine Persons who are jointly the Creator.

All Christian believers are one in faith and baptism. Their unity reaches still further since baptism includes a desire for the Eucharist and for the Eucharistic sharing of Christ. The further unity of believers in one visible

Communion of communions is part and parcel of the hope that is inseparable from the faith. As the Christian faithful contemplate the prospects and imagine the conditions of their eventual reconciliation and reunion, they should enter into doxological adoration. God, through Christ, in the Holy Spirit, is the Master of history no less than the Creator of the world. The Churches should pray that they themselves and their members be made instruments of mutual reconciliation and of peace, even though the means of such a reconciliation still elude them and the times and moments of its eventuality are still hidden in God.

For Further Reading

John Oesterreicher, *Seeds of Hope: Five Sermons on the Mystery of Israel. 1945-1949.* St. Louis: Pio Decimo Press, 1950.

George H. Tavard. *Two Centuries of Ecumenism.* Notre Dame: Fides Publishers, 1960.

Henri de Lubac. *The Church: Paradox and Mystery.* New York: Alba House, 1970.

Heinrich Fries and Karl Rahner. *Unity of the Churches: An Actual Possibility.* New York: Paulist Press, 1985.

Roman Catholic/Lutheran Joint Commission. *Facing Unity: Models, Forms and Phases of Catholic-Lutheran Church Fellowship.* Geneva: Lutheran World Federation, 1985.

Paul Van Buren. *A Theology of the Jewish-Christian Reality,* 3 vol., San Francisco: Harper and Row, 1988.

12

The Dialogue with Religions

The ecclesial dialogue, which Paul VI related to the very being of the Church, should extend beyond the boundaries of Christianity. In one form or another it has always done so, but oftentimes in conflictual ways that are not in keeping with the ecumenical approach of our previous chapter. Friendly or hostile, however, relations with other religions have to take account of the minority status of Christians in the world. In spite of the Church's growth over the centuries, the disciples of Jesus are a minority. Both as a group and as individuals, they live side by side with the faithful of other religions and the followers of several quasi-religions. And as the mass media of communication and the modern means of travel bring all human groups in contact with all other groups, the dialogue between religions becomes, for the Church, more urgent than ever before.

The Apostolic Fathers held the religious culture of the Greco-Roman tradition in high regard. The strictures of Christian polemicists and apologists bore on attempts at syncretism, as were common among the Gnostics, rather than on the ancient religions. The mentality began to change, however, among the great Fathers of the fourth and fifth centuries. St. Ambrose (c. 340-397) entertained nothing but contempt for the old religion of the empire, as he showed in two letters of 384 to Emperor Valentinian II: the bishop of Milan strongly objected to the official privileges that were still enjoyed by the old paganism and violently criticized the venerable institution of the vestal virgins.[1] With the later invasions of the Byzantine Empire and of Northern Africa by the armies of Muhammad's followers, Islam was naturally seen as the enemy from outside. And the armed struggle with Islam altered for the worse the Christian outlook on Judaism: Jews were seen as a fifth column within Christian society.

[1]St. Ambrose, *Letters XVII* and *XVIII to Valentinian II,* in PL, 16, 1001-1024.

Although the time of crusades and holy wars is over, new difficulties have arisen. In the nineteenth century, the gospel was preached in the wake of colonial conquest. This came to an end after World War II. The coexistence between Christians and other believers is now universally accepted. But reluctant coexistence is not friendship. Mere coexistence can of course be practiced for a long time. Because it seems relatively safe, it may well be preferred by the more conservative or timorous leaders of the Churches. But the educated faithful are bound to feel more and more impatient with peaceful coexistence. Mutual knowledge has begun to spread. And it is not unrealistic to think that out of knowledge there will come mutual enrichment and friendship.

The World Context

Like those of all religions, the future prospects of the Christian Church will depend on the evolution of the world as the human habitat. Shall it last only a few more years or decades, as various apocalyptic prophecies would have it? Or shall the inhabited world go on for an immense period of time which, as Teilhard de Chardin thought, could reach to many more millenia?

The first scenario finds support in the population explosion, the human race increasing beyond its present capacity to feed itself, and in the growing evidence of air and water pollution that is bound, in the long run, to remove the conditions that made life possible in the first place. In addition, given the number of nuclear weapons in existence, the extinction of the human race at its own hands is a distinct possibility. The second scenario argues that humankind has lasted a very short time compared with the duration of the universe and even with the age of the dinosaurs, that it has only begun to explore the solar system, and that the technological advances that have taken humankind to the brink of nuclear suicide may also lead to new sources of energy and thereby to yet unsuspected uses of the available resources.

In the first case, the Church will not last much longer, and it is time for its members actively to prepare for the "second coming" of Christ and the "final judgment." A de-emphasis on human power, total reliance on divine grace, and the imminence of the kingdom of God should be primary themes of preaching. Education should prepare the younger generations for a joyful or at least an accepting welcome of death as the ultimate means of spiritual transformation. Theological reflection should bear chiefly on eschatology, and the most obvious topic for debate ought to be whether the kingdom should be expected on this earth or beyond the present form of the physical universe. Whatever answer is given to this question, the faithful should be made to realize that henceforth they constitute indeed the community of the "latter-day saints."

In the second case, the Church's future will last infinitely longer than the Christian tradition used to think when the universe was assumed to be little more than four thousand years old. As a new vision of the universe emerges from modern astrophysics, a different sense of time and temporality will gain ground. Theology will need to take account of this. And already one question is urgent: how should the Church's mission to proclaim the gospel to all nations be adapted to the true size of the universe and to the new history of time?

Such a reflection has begun. Yet there is still little consideration of the theological implications of the contemporary technical revolution. The views of Teilhard have not ceased to be inspiring in their generality, although much is already obsolete in their specific details. And theology itself is in urgent need of a drastic review. The purpose of creation is in question. For if neither the earth nor the solar system lies, by God's doing, at the center of the universe and they are located on the outskirts of a small-size galaxy that floats in a magma of a hundred billion galaxies, then the emergence and development of humanity cannot be convincingly described as the purpose of creation, and what has been seen since the Epistle to the Colossians as the cosmic dimension of Christ, should be redefined. By implication, the question of God's attributes is acutely raised by the new sense of space and of time: what is the Creator like, if the physical universe is an ocean of uninhabitable galaxies?

This world context is the current backdrop for the question of the religions.

The Question Raised by the Religions

The conditions of the world after the Second World War opened the Christian Church to a greater awareness of the religious dimension of non-Christian civilizations. Given the spiritual depth and the cultural impact of the great religions of the world, especially those of Asia, the feeling grew in some circles that the exclusivist assertions of Christian theology concerning salvation could not be maintained. This question is increasingly being asked. It is primarily Christological. Jesus the Christ is indeed, in the eyes of faith, the eternal Word of God who was made flesh and became man for the salvation of the world. But in the eyes of history, he is only a somewhat unorthodox rabbi of Palestine under Roman occupation, who was marked by the culture of his times and who was said by his disciples to have risen from the dead. As long as the Christian mission did not reach much further than the original world of pagans and Jews where it had seen the light, the central message did not cause much of a cultural shock among its hearers. The adaptation of the message was relatively easy. But the situation changed radically when Christian missionaries branched out beyond the civilization of the Mediterranean and of Europe into the great cultures of Asia that had been built around other concepts of salvation. Can Jesus Christ still be presented to the whole world as the only Savior for all humanity? Is the name of Jesus

truly the only one by which women and men can be saved when so many
have believed themselves to be saved, in one or the other sense of the word,
by calling on the names of other prophets, seers, and teachers? Further, can
the Trinitarian name for God—Father, Word, and Holy Spirit—still be
regarded as God's true name? Many, possibly most, of our contemporaries
share the view of Senator Aurelius Quintus Symmachus (c. 340-402) who
in 384 pleaded against the removal of a statue of the Goddess Victory from
the Roman senate: "We cannot arrive by one and the same path to so great
a secret."[2] Should they be right, then the exclusive message of Christianity—
that there is only one Mediator—is wrong. But even if they are mistaken,
the message is so worded as to seem implausible.

Moreover, the Christological question cannot avoid being also ecclesiological. Given the growing desire for inclusive perspectives, one may wonder
how long it will take before the awareness of being the Church is judged in-
compatible with the claim that the Church is indeed the exclusive realm of
salvation, or the one corporate and universal instrument of salvation, or the
society in which alone the word is preached and the sacraments administered.

Faith and Religion

Admittedly, this line of questioning is not self-evident. In fact, it was pre-
empted by the theology of Karl Barth who has undoubtedly been the most
impressive Protestant theologian of the twentieth century. Barth strongly
reacted against the liberal theology that had grown out of the writings of
Friedrich Schleiermacher (1768-1834). He rejected Schleiermacher's basic
principle that the meaning of religion in general and of Christianity in particular may be obtained by drawing out the implications of human self-
consciousness and of its vague awareness of dependence upon an ultimate
principle beyond itself. Precisely, the religions of the world are mythological
expressions of this awareness. Each one of them attempts to sketch the out-
lines of a total system of the universe that would be self-explanatory, and to
provide correct rules of behavior for living in harmony with that system.
Since, however, myths and religions are engendered by human experience,
reflection, and imagination, they are no more—at the level of doctrinal
speculation—than human constructs. One may then regard them as interesting artistic hypotheses or, in a more ethical line of thought, as illusory attempts at self-salvation.[3] Ludwig Feuerbach (1804-1872) concluded that

---

[2] *Relatio III*, n. 10 (PL, 18, 303), quoted in J. Stevenson (ed.), *Creeds, Councils and Controversies: Documents Illustrative of the History of the Church, A. D. 337-461* (New York: Seabury
Press, 1966, p. 122).

[3] Karl Barth, *Church Dogmatics*, vol. 1/2 (Edinburgh: T. and T. Clark, 1970), p. 280-361;
Ludwig Feuerbach *The Essence of Christianity* (New York: Harper, 1957).

the idea of God is only a projection of the wish for salvation and happiness. As he denied this conclusion, Barth nonetheless accepted Feuerbach's starting point: religion is man-made. But a merely human effort to handle the divine is idolatry and, at bottom, unbelief. In order to be saving, Christianity must be God's own construct, the fruit of divine grace. It must be faith. And faith is not a projection: it has no human source.

Yet even if it is faith, Christianity, like the native Judaism which it outgrew, presents the features of a religion. In both Judaism and Christianity, there are myths concerning the origin and shape of the universe, and there are laws that define the creature's proper relationship to God in terms of rites, sacrifices, the practice of virtue, and the performance of good actions. Even where divine inspiration is claimed, as is the case with the Scriptures, the admixture of merely human elements is undeniable. Whether in the Law, in the Prophets, or in the Writings, it is difficult, if not impossible, to sort out the Word of God from human words. Likewise, in the gospels and the epistles, one cannot ascertain what are the actual words of Jesus and the real events of his life, and what are the rhetorical and historical reconstructions by the authors of each book. Nonetheless, Christianity is saved from being an ineffective human construct by the fact that it is, first of all, faith. Being a total reliance on God and no one else, faith does not come from humans; it is "acquitted . . . only by the grace of God, proclaimed and effectual in His revelation." Insofar as Christianity is a religious construction, it may be studied with the methods of comparative religion, and it may itself enter in dialogue with other religions. But in neither case is the heart of Christianity involved. This heart is faith in God's only self-revelation that was given in Jesus Christ. As faith, Christianity can enter in dialogue neither with the religions nor with the unbelieving world. For dialogue presupposes discussion *par cum pari*,[4] on an equality of terms that would be unthinkable between human constructs and God's self-revelation.

Barth's basic ideas were applied to missiology by Hendrik Kraemer (1888–1965). Himself a student of comparative religion, Kraemer did not think that the Church had anything to bring to the great civilizations of Asia if it only gave them another religion. Yet these civilizations, in their own religious dimension, miss the word of God which is addressed to all humans in Jesus Christ alone. Mission is therefore proclamation of the word of God to those who have not heard or recognized it. It is not dialogue.

Barth's theology, and Kraemer's version of it, found a favorable hearing in the World Missionary Council before the creation of the World Council of Churches, especially at the meeting of Tambaram in 1938.[5] Yet their im-

---

[4]As in the conciliar decree UR, nos. 4 and 9.

[5]Kraemer's major study was composed in preparation for the Tambaram Assembly: *The Christian Message in a Non-Christian World* (New York: Harper, 1938); the theses were somewhat modified in a later book: *Religion and the Christian Faith* (London: Butterworth Press, 1956).

pact would have been limited to a few seminaries and to students of missiology, had it not been for their oversimplification in a series of letters written in 1944 by Dietrich Bonhoeffer (1906-1945) while he, in prison, was waiting for what could only be his execution. The pithy formulas of these letters were later haloed by Bonhoeffer's martyrdom. The context is provided in part by the practical atheism of the modern world, by the seeming triumph of evil, and by the challenging proposal made by Rudolph Bultmann (1884-1976) in 1942 to "demythologize" the Christian message in order to make it existentially effective. Now that the world is culturally adult, that is has "come of age," it has become "religionless." So should Christianity be if it is to communicate with the world. God and Christ should now be preached "without religion." Christ himself "is not an object of religion but something quite different, indeed and in truth the Lord of the world." While the whole of Christianity should be preserved, including its "mythological concepts," these should be "interpreted in such a way as not to make religion a precondition of faith."

The outcome is clear. Dialogue is possible to the extent that Christianity submits to comparison. The Christian faith, however, may be contrasted, but cannot be compared, with the stance of the religions. A Christianity that is comparable is religion, not faith. And the Christian religion, being like all religions, man-made, is not true to its Lord or to its faith. Authentic Christian dialogue with the religions is therefore impossible. This remains the position of fundamentalist Churches even in the absence of a sophisticated Barthian basis for their theology.

The Discovery of the Religions

In spite of the depth and passion behind Bonhoeffer's formulas and their widespread appeal, the refusal of religious dialogue has not been able to withstand the enthusiastic discovery of the great religions.

In the Catholic world, the work of Wilhelm Schmidt (1858-1954) had a decisive impact in arousing interest in the religions of the world even though the heart of his theory has been universally abandoned. In a twelve-volume study, Schmidt tried to demonstrate that monotheism preceded the degeneration of religions into polytheistic cults. But Schmidt's thesis could not be satisfactorily proven. Theories regarding primitive prehistoric religions can only be extrapolated from the historically known Animist religions. Even in the best of cases, the documentation is too scant to allow for a valid reconstruction of the origins.

As more scholars have entered the fields of anthropology and ethnology, they have come to renounce the ambition of describing with any degree of certainty the shape of the primitive religions. While the existence of religious notions from the very beginnings of *homo sapiens* seems certain on the basis of the oldest cave paintings that are known today, the developed mythologies of all religions are so varied, in spite of similar structures, that no extrapolation concerning original teachings and rituals can be regarded as valid. But a detailed knowledge of the past is not indispensable. Whatever the past may have been, a dialogue is feasible only among the adepts of living religions. The descriptions of many aspects of the world religions that were made, among others, by R. C. Zaehner (1913-1974) and Mircea Eliade (1907-1986), had a powerful influence on changing assessments of the religions by Christian theologians.[6]

From the standpoint of such a dialogue, a certain number of common elements characterize all religions: in each one of them there are teachings on the nature and purpose of the world and on the nature of humanity and the purpose of its sufferings, these teachings being usually couched in the shape of myths and tales; there are rituals of propitiation and prayer that are not always organized around a caste of priests; there are methods of meditation and interior journeying into the recesses of the mind and the soul; and there are teachers, prophets, and mystics who speak for God or who obtain insights into Ultimate Reality. The researches of Claude Lévi-Strauss into structural anthropology have also shown that there is an intriguing correspondence between the structures of society, the structures of kinship, and those of religious ritual. This tends to show that religion is as fundamental to the human mind as are family ties and the need to live in society.[7]

The Mystical Element of Religion

Even before the progress that was made by anthropology in the second half of the twentieth century, interreligious dialogue was urged upon theologians by the discovery of what Baron Von Hügel (1852-1925) called the "mystical element of religion."[8] The discovery of Hinduism and Buddhism by Westerners in the nineteenth century had revealed the writings of mystics who, though outside of Christianity, could be regarded as having obtained a high experience of God or, where God is not named as such, of the Ultimate. The Upanishads and the *Bhagavad Gita* on the one hand, the traditions concerning the Buddha on the other, suggested that no religion has a monopoly on the perception of the Holy. Life in Buddhist monasteries was not essen-

[6] Mircea Eliade, *The Sacred and the Profane: The Nature of Religion* (New York: Harper and Row, 1961); *Patterns in Comparative Religion* (New York: Meridian Books, 1968); R. C. Zaehner: *Christianity and Other Religions* (New York: Hawxthorn Books, 1964); René Girard, *Violence and the Sacred* (Baltimore: Johns Hopkins University Press, 1981).

[7] Georges Charbonnier, *Conversations with Claude Lévi-Strauss* (London: Jonathan Cape, 1969).

[8] *The Mystical Element of Religion, as studied in St. Catherine of Genoa and her Friends*, 2 vol. (London: J. M. Dent, 1909).

tially different from life in Christian monasteries. In addition, the translation into European languages of the poetry of the sufis of Islam and a growing familiarity with studies of the Kabbalah by Jewish scholars imposed on many Christians the conclusion that mystical contemplation, and therefore mystical grace, have been experienced in all the great religions of the world.

Yet the recognition that there is authentic mystical experience among Hindus, Buddhists, and Muslims is one thing; the modification of Christian attitudes toward other believers is another. The latter is conditional upon an antecedent acceptance of mystical contemplation as a genuine Christian experience. By and large, the Lutheran and the Calvinist traditions have not been persuaded of this, in spite of Luther's endorsement of the *Theologia germanica* (an anonymous mystical writing of the fifteenth-century which Luther found and published in 1516 and 1518) and of the Augustinian focus that Calvin deliberately chose for his theology: the joint knowledge of God and of self.[9] In Lutheran and Calvinist circles, the distinction between two types of faith is widely accepted: prophetic and priestly, Abrahamic and Mosaic, the former being that which justifies, the second that which lives and sanctifies through charity.[10] The force of this distinction, however, is not conclusive. For the prophets of the Old Testament themselves would have had nothing to say unless God had somehow impressed his message upon them. And this is precisely the heart of the mystical experience.

If there is some sense in which mystical contemplation as authentic experience of God does take place outside of biblical religion and of Christianity, then the problem of salvation outside the Church should be put in other terms than it was in the past. For the experience of non-Christian mystics cannot be dismissed as entirely man-made. The religions could be understood and appreciated as authorized, if not revealed, ways to God. Their rituals should not be condemned as false worship. Their beliefs should not be dismissed: they do include elements of true faith. In consequence, the Church's missionary urge could still be justified by the altruistic desire to bring all the means of salvation to all of humankind. At the same time, however, the Christian Church should enter into a new relationship with religions. Recent studies of the Animism of Africa and of Native American religions have reinforced these conclusions.

Two Approaches

One outcome of the discovery of the great world religions was the emergence of the academic discipline of Comparative Religion. If religion is taken

---

[9] *The 'Theologia Germanica' of Martin Luther* (New York: Paulist Press, 1980); Calvin, *Institutes of the Christian Religion*, bk 1, ch. 1.

[10] Martin Buber, *Two Types of Faith* (New York: Harper and Row, 1961); Franz L. Leenhardt, *Two Biblical Faiths, Protestant and Catholic* (Philadelphia: Westminster Press, 1964).

as a general category, each concrete religion can be assigned a place under that category. The many religions of humanity can then be compared, and scholars can propose interpretations and elicit conclusions that need not assume any supernatural or revealed element at the origin or in the history of religions, but that throw light on a particular dimension of human experience and of the human mind, the religious dimension. When such conclusions began to be systematically organized, the additional discipline of Philosophy of Religion came into being. In turn, the Philosophy of Religion has had an impact on the way some Christian theologies have envisaged the relationships between Christianity and other religions.

A case in point is the theology of Paul Tillich (1886–1965). Because Tillich has defined faith as the experience of an "ultimate concern," he is able to discover faith in all religions and quasi-religions. And because he has interpreted justification as God's gift regardless of both intellectual doubt and moral effort, he is able to conclude that the faith of all religions and quasi-religions is already justifying and salvific. Then the encounter of religions brings together diverse experiences and formulations of ultimate concern and of saving faith. In this encounter there should always be "a dialectical union of rejection and acceptance."[11] In Tillich's mind, this does not do away with the specificity of Christianity as the religion that is focused on the only Savior. Rather, it means that contemporary Christians can share the conviction of the early Church when Christianity "did not consider itself as a radical-exclusive, but as the all-inclusive religion in the sense of the saying, 'All that is true anywhere in the world belongs to us, the Christians.'" In thus asserting the universal meaning of the Christ, Christians must also apply to their religion the meaning of the cross of Christ: through abandonment of the self one has access to the true meaning of the self. Hence the possibility that Christ and salvation are present and active in all religions. What is needed is a descent into the mystical core of all religions: "In the depth of every living religion there is a point at which the religion itself loses its importance, and that to which it points breaks through its particularity, elevating it to spiritual freedom and with it to a vision of the spiritual presence in other expressions of the ultimate meaning of man's existence."

In the theology of Karl Rahner, the possibility of a salvific relationship to God is inscribed in the structure of the human person.[12] Firstly, there exists "a universal and supernatural salvific will of God which is really operative in the world." Secondly, there is "supernatural revelation" as soon as "transcendentality"—"the presence of absolute mystery" in human life—is made manifest by grace. And there is saving faith as soon as the free human re-

[11]Paul Tillich, *Christianity and the Encounter of World Religions* (New York: Columbia University Press, 1961), p. 29 and 35; *The Future of Religion* (New York: Harper and Row, 1966); *What is Religion?* (New York: Harper and Row, 1969); George H. Tavard, *Paul Tillich and the Christian Message* (New York: Scribners, 1962).

[12]*Foundations of the Christian Faith* (New York: Seabury Press, 1976), *passim.*

sponse—loving acceptance of the mystery—is elevated by grace to the supernatural order. Thirdly, it follows that the religions are ways, even though
man-made, in which what is "unthematic" in humanity as such becomes
"thematic." The presence of the divine mystery and its acceptance are concretely formulated in the religious myths of humankind. At one step of his
reflection, Rahner used the phrase "anonymous Christians" to cover this
situation. The expression is meant to safeguard the universal salvific mission
of Christ as the only Mediator. Yet its imperialistic undertones are unfortunate, so that if one uses it one should be ready to admit that Christians
may also be, in Buddhology, anonymous Buddhists. But there is a more
basic difficulty to Rahner's line of thought. Should it be pursued to its logical
end, it would lead to the point where all religions are implicit in all others.
And this would ultimately imply the irrelevance, before the awesome mystery
of the Absolute, of each religion's specificity, including that of the Christian
Church.

Vatican Council II

These and similar questions were faced by the Catholic Church at Vatican
Council II. Four documents of the council are relevant.

In the constitution on the Church, after describing the people of God, the
council turned to "those who have not yet accepted the gospel," yet "relate
to the people of God in diverse ways" (LG, n. 16). It mentioned Jews and
Muslims, and then made the following statement: "Those who are ignorant
of Christ's gospel and of his Church through no fault of their own but who
seek God in sincerity of heart and try with the help of grace to carry out in
their actions his will as known to them by the dictates of their conscience
can attain salvation." Such a text does not go very far. It simply recognizes,
with St. Paul (Rom 1:20), as understood in the natural law tradition of Scho-
lasticism, that a natural knowledge of God is implicit in following one's
conscience. In keeping with the doctrine of the fifth council of Orange in
529, on the necessity of divine grace for salvation, it also implies that God
is at work in all of humanity. The religions as such are not considered, except
perhaps negatively, in this allusion to idolatry: "Often, men, deceived by the
Evil One, . . . have exchanged the truth of God for the lie, serving what is
created rather than the Creator. . . ."

The council's approach is more positive in the decree *Nostra aetate*. The
text opens on the basic statement that all nations and peoples form one community and that all humans are oriented to the same final end which is God,
"whose providence, manifest goodness, and designs of salvation extend to
all until the elect are united in the Holy City. . . ." (NA, n. 1). The Church's
desire to promote all that contributes to human unity and harmony is affirmed. The religious experience of humankind is then described in broad

yet positive terms: "From antiquity down to our own days there is found among the diverse nations some perception of that hidden Power which is present in the unfolding of reality and in the events of human life, and at times there is even a recognition of a Supreme Numen and even of a Father. Such perception and recognition steep their life in an intimate religious feeling" (n. 2). The religions as such are recognized: "In keeping with the progress of their culture, the religions try to answer the same questions with more advanced notions and a more studied language." After a summary description of Hinduism and of Buddhism, seen as the most developed religions of this kind, the text goes on: "Thus, the other religions too that are found in the whole world try to respond in various manners to the disquiet of the human heart, as they propose ways that include doctrines, precepts of life, and sacred rites."

The council is not content with description. It puts forward the principle of what could be (though it is not so called at this point) a new relationship: "The Catholic Church rejects nothing of what is true and holy in these religions. With sincere interest it regards those modes of action and life, those precepts and doctrines, which, though they differ in many things from what it itself holds and proposes, not seldom reflect a ray of that Truth which illumines all human beings." On this basis, the council exhorts the faithful to "dialogues and collaboration with the followers of other religions."

As a complement to this positive though excessively general assessment of the religions of the world, the council affirms "the right of the person and the communities to social and civic freedom in religious matters." This is the topic of the declaration, *Dignitatis humanae*. Here, the right to religious liberty is based on the intrinsic dignity of the human person (DH, n. 2), on the responsibility of the individual conscience as the proximate norm of morality (n. 3), and on the nature of saving faith as a divine gift that should be appropriated in an uncoerced and unimpeded human act.

The Church's Mission

In the perspective of Vatican II, the beginning of a dialogical relationship with other religions does not put an end to missions. For the Church is missionary in its very essence: it is sent by the Lord to preach the gospel. This is at the heart of its life. In *Nostra aetate*, mission is justified by traditional Christology: the Church "preaches, and is bound unceasingly to preach Christ, who is 'the way, the truth, and the life,' in whom humans find the fullness of religious life, in whom God reconciles all things with himself" (NA, n. 2).

This is also the starting point of the decree on the Church's missionary activity, *Ad gentes*: "The Church is missionary by virtue of its pilgrim nature, as it has its origin in the mission of the Son and the mission of the Holy Spirit according to the design of God the Father" (AG, n. 2). This makes the Church "the universal sacrament of salvation" (n. 1). Having said this and having related the task of preaching the gospel to the missions of the Word and the Spirit which themselves originate in God's Trinitarian life, the council turns to the younger Churches of Africa and Asia that were officially considered mission territories until recently. In principle, a land ceases to be considered a mission territory when it receives a normal Catholic hierarchy and is no longer in the care of the Roman Congregation for Missions (the former *Congregatio de Propaganda Fide*). Likewise, Protestant mission outposts become full-fledged Churches when they obtain autonomy of government. Then, preaching the gospel becomes the primary concern of local Christians. The gospel ceases to be a foreign import.

However important the communication of the gospel is for Christian authenticity, the Church's dialogical nature should not be left out of consideration. The relations of Christians with the adepts of other religions cannot be reduced to informing and persuading others with a view to their conversion. In any modern society, Christians and others should be involved in many-sided cooperation: association for the defense of religious liberty against oppressive ideologies and governments, mutual assistance in the service of the poor and the sick, common defense of the rights of women in the face of male hegemony, joint efforts to make social structures more just and responsive to the needs of the citizens, the elaboration of social projects regardless of race and religion, the promotion of nonviolence and peace. After Vatican II, Pope Paul VI drew a further consequence of his understanding of dialogue: the relationships of the Church outside of itself should be dialogical on the model of its internal relationships. Parallel to the Secretariat for Promoting Christian Unity, Pope Paul created a Secretariat for Dialogue with Non-Christian Religions and another for Dialogue with Non-Believers. Similar concerns for dialogue have been expressed in the World Council of Churches. In both Protestant and Catholic circles, these concerns have inspired new theological approaches to the question of the salvation of unbelievers and to the nature of the great world religions.

The People of the Book

A principle that is stated in the Koran is now generally recognized: Jews, Christians, and Muslims belong together in one category; they are the *Ahl al Kitab*, the People of the Book. Judaism, especially in its Old Testament form, is focused on the Bible, Christianity on the Bible and the writings of the New Testament, Islam on the Koran which incorporates a certain number of notions and stories from both the Bible and the New Testament. Some authors add to them the religion of Zoroaster which is focused on the *Gâthas*, poems attributed to its founder, but whose connection with the Old Testament is extremely remote or non-existent. Besides the conviction that God has spoken through certain prophets and that the essentials of the message have been consigned in a book, these religions share the belief that God is One, and they endow this God with the attribute of personality.

Christian theology has traditionally distinguished between God's public revelation, which was made off and on in the course of the Old Testament and which culminated in Jesus the Christ, and private revelations, which God is free to make to a chosen few. Whatever theologians may think of their authenticity, the Church does not endorse private revelations even when it tolerates certain types of popular devotion or when it authorizes pilgrimages to certain shrines considered particularly holy because they have been associated with alleged apparitions and revelations. Such an endorsement would blur the distinction between public and private, obligatory and optional; and it would be, in the long run, confusing. The public revelation is the one that the Church was charged by the risen Lord to make known to all nations. Private revelations, if they do take place, are for the spiritual advancement of those who receive them or for a specific prophetic task. They are to be assessed theologically according to standard rules for the discernment of spirits.

However, the study of other religions suggests that few, if any, peoples have been left without prophets. One ought to recognize a third category, namely, a revelation made to one person for the spiritual advancement of an entire group. The Church has an immemorial practice of not endorsing private revelations. There is therefore little likelihood that the Church, speaking officially, would endorse such a revelation. Yet, by the same token, there is nothing that should stop theologians from expressing a favorable judgment concerning the prophets of the world religions.

Nonetheless, just as Christians should decide whether they will look at Jews as the still chosen people of the Mosaic revelation or only as the first people of the Book, so they need to determine to what extent they share and recognize the revelation proclaimed by the Prophet of Islam.

The Prophet of Islam

The revelation to Muhammad is a case in point. One can hardly doubt that the Prophet of Islam did teach the Lordship of God, Allah, in the oneness of the divine nature and the multiplicity of its attributes, and the proper attitude of adoration and submission to the divine will on the part of the faithful. This is especially manifest in the sourats (chapters of the Koran) composed at Mecca, which deal with the faith (*'aqida*), the later sourats of Medina being more concerned with the organization of the believers' community and the legal aspects (*shari'a*) of its life. This revelation was brought by the Prophet and his companions and successors to the Arabian tribes and to the other peoples who accepted the Koran in Asia, Africa, and Europe.

Vatican II took a positive step in this direction when it selected Islam for special mention: "The Church regards with esteem the Muslims: they worship the one God, living and subsistent, merciful and almighty, the Creator of heaven and earth, who spoke with men; they seek with their whole soul to submit even to his hidden decrees, on the model of Abraham, who submitted himself to God, and to whom the Islamic faith willingly relates" (NA, n. 3). The council noted the place in Islam of Mary the Virgin, the Mother of Jesus; the expectation of the day of judgment and of the resurrection; and the traditional moral concerns of Muslims. It cited three of the five "pillars of Islam:" prayer (*salat*), almsgiving (*sadaqa*), and fasting (*sawm*).

Two pillars, however, were omitted: the testimony (*shahâda*) and the pilgrimage (*hadj*). Presumably, this was because they imply precisely the points where the Koranic teaching differs the most from the Christian faith. These omissions are significant. They point to inherent difficulties in a theological dialogue with Islam. Yet Christian theologians find a remarkable convergence between the Koranic and the biblical teachings on the oneness and unicity of God. Many of them also think that the sufis or mystics of Islam have often obtained, by divine grace, a loving intimacy with the true God and, exceptionally, as in the case with Husayn ibn Mansûr al Hallâj (c. 858-922), who died crucified in Bhagdad, with Christ crucified.[13] Yet the Koran excludes the incarnation, and it argues against the Christian belief in Three divine Persons. Furthermore, the sufis have often been actively persecuted largely because they have tended to place love above faith, or love within faith, and interior religion above external observances, the pilgrimage in the heart above the pilgrimage to Mecca.

Vatican II also called for mutual esteem between Christians and Muslims and for the joint pursuit of social justice, public morality, and peace and freedom instead of the disagreements and struggles of the past. But it did not suggest dialogue. At this point, the council presumably practiced the delicate diplomatic art of not proposing more than can be obtained. A dialogue of equals, *par cum pari*, on religious doctrines would not be compatible with the islamic teaching that Muhammad is "the Seal of the Prophets." Furthermore, a dialogue between theologians presupposes personal speculation (*ijtihad*) about the divine revelation, a pursuit that has seldom been in official favor in Islam.

Given this situation, the awareness of being the Church may well include gratitude for walking part of the human pilgrimage with the followers of the Prophet. But it cannot ignore the separation at the point where Christians

---

[13]Reynold A. Nicholson, *The Mystics of Islam: An Introduction to Sufism* (New York: Schocken Books, 1975), p. 149-160; the classic study is by Louis Massignon, *Al-Hallaj martyr mystique de l'Islam*, 2 vols. (Paris: Geuthner, 1922).

worship the Father through Christ in the Holy Spirit and Muslims directly worship Allah, who is said in the Koran not to be Father for he has "no consort."[14]

Many Prophets and Many Ways

A number of theologians have further broadened the ecumenical horizon and the dialogical structure of the Church by extending the dialogue to the great religions of Asia. Vatican II recognized the possibility of such a dialogue as it described the main religions of India: "In Hinduism, men scrutinize and formulate the divine mystery in an unexhausted fecundity of myths and in acute philosophical efforts, and they seek liberation from the anxieties of our condition through some forms of ascetic life, through deep meditation, or through finding shelter in God in love and trust" (NA, n. 2). These are the three ways of *yoga* (especially the *râja-yoga* of Patañjali), *jñâna*, and *bhakti*. A religious dialogue with Hinduism may be focused on any of these three ways. But it ought to lead to a more advanced stage. The difficulty lies in that Hinduism generally recognizes God as Being but not as Person. Yet a dialogue in stages may be possible. Starting with the attributes of the divine Being, especially the attribute of eternity, perception of which may be obtained by interior contemplation, one could go on to discuss the human sharing in these divine attributes and, one more step removed from the deluded experience of the world, the sharing in the very Being of God.

The description of Buddhism by Vatican Council II is more hesitant: "In Buddhism in its varied forms, the radical insufficiency of this changing world is recognized, and a way is taught by which humans, with devout and trusting heart, may obtain a state of perfect liberation or, whether by their own efforts or with the assistance of higher help, may attain to the summit of enlightenment" (NA, n. 2). The problem lies in the fact that Buddhism recognizes neither God as Being nor any being that could be called God in the absolute sense. Yet the apophatic experience of God by a number of Christian mystics of both East and West offers a point of contact with the negativities of Buddhism. There is a Christian negative theology which, however tentatively, has drawn on apophatic mystical experience. If God is so entirely Other that human language is always inadequate, the Buddhist refusal to name the Transcendent is itself entirely proper. The awareness of being the Church of God includes the conviction that all created forms and dimensions of this Church, including theological speculation about God, are destined to vanish in a mystery that lies beyond all understanding.

Because Hinduism and Buddhism present themselves as ways of salvation from the world and from illusion, there are Christian theologians who wish

[14] *The Koran*, sourat VI ('Cattle'), v. 101 (A. J. Arberry, *The Koran Interpreted* [New York: Macmillan, 1955], p. 161).

to recognize them also, along with Judaism and Islam, as God-given ways. The theory would be that the divine self-revelation has been tailored to each people's culture. What God has revealed in many revelations to the prophets of all religions is not actually the divinity in its Person(s), its Being, and its Non-Being, but the path or several paths to the divinity. Languages and metaphors vary, yet the convergence is remarkable: Hindus follow a *marga*, Buddhists follow the *tao*, or are carried in a *vehicle*, Hebrews and Jews follow their *derek*, Christians their *odos* or *via*. The People of the Book will be saved by worshiping the one God in unreserved faith—Muslims according to the Koran, Jews according to Torah in its varied interpretations, Christians according to the gospel.

These proposals run counter to the central Christian tradition for which Jesus the Christ is the only Mediator for all nations and the Lord, not of heaven only (as was thought in China when the early Catholic missionaries began to call God *T'ien chu*, "Lord of Heaven") but of all the universe. Their proponents need to take seriously the threat to the Christian message that is inherent in such theories. The scriptural call to preach the gospel to all nations is neutralized, if not nullified. And one wonders if the Christian awareness of being the Church of God does not also become subjectively hesitant and objectively inconsistent. Problems of this kind stand behind the reticence of most theologians and Churches to follow this line of thought.

The Trinitarian Way

After this reflection on the dialogical relations of the Christian Church with the religions of the world, I stand by the interpretation of the religions that I formulated in a previous volume.[15] All religions indeed have an active relation to the Christian revelation of the Three Persons. Some of them derive from a perception, more or less distinct and clear, of the attributes and the depths of the Divinity, which Christian experience and reflection have associated with the *ousia* that is common to the Father, the Word, and the Spirit. This is generally seen by Oriental theologians as the *ousia* of the First Person; and in the common Western theology it is appropriated to the Father.

Other religions find their balance in a search for a scale of mediations and mediators between God and creation, thus placing their adepts in the path of the one Mediator, the Word Incarnate. Others, still, have discerned the divine Spirit as being present and at work in the universe and above all in human hearts and lives. But there is no authentic perception of God that is not given by God. Therefore, without claiming anything for themselves, Christians may confess that in all religions the one Mediator, Jesus Christ,

---

[15] *La Religion à l'épreuve des idées modernes* (Paris: Le Centurion, 1970); these lectures were originally delivered in English at the University of Nottingham, as the Firth Lectures for 1968.

has been at work, prophets have been called and instructed by the Spirit, hearts have been transformed by divine gifts that are to be counted among "all good giving and every perfect gift" that "come from above, from the Father of the lights of heaven" (Jas 1:17). There is only one New Testament, given in hellenistic Greek, and there is one Old Testament, given in Hebrew and Aramaic, that were its historical cradle, but there are many propedeutic Old Testaments, given in many languages, that also foretell something of the Christ.

The key to the encounter of religions and to the outer aspect of the Church's dialogical structure was given in Jesus Christ whose dying and rising unveiled to the apostles the inner source of his life and teaching. Through Himself as the Word, in the Holy Spirit, the believers are led to the hidden Father, "the one who is in heaven" (as in Luke's version of the Lord's Prayer). God is One in *ousia* and Three in Persons. It is precisely the Church's opportunity in its dialogue with the religions to discover and to give thanks for the many ways in which the Spirit and the Word have been at work in humankind, leading women and men to God the Father.

For Further Reading

Anita Röper. *The Anonymous Christian*, New York: Sheed and Ward, 1966.

Andrew Chih. *Chinese Humanism: A Religion beyond Religion,* Taipeh: Fu Jen Catholic University Press, 1981.

Paul Knitter. *No Other Name? A Critical Survey of Christian Attitudes toward the World Religions.* Maryknoll, N.Y.: Orbis Books, 1985.

Choan-Seng Song. *Third Eye Theology: Theology in Formation in Asian Settings.* New York: Orbis Books, 1979.

F. Eboussi Boulaga. *Christianity without Fetishes: An African Critique and Recapture of Christianity.* New York: Orbis Books, 1981.

Kenneth Cracknell. *Towards a New Relationship: Christians and People of Other Faiths.* London: Epworth Press, 1986.

Peter C. Phan (ed.). *Christianity and the Wider Ecumenism.* New York: Paragon House, 1990.

13

An Ongoing Pentecost

The consciousness of being the Church is being enlarged in this last decade of the twentieth century to the full ecumenical horizon. This is a major lesson of our times. Other options still have been set before Christian believers by the contemporary situation of the Churches. One may appeal to the pneumatological dimension of the communion. Since the Holy Spirit is to guide the disciples "into all the truth" (John 16:13), one may hope at any time for a new outpouring of the Holy Spirit.

The awareness of the Spirit's presence and guidance belongs to the awareness of being the Church. It has from time to time in the past inspired specific conceptions and prophecies of the Spirit's future actions. Most such prophecies were disproved by the facts. But this has never restrained the enthusiasm of later prophets. Our analysis of the ecumenical horizon has revealed the emergence among many believers of such a new awareness of the Spirit. The Pentecostal Churches have introduced the necessity of a, so to say, triangular ecumenism between the Churches of the Catholic, of the Reformation, and of the Pentecostal traditions. The three sides are reduced to two if one admits that the Catholic and the classical Protestant Churches find their primary ground in Christology while the Pentecostal urge is nurtured by pneumatology. In the best of the tradition, however, Christology and pneumatology do not give rise to different doctrines of the Church. At the most, they highlight two aspects of the community of salvation.

The Spirit and the Bride

Ever since the apostolic period, the principle has been recognized that the Church as the communion of the believers stands in a very special relation to the Holy Spirit, the Third Person. This goes back to the writings of the

New Testament. The author of the Book of Revelation ended his work with the words, "The Spirit and the Bride say, 'Come.' Let the one who hears say, 'Come.' Let the one who thirsts come; and the one who wills receive the water of life, freely" (Rev 22:17).

There are two movements in this text. First, the bride who, in the light of the preceding verses, must be identified with the Church is in a spousal relationship with the Spirit. Their calling to each other is a nuptial dance that will climax in their union. Second, the image that is proposed by the author is no mere metaphor. Rather, it directly expresses a central Christian experience. Those who are thirsty and accept the water of life are the neophytes who in baptism are plunged in the bath of regeneration. Those who address the Spirit in bridal language are already full members of the Church. Like the Church and the Spirit, the Christian and the Spirit are engaged in a nuptial relationship of unreserved mutuality. Each is for the other and each is in the other. At any moment in the Christian life, the grace of baptism may therefore be reawakened. Then, the believer who "hears" the call of the Spirit and who "thirsts" for a nuptial encounter with the Beloved joins the Church's bridal dance. Along with other biblical texts such as the Song of Songs with its erotic images, the parables of the wedding feast (Matt 22:1-14; Luke 14:15-24), the ecclesial symbolism of marriage (Eph 5:22-32), these verses of the Book of Revelation justify the rich use of matrimonial images in the Christian tradition, notably in relation to the Spirit. Thus St. John of the Cross, mystic and poet, took the Song of Songs as the chief model for his own poem, *The Spiritual Canticle*; and in *The Living Flame of Love* he sang of the soul's mystical encounter with the Holy Spirit who awakes in it. Given the totality of mutual sharing that is implied in the nuptial image, the Christian tradition has applied to the Church and the Spirit, by analogy, the verses of Genesis: "Bone from my bones, flesh from my flesh!" (Gen 2:23) and "That is why a man leaves his father and mother and is united to his wife, and the two become one flesh" (Gen 2:24). The Church and the Spirit are one.

In the Catholic tradition, the nuptiality of the Church and the soul's experience of spiritual marriage have been projected upon the image of the Virgin Mary Theotokos, the Bearer or Forthbringer of God. Mary's maternal intimacy with the Lord derives from her close union with the Spirit who "overshadows" her at the annunciation (Luke 1:35). Christ, filled with the Spirit, is God's Uncreated Wisdom. For this reason, the great church built by Emperor Constantine in Constantinople was called Haghia Sophia and dedicated to Christ as Eternal Wisdom. But when the Virgin is seen as God's highest creation, the creaturely paradigm of all that is, she becomes God's Created Wisdom. And so the cathedral of Kiev, built in the eleventh century, was called Haghia Sophia and dedicated to the Theotokos.[1]

---

[1]David Talbot Rice, *Art of the Byzantine Era* (New York: Frederick Praeger, 1966), p. 47-55; Tamara Talbot Rice, *A Concise History of Russian Art* (New York: Frederick Praeger, 1967), p. 16-26.

The Church is the bride of the Spirit. So is the soul. Awareness of being in the Spirit and of having the Spirit belongs to the awareness of being the Church. With Calvin, one may say that those who hear the Word of God respond to the interior testimony of the Spirit concerning the Word. Likewise, those who receive divine grace in the sacraments have been led to them by the Spirit. And as they face the difficult problems of life, one may recognize, with Thomas Aquinas, that the faithful are guided by an *instinctus* that is from the Holy Spirit. By the same token, and all the more because of her intimacy with the Lord in her task as the Theotokos, so is the Virgin Mary.

Traditional Accents

Orthodox theology has generally conceived ecclesiology in keeping with its standard doctrine of the procession of the Holy Spirit from the Father alone, rather than, as in the West, from the Father and from the Son. That is, the presence and the action of the Spirit, who "reposes" upon the Logos, do not simply follow and complement Christ's presence and action. The Church is the Church of the Spirit through whom Christ himself is present in this world in his risen body. It is led by the Third Person as it lives its experience of *sobornost* in the harmony of its diverse members, functions, and tasks. If the ecclesial basis of the *Koinonia* is given by God in the incarnation of the divine Wisdom, the believers' life and cohesion are given in the Third Person who leads them in doctrine and prayer, whence the harmonious coexistence of the monastic and the hierarchic principles, the inseparability of the bishop from his synod, the relative autonomy of the charisms of prophets and saints, and the predominance of the spiritual dimension over the magisterial. The shape of the divine liturgy gives prominence to the "epiclesis." In this prayer which follows the account of the Last Supper, the Lord, that is, the Father, "who sent the Holy Spirit on the apostles," is asked "not to take Him from us, but to renew Him in us," and to "make this bread the precious body of His Christ," and "that which is in the chalice the precious blood of His Christ."[2] The numerous Orthodox monasteries that flourished in times past were the guardians of this ecclesiology. In spite of the recession of the monastic life in Orthodox lands, this ecclesiology is as much alive today as it formerly was.

By the same token, the conciliarity of the Church being impaired by the separation between Rome and the Oriental patriarchates, the epiphany of the Spirit in a truly ecumenical council has become provisionally impossible. At the present time, the Orthodox Churches are involved in a process of consultation toward holding a "Great and Holy Council" in the future. They have also engaged a wide-ranging dialogue with the Catholic Church. In both

---

[2] *Liturgy of St. John Chrysostom.*

cases, however, no final decision can be reached until it becomes evident that these initiatives are led by the Spirit.

The Trinitarian theology of St. Augustine has had the unforeseen result that the pneumatological principle has been largely neglected in the Latin Church. On the one hand, Augustine's doctrine of appropriation attributes to the divine nature as such all the creative actions of God, so that nothing in creation is revelatory of any one of the divine Persons. On the other hand, if indeed the Father and the Word are eternally the joint origin of the Spirit who proceeds from them both as from one principle, then Christ and the Spirit always act jointly. If one says that the Spirit acts, this is only a manner of speech as a common deed of the Three is appropriated to one.

Yet the Holy Spirit does have a place in the Western consciousness of being the Church. The Spirit is given by the Father through Christ, with the instrumentality of the Church and its ministers, in the sacraments. And the Spirit in turn testifies to Christ, thus subordinating all charismatic manifestations to the magisterial judgment of the hierarchy. In the Latin liturgy, the stress has been placed on the consecration of bread and wine through the words of Jesus at the Last Supper; and this was further underlined during the Berengarian controversy (eleventh century) by the elevation of the host and the chalice and the ringing of bells.[3] Accordingly, the epiclesis has mostly disappeared. And when, in the sequel to Vatican Council II, attempts were made to restore it in the new canons of the Mass, it was not always located at the proper place. When it is enshrined between the preface addressed to the Father and the consecration commemorative of the Second Person Incarnate, the epiclesis of the Holy Spirit does not respect the order of the divine processions. While priest and people invoke or evoke the Third Person before the narration of the Last Supper, they also ignore its Trinitarian specificity. All this undoubtedly reflects, and in turn fosters, a lesser awareness of the Spirit than is common in the Eastern Church.

It is presumably to compensate for this lack in Western piety that the action of the Spirit has been sensed by many in such parasacramental experiences as private revelations and visions. In medieval devotion, such visions were chiefly of lesser saints and angels, though visions of the Virgin are mentioned from time to time. Beginning in the sixteenth century with the story of Guadalupe in Mexico, visions have been closely dependent on devotion to the Virgin Mary whose alleged apparitions have often coincided with times of special trouble and turmoil. The image of the Virgin has acted, in popular piety, as a substitute for the Holy Spirit. Even in more knowledgeable spiritual authors, devotion to the Virgin has taken forms that are primarily suitable to the Holy Spirit, as when Louis-Marie Grignion de Montfort (1673–1716) recommended vowing to be Mary's slave or when the poet Gerard Manley Hopkins (1844–1889) compared the Virgin Mary to "the air

---

[3]Hubert Jedin (ed.), *History of the Church* (New York: Seabury Press, 1980), vol. 3, p. 467-68.

we breathe." Admittedly popular pilgrimages to the Virgin, as at Lourdes or Fatima, often attempt to redress the devotional imbalance. But this is done by stressing the ties of Mary to Christ and the Christological dimension of marian doctrines. And this is itself an indirect testimony to a discomfort with pneumatology.

"One Person in many persons"

The ecclesial symbolism of nuptial unity has inspired another image that has been used from time to time in Western theology, and never as much as in the twentieth century, to designate the close union of the Church and the Spirit: the Church is *una persona in multis personis*, "one person in many persons." There is no hesitancy about the identity of the "many persons" of this Scholastic expression: they are the faithful. But the other term of the proposition has been interpreted in at least three senses.

Firstly, the one Person is the Church itself. The Church gathers the faithful in unity or, in the words of St. Augustine who borrowed the idea from the Donatist Tyconius, the Church constitutes the "total Christ," the head with the members. The Church is the Person, but its personality is rooted in that of Christ. Christ who is the Head is also the Person of the Head. And since there can be but one person for both head and body, he is by the same token the "Person of the body." So did Thomas Aquinas understand the mystical body of Christ: Christ and the Church add up to *quasi una persona*, "as it were one person."[4] In this context, the word "mystical" designates an analogy modeled on the spiritual senses of Scripture and also a "mystery" that is experienced in the Eucharist, the liturgical mystery par excellence. Precisely for this reason the adjective "mystical" came to be applied to the body of the Church: before the eleventh century it designated the Eucharist.[5]

Or, secondly, the *una persona* is directly the divine Person of the Incarnate Word, acting as the head (*caput*) that infuses divine grace into his mystical body. So could many Pauline texts be understood, as when the faithful are said to be "in Christ" (Gal 3:23) and are destined to form with him "one perfect man, the measure of age of the fullness of Christ" (Eph 4:13). The language of Tertullian for whom a Christian is made, through baptism, *alter Christus*, "another Christ," or, better, "the other Christ," fits this perspective: a member of the body is not "other than" the head, not *alius*, but *alter*. It shares the substance that is common to the body and to the head, yet according to its own function and shape. Thus, the divine Person that is manifested in the Church and shares its life is the Person of Christ. This was the teach-

[4]*Summa Theologica,* III, q. 49, a. 1; see above, ch. 5, p. 85 and note 4, ch. 10, p. 183 and note 8.

[5]Henri de Lubac, *Corpus Mysticum: L'eucharistie et l'église au moyen âge* (Paris: Aubier, 1944). This was one of the influential publications that heralded Vatican II.

ing of Pope Pius XII in the encyclical *Mystici corporis*: Christ is one Person who resides in the many persons of his mystical body.

Or thirdly, the *una persona* is the Person of the Holy Spirit acting as "soul" of the Church. This image must not be taken in the Aristotelian sense that sees the human compound as comprised of "form" and "matter," the soul being the form of the body, the body the matter of the soul. What could be acceptable to the philosophy of the Greeks is indefensible in Christian theology. In theology, the Spirit cannot be the form of the Church for in that case the Church, being the Spirit's matter, would be hypostatically united with the Third Person. Soul, here, is therefore not tantamount to form. It designates symbolically the source and origin of life. The life of the Church, and of all the believers who are gathered in it, is given by the Holy Spirit; it is undeserved grace flowing into the faithful from the merits of Christ the Savior by the action of the Spirit who may then be called, as in *Mystici corporis*, "the Uncreated principle" of the unity of the Church. This is the line followed by Heribert Mühlen's ecclesiology: within the mystical body of Christ the Holy Spirit is "one Person in many persons."[6] The first and highest of these persons being the Word incarnate, it is by the salvific mission of the Holy Spirit that Christians are made one Person with Christ. Whatever the eloquence of the formula and the beauty of the perspective that is thus opened, the danger of this line of thought is patent: if the faithful are one Person with Christ and Christ as such is one and not many, then it would seem logical to conclude that the faithful are the Person of Christ. This conclusion had in fact been reached by some theologians of Germany when Pope Pius XII wrote *Mystici corporis*, in part to protect the integrity of Christological doctrine.

Aberrant conceptions of salvation have at times inspired similarly deviant views of the presence and role of the Spirit in the Church. In 1951, André Malraux, himself a profoundly religious person though not a Christian believer in the formal sense of the term, put his finger on a latent yet active characteristic of modern religious sensibility. As he analyzed the "voices of silence" of art, he remarked that unlike their medieval forerunners modern painters seldom depict Christ or specifically religious topics: this is because in modern art it is the artist who is the Christ, and the artistic craft is the saving act. This came out into the open along a more theological line in the controversy about "the death of God" that flared up in the wake of the "Honest to God" debate of 1963. Thomas Altizer put forward the peculiar notion that the divine presence on earth is no longer mediated by Christ; it is from now on directly in the people: the people are the Spirit. After being Father in heaven, and then Son in Jesus Christ, God has now become Spirit in hu-

---

[6] *Una Mystica Persona: Eine Person in vielen Personen* (Paderborn: Ferdinand Schöningh, 1964); here, the "one Person" is the Spirit; in *Mystici corporis* it is the Word.

mankind.[7] In this case, the act of salvation is easily identified with the struggles and sufferings of the people. Thus also, but in a different vein, the mariology of Leonardo Boff introduces a confusion between the created person of the Virgin and the Uncreated Person of the Spirit: though not identical, as would be the case in an incarnation, their two Persons are, according to Boff, ontologically united in inseparable union, the Virgin Mary being thus given a unique metaphysical status in creation: she is, if not Spirit as such, at least Spirit-for-us. This is not unrelated to the characterization of the struggles and sufferings of the people as themselves salvific and liberating.[8]

It is not necessary, however, to opt between these three broad interpretations of the one Person who is in many persons in the Church. It is not even necessary to accept the idea that the Church is in some sense one Person in many persons. This notion is in fact proper material for the use of "Ockham's razor." This is the principle formulated by John Duns Scotus that, in theology, entities (and, by the same token, doctrines) ought not to be multiplied unnecessarily. The doctrine in question is by no means needed to account for the unity of the Church, for the multiplicity of the faithful, and for the oneness of the life of grace that comes from God through Christ and is given by the Spirit.

"One Person in many persons" is itself a symbolic formula in which the word "person" does not apply in the same sense to Christ as the Word Incarnate and to the human persons who believe and are members of his mystical body. The symbol has been useful. For it has emphasized the principle, held since the apostolic period, that the Church as the communion of the believers stands in a very special relation to divine grace and therefore to Uncreated Grace, the Holy Spirit, the Third Person. When Martin Luther insisted that the Church is *creatura verbi*, the creature of the Word, he had in mind both the word of preaching by which the gospel is announced and proclaimed and the Word incarnate without whom there is no word on earth that is from God. Thus the Church is the Word's creature. And it is also the Spirit's beloved. A pneumatological ecclesiology is ultimately grounded in the doctrine of the Trinity. But it is easily misunderstood once the symbolic dimension of theological language is forgotten. For then the traditional formulas are taken in a literal sense that is alien to their fundamental intent.

The Dream of a Church of the Spirit

One should learn a lesson from history. The heart of the Christian faith is focused on the doctrines of the Trinity and of the Incarnation. In practice,

---

[7] *The Gospel of Christian Atheism* (Philadelphia: Westminster, 1966).

[8] Leonardo Boff, *Je Vous Salue Marie: L'Esprit et le féminin* (Paris: Le Cerf, 1980), p. 36, note 4.

however, the believers' human minds do not cease to be at work. Belief in the Trinity of God and in the redemption that was wrought by the Lord Incarnate does not erase the dilemmas of existence. To confess the Lordship of Christ is one thing; to trace all human events to divine guidance is something else. When the faithful are puzzled by circumstances, they are tempted to shift attention from the familiar and distinct focus of faith on the Second Person Incarnate to a less explored and more ambiguous focus on the Third Person. This has happened time and time again.

Out of the persecutions of the second and third centuries, there grew the Montanist movement. Around the year 150, Montanus and his followers, the Cataphrygians (named after the province of Phrygia, the birthplace of the movement) believed that a new age of the Spirit had dawned; he and several prophetesses went around proclaiming the advent of "the new prophecy." Even the great theologian of North Africa, Tertullian (c. 150–230), blamed and even condemned the main Church for failing to recognize the new prophecy and to follow the Spirit.

At the end of the twelfth century, Abbot Joachim of Fiore (c. 1135–1202) started another prophetic movement. He announced the coming of the last age of the world, the imminent end of the time of the Word Incarnate, of the New Testament, and of the clerical Church: they were soon to be replaced by the time of the Spirit, the revelation of "the Eternal Gospel," and the monastic Church. This was to be heralded by the foundation of a new religious order, the order of the end-times, or, so to say, the latter-day saints. This kind of speculation would have remained a dead letter confined within Joachim's writings and within the walls of his monasteries had it not been for the turmoil that followed the spread and the violent destruction of Catharism ("the Church of the Perfect") in southern France: the Cathars believed that they were the latter-day saints. And the new religious order of St. Francis of Assisi (1181/82–1226) was taken by some of its members to be the order of the end-times that had been foretold by Joachim. This identification was upheld by the third successor of St. Francis at the head of the order, John of Parma (d. 1289). And a young theologian, Gerard da Borgo San Donnino (d. 1275), in his *Introduction to the Eternal Gospel*, equated Francis of Assisi with "the angel of the sixth seal" (cf. Rev 3:7–13) and the Franciscans with the Latter-day saints. This became the doctrine of the "Spirituals." It split the Franciscan order. It threatened the centrality of Christ in the Church as the center shifted to the Spirit.[9]

In 1259, St. Bonaventure (1221–1274) succeeded John of Parma as Minister General of the order. He was elected because he did not share the most elitist and divisive orientations of the Spirituals. Yet he followed the general

---

[9]Henri de Lubac, *La Postérité spirituelle de Joachim de Flore*, 2 vols. (Paris: Lethielleux, 1978, 1980); Joseph Ratzinger, *The Theology of History in St. Bonaventure* (Chicago: Franciscan Herald Press, 1971).

lines of Joachim's view of Church history which were never officially condemned, and he also held that a new age of the Spirit was about to dawn.
This was the topic of his last major work, the *Conferences on the Six Days*,
delivered at the university of Paris in 1274. The six days of creation are six
visions or insights into the mystery of the Word Uncreated, Incarnate, and
In-Spirited (present through the Spirit in the Church and in the soul). They
symbolize the ages of the world. The sixth day—when the creative work is
about to be done and the day of rest draws near—serves as a prophetic image
of the sixth age of the world when the highest gifts of the Spirit (understanding
and wisdom) are poured on the faithful. It runs concurrently with the seventh
which is the passage from this world to the next when the saints rise in Christ
and already reign with him. The eighth day will be the final day, eternity.

At the end of the sixth age of the world, the Church will be transformed.
There will be a mutation of the Church from the "active" to the "contemplative" state. St. Francis already has a symbolic function in this regard, for in
him the seraphic order that will lead the Church into contemplation and prepare it for the end-time is already present. After a period of tribulation that
is still to come, there will be a special revelation. This will not add anything
to what has been revealed once for all in Christ. Rather, it will be a fresh insight into the words and deeds of Christ, the "key of David" of Apocalypse
3:7. The Savior is indeed the center of history. But he still has to open the
gate of the future kingdom of God. To whom will this new insight be imparted? Given the option of a selective prophecy entrusted to one person or
of a populist access of all the faithful to all the truth, Bonaventure chose the
latter. The reporter of the *Conferences on the Six Days* wrote: "And he said
that 'there will be given the understanding of Scripture, a revelation, or the
key of David: to a person or to the multitude; and I rather believe to the multitude.'"[10]

The end-time will introduce the Church into the seventh period, beyond
history, the period of the eschatological transformation of all and the gate
of eternity. In spite of this charismatic-eschatological view of the future, however, Bonaventure parts with the Spirituals. He does not identify the Franciscans with the seraphic order of the end-time, of which Francis of Assisi is
the only member. Along with the Dominicans, the Franciscans constitute
the cherubinic order. They function at the level of *speculatio* and look at the
heavenly realities "through a mirror, darkly" (1 Cor 13:12). The ultimate
level of insight is still to come when heaven will be contemplated (*contem-
platio*) through mystical uplifting (*sursumactio*).

The eschatological theology of St. Bonaventure has been mostly forgotten
even in the Franciscan order. To those who know it, it evokes the attraction
that is still exercised on the Western mind by Joachim's apocalyptic visions.

---

[10]*Collationes in Hexaëmeron*, XVI, 29; José de Vinck, tr., *The Works of Bonaventure*, vol. V
(Paterson, NJ: St. Anthony Guild Press, 1970), p. 249.

This attraction is heightened from time to time by what seem to be the cata-strophic conditions of the world.

The Great Fear of the Twentieth Century

When it started in July 1789, the French Revolution inaugurated a new age for humanity. This age has distinct characteristics. In politics, the Revolution rejected the older forms of monarchic and aristocratic government. In the social order, there has taken place a progressive predominance of technological civilization centered on mathematics, over the classical culture inherited from Greece and Rome; public life and government are focused on the administration of finance through banking; natural resources are harvested by methods of macroagriculture and of mass production that have replaced family farming and individual craftsmanship. Individualism has largely taken the place of tribal consciousness and family loyalty.

The modern age is child to the philosophies of the Enlightenment. In the United States, these were responsible for the principle that is embodied in the Declaration of Independence: "All men are created equal." Yet philosophy, manipulated by politicians, was not taken to its logical conclusion. The principle of equality was applied only to the white races. It ran parallel to the continued subservience of women to men, to the enslavement of the black races, and to the genocide of the red men. In the successive regimes of the French Revolution, the equality of all races, the immediate abolition of slavery, the equality of men as "citizens" were duly proclaimed; yet the legal subservience of women continued. There was at the same time a progressive and eventually total rejection of the Church. At first, the Civil Constitution of the Clergy, voted by the Constituent Assembly in 1790, reorganized the French Church on Gallican principles; but it was replaced in 1794 by a deistic cult of "Supreme Being" and "Goddess Reason."

In the settlement that prevailed in Europe after the Great Revolution, the most blatant excesses came to an end. But the anterior situation was not restored. The Catholic Church came out of the revolutionary turmoil weakened by persecution and confused by a latent conflict: those clergy who had rejected the Civil Constitution of the Clergy did not look favorably on those who had taken an oath of allegiance to it. Above all, institutions of theological learning having been destroyed, the Church of the early nineteenth century faced huge problems of reconstruction without adequate theological guidance.

Secularism

The new social and political regimes of continental Europe were in immediate tension with the Christian Church. The medieval Church had condemned usury on the principle that money, being only a means of exchange, does not breed money. But banking and investments have proven that money can be so manipulated that it will bring in more money. The wealthy become wealthier.

The *Decree* of Gratian and the *Decretals* of Gregory IX show to what extremes the medieval Church went in its attempt to moderate the evils of war. It outlawed war on most days of the week. But the "nation under arms" that was created by the French Revolution when the country was threatened with invasion by foreign armies was itself based on the monarchic principle of the *raison d'état*: whereas kings had claimed to exist by divine law (*de divino jure*), the new type of nation was convinced of being entrusted with an essential mission, a "manifest destiny." Being equally jealous of its sovereignty, the nation admits no religious interference with its right to wage war. From the nation under arms, the modern world went on to "total mobilization" (World War I) and hence to "total war" (World War II). The Church, which used to be the guarantor of *jus gentium* or international law, is no longer considered relevant in the councils of nations.

Culturally, the progressive relegation of Greek and Latin to the status of dead languages has displaced the center of education and taken away from theology its former status as "queen of knowledge." Since, in addition, the Church and the State have been either progressively or brutally "separated" in most countries of advanced civilization, priests and ministers have lost their central place in the village, the bishop his place of honor in the city, and theology its dominant place in the university.

The resulting situation is often called "secularism." The secularist society is, as a matter of principle, indifferent to religion and, by the same token, to the religious foundation of ethics. It creates a non-religious environment for the Christian Church as for all organized religions. Yet it is in this environment that the Church must endeavor to teach religious principles to its members. As a result, there necessarily is, if not an opposition, at least a disharmony between society and the Church that lives in it.

Pope John XXIII and the "New Pentecost"

When Pope John XXIII invited the bishops of the Catholic Church to a general council, the first since 1870, he expressed the wish that this council would turn out to be "a new Pentecost." The decision to call a council was prompted, as John XXIII admitted, by a sudden intuition. And since the pope identified *aggiornamento*, updating, as the central task of the council, his intuition must have been related to the feeling that the Church has not yet properly adjusted to the conditions of the modern world and that it would take nothing less than a special prompting of the Spirit for such an adaptation to take place. Vatican Council II attempted to describe the discrepancy between the Church and the modern world in the pastoral constitution on the Church in the Modern World, *Gaudium et spes*.

The text spoke of the "hope and anguish" felt by Christian believers, and indeed by all human persons, in modern times as a new world is striving to be born after the series of major wars that followed the French Revolution (GS, n. 4). It cited the "profound mutation" of the social order (n. 6) that has been largely engineered by technological progress (n. 5), the ensuing "psychological, moral, and religious mutations" (n. 7), and the lack of balance that such developments have brought about in humanity (n. 8). This analysis enabled the council to list among the fundamental "signs of the times" what it saw as the "universal aspirations" of humankind toward more justice (n. 9) and the "deep interrogations" of the human heart concerning the meaning of life (n. 10). The council went on to describe the basic attitude that ought to be adopted by Christians in such a situation. They should renew their total commitment to Christ by faith. Indeed, the Church believes that "the key, the center, and the end of all human history are found in its Lord and Teacher" who is Christ, "the Image of the invisible God, the Firstborn of every creature."

The problem comes, however, when one attempts to determine which concrete types of behavior ought to mark Christian believers in the modern world. The pastoral constitution was in fact drawn up in the optimistic perspective that marked the flowering of the Church in France after the Second World War. Yves Congar wrote of this period: "Anyone who has not lived through the years 1946 and 1947 of French Catholicism has missed one of the finest moments in the life of the Church."[11] In keeping with the mood of those times, *Gaudium et spes*—the only document of Vatican Council II whose first version was composed in French—affirmed a general trust that "the human values that are most esteemed today" are themselves religious since they can be shown, in the light of faith, to have "a divine source" (n. 11). It therefore saw the signs of the times as wonderful occasions for Christianity to display its divine dimension to a grateful humanity.

This optimism, however, was not vindicated by the aftermath of the council. Some of the scientific findings of the post-conciliar decades have shown that the perspective of *Gaudium et spes* was not critical enough. The attention of the media has been directed to the destruction of the environment through technological applications, the pollution of water and air, the risk of poisonous radiation from nuclear plants, the break up and thinning of the ozone layer that protects the earth from the sun, the burning of the last remaining rain forests that control the amount of carbon dioxide in the atmosphere, the dying out of numerous animal species that follows the destruction of their habitat: nothing of this was foreseen at Vatican II. The

---

[11] *Dialogue between Christians: Catholic Contributions to Ecumenism* (Westminster: Newman Press, 1966), p. 32.

bishops and *periti* who authored the text took for granted the broad lines of the optimistic vision of the world presented in the writings of Pierre Teilhard de Chardin, without paying enough attention to Teilhard's warning that the ascent to Point Omega will not take place automatically and may well be impeded by sin. Nonetheless, the optimism of Vatican II and particularly of *Gaudium et spes* was also grounded in the traditional doctrine that relates the Church closely to the Holy Spirit: the Spirit who has guided the Church so far should be trusted to continue in the same salvific line.

The Charismatic Explosion

Whatever Vatican Council II intended to do and did, it did not suffice to restore the sense of the Holy Spirit to the awareness of being the Church. A gap was left between theory and practice that was filled in part by the improperly called "charismatic movement." I say *improperly* because gifts of the Spirit (charisms in the traditional sense of the term) are always at work in the Church at large, even apart from any "movement." The priesthood of all believers, the ministerial and magisterial functions at all levels are themselves charisms of the Spirit. And all the faithful have received manifold natural talents and spiritual gifts that also come from the Spirit.

Be that as it may, what is popularly known as the charismatic movement entered the post-conciliar Catholic Church suddenly and without any apparent cause. It started in 1967 at Duquesne University in Pittsburgh, Pennsylvania, in the course of an entirely traditional retreat whose priest-leader was as startled by the happening as were the few students who began to "speak in tongues." This is hardly the place to discuss the nature and the spiritual authenticity of glossolalia and of other "charismatic" happenings. Yet two remarks need to be made.

On the one hand, the great mystical tradition of Christianity as embodied in the works of St. John of the Cross has always frowned upon external manifestations of the Spirit. For as John of the Cross explained it in *The Ascent of Mount Carmel,* it is "faith" and not feelings, and still less gestures and words, that is the "proper and proportional" means of union with God.[12]

On the other hand, the movement should also be known by its works. The main work that is done spontaneously with no previous planning is that it fills a gap and specifically the gap that is left by the absence of a popular awareness of the Spirit. From this point of view, the emergence of the Pentecostal or charismatic movement in the Catholic Church in the years that followed Vatican II was not an extraneous phenomenon. A new form of the unconscious wish for a vivid experience of Christ and the Spirit has always been

---

[12]*Ascent of Mount Carmel,* part 2, ch. 9; George H. Tavard, *Poetry and Contemplation in St. John of the Cross* (Athens, Ohio: Ohio University Press, 1989), ch. 6.

at work in the phenomena of visions and apparitions. This may have more or less subterranean links with Messianic hopes in a national-religious revival, with utopian expectations of a millennium or of an age of the Spirit, and with a longing to escape the ambiguities of history in a kingdom of God on earth. Through forms, actions, and statements that are often ambiguous, the works of the charismatic movement amount to a long overdue recovery of devotion to the Third Person. In some countries, the movement has inspired a renewal of the monastic and the religious life that is not without promise for the future shape of the monasticity of the Church. New communities have sprung up.[13]

Some of them, as for instance the "Community of the Lion of Juda and the Immolated Lamb" (founded in 1973), have been remarkably creative in their conception and practice of the common life as a life of prayer and contemplation consecrated to God and neighbor, in warm adoration and imitation of Christ, under the personal inspiration of the Holy Spirit, and on the model of the Virgin Mary, "bride of the Spirit." Not only the Catholic Church but the classical Protestant Churches also have been affected by the charismatic wave. This in turn does not go without creating tension, for the Churches of the Reformation have generally remained faithful to the stance of Luther and Calvin. Both Reformers heatedly condemned *die Schwärmer* and *les fanatiques*, whose behavior was often undistinguishable from that of post-Vatican II charismatics while their doctrines clearly departed from the great doctrinal tradition.

The Year 2000

It is often believed that the proximity of the end of the first millenium after Christ gave rise, in the Europe of the time, to widespread fears that the alleged prophecies of the Apocalypse were about to be fulfilled. This has been called "the great fear of the year 1000." Although the tenth century was one of the darkest in the history of the Church and of the papacy, there is in fact no basis for this belief: no trace of such a great fear can be found in the literature of the period. As we come to the year 2000, however, we may well wonder if our predecessors of the year 1000 were not more enlightened than we are. Not only have the last decades of the twentieth century, like those of the nineteenth, begotten a rash of social unrest with violence in the streets, kidnappings, bombs, terrorism. There is also a widespread fear of overpopulation, of famine, of earthquakes and other natural catastrophes, which contributes to an atmosphere of distrust and discouragement. Yet it also gives rise to great hopes for the third millenium. The year 2000 is acting

---

[13]Pascal Pingault, *Renouveau de l'Eglise: Les communautés nouvelles* (Paris: Fayard, 1989). Most of these communities have no formal vows and include both married and single members.

like a magnet, drawing to itself a new utopian vision of the Church and its future.

There is no more eloquent instance of the extent of this fascination with the year 2000 than its inclusion in the vision of the world that is proposed in the writings of Pope John Paul II. Pope John XXIII envisioned a "new Pentecost." It is safe to say that it has not arrived yet. But is it possible to think that it may come with the nearing new millennium? Pope John Paul II has written: "This time, in which God in his hidden design has entrusted to me . . . the universal service connected with the Chair of St. Peter in Rome, is already very close to the year 2000. At this moment it is difficult to say what mark that year will leave on the face of human history. . . . For the Church, the People of God spread, although unevenly, to the most distant limits of the earth, it will be the year of a Great Jubilee. We are already approaching that date which . . . will recall and reawaken in us in a special way our awareness of [the incarnation and the redemption]. . . . We are in a certain way in a season of a new Advent, a season of expectation. . . ." (Encyclical *Redemptor hominis*, 4 March 1979, n. 1).

In a more subdued mode, as the pope refers to God the Father who is "rich in mercy," he remarks that in the Second Vatican Council "we can rightly see a new phase in the self-realization of the Church, in keeping with the epoch in which it has been our destiny to live. . . ." (Encyclical *Dives in misericordia*, 30 Nov. 1980, n. 15).

It is, however, in the encyclical on the Holy Spirit, *Dominum et vivificantem*, that the fascination of the year 2000 reaches its acme. This encyclical was issued on the feast of Pentecost, 18 May 1986. As Pope John Paul II brought the attention of the Catholic faithful to the Holy Spirit, he indulged in a deep and bold theological speculation on the Third Person. Uniting the individual and the collective perspectives, he unfolded many scriptural statements and allusions in a meditative reading that enhances the permanent presence and action of the Spirit in the Church. The humanity of Jesus was shown as being itself imbued with the Spirit. The Scriptures were interpreted symbolically as keys to life in the Spirit. It is in the Spirit that "the salvific self-giving of God" (*DVif*, n. 11) takes place. The Spirit is given to, and experienced by, the whole communion and each of the faithful. "The Church feels herself called to the mission of proclaiming the Spirit; while together with the human family she approaches *the end of the second Millennium after Christ*, . . . as she prepares to celebrate . . . the great Jubilee which will mark the passage from the second to the third Christian Millennium" (n. 2).

This is a recurrent theme of the pope's meditation: "We await the end of the second Christian Millennium" (n. 62); we are "in this phase of transition from the second to the third Christian Millennium" (n. 64); we live "in the prospect of the transition from the second to the third Christian Millennium" (n. 67). Furthermore, the year 2000 carries special theological import: "*The Church's mind and heart turn to the Holy Spirit as this twentieth century draws to a close and the third millennium* since the coming of Jesus Christ into the world *approaches. . . ."* (n. 49). "The *Great Jubilee* at the close of the second Millennium, for which the Church is already preparing, has a directly *Christological aspect:* for it is a celebration of the birth of Jesus Christ. At the same time it has a *pneumatological aspect* since the mystery of the Incarnation was accomplished 'by the power of the Holy Spirit'" (n. 50). In order to understand the full meaning of the Great Jubilee that is imminent, one must "go beyond the historical dimension of the event considered at its surface value. Through the Christological content of the event we have to reach the pneumatological dimension, seeing with the eyes of faith the *two thousand years of the action of the Spirit of truth. . . . We need to go further back*, to embrace the whole of the action of the Holy Spirit even before Christ—*from the beginning,* throughout the world, and especially in the economy of the Old Covenant" (n. 53).

The perspective of a new effusion of the Spirit is thus kept before the eyes of the faithful. Where Pope John had looked to the council, John Paul II looks to the end of this century: "In the time leading to the third millennium after Christ, while 'the Spirit and the bride say to the Lord Jesus, Come,' this prayer of theirs is filled, as always, with an eschatological significance, which is also destined to give fullness of meaning to the celebration of the great Jubilee. . . . *this prayer is directed toward a precise moment of history* which highlights the 'fullness of time' marked by the year 2000. The Church wishes *to prepare* for this Jubilee *in the Holy Spirit*, just as the Virgin of Nazareth in whom the Word made flesh was prepared by the Holy Spirit" (n. 66).

As one might expect, the theme recurs in the encyclical on the Virgin Mary, *Redemptoris Mater*, of 25 March 1987 (feast of the annunciation). Prompted by *"the perspective of the year 2000,* now closing in on us" (RM, n. 3), this document announced a marian year—from Pentecost 1987 to 15 August 1988—that would celebrate the birth of the Virgin "in the period preceding the conclusion of the second millennium after the birth of Christ" (n. 48). From 1987 to 2000 there are of course thirteen years, the approximate age of puberty among Palestinian girls at the time of Jesus.

One may interpret these texts mildly. It is part of the awareness of being the Church to entrust oneself to the Spirit and to count on the spiritual gifts of unity and truth. The daily sessions of Vatican II began with a prayer to the Spirit that included the words: "Unite us to Thyself effectively through the gift of Thy grace alone, that we may be one in Thee and never deviate from the truth." The believers' concrete expectations may well reflect the culture of their time and place. That of Karol Wojtyla, poet, playwright, and bishop, was marked, as is the case with all Polish intellectuals of our times, by the national and religious Messianism of Adam Mickiewicz[14] (1792–1855),

---

[14]Mickiewicz was himself influenced by the ideas of Joachim of Flora: Henri de Lubac, l.c., vol. 2, p. 235-259.

the intellectual mentor of modern Poland. This vision draws new life from the events of the Second World War and from the experience of life under an oppressive political system. Such a Messianism must be carefully controlled by its Christological references. Yet as with all utopias, one may fear future disappointment. All similar expectations and prophecies in the past have come to naught. I perceive no sign that the passing of the year 2000 will be any different from that of the year 1000.

Perspective

The world in which we now live, in the last decade of the twentieth century, is a hotbed of new sects and cults. Some have grown out of old Christian soil. The "Gospel given at Arès" is claimed by an apostate Orthodox priest to be a new gospel, superior to the old ones. The "Christ of Mont-Favet" was believed by his followers to be the authentic Christ. Some movements have developed in Asia. The "Holy Spirit's Association for the Unification of World Christianity," popularly known as "the Moonies," was born in Korea. Itshiren Shoshu has been imported to the West from Japan. Others like the Transcendental Meditation of the Maharishi ("TM") and the Krishna Consciousness have, with considerable simplifications, adapted Hindu insights to the inadequacies of the Western mind, in what is taken by Hindu mythology to be the decadent end of an eon. Others still claim to have restored a pre-Christian religion of Europe, as in Wikka, or even some ancient religions of the Middle East, as in the feminist "Cult of the Goddess." In addition, "New Age" expects the advent of a more advanced religious period of humanity in which ecology, astrology, magic, and individual mysticism will share the limelight. Even the drug subculture of certain sections of society testifies to a deep desire for newness of vision.

Some of these movements have attracted favorable attention from a number of devoted Christians. "Creation spirituality," coping with questions raised by the ecological dilemma of technological society, hopes to use the forces of cosmic nature for spiritual advance. In a different vein, "Liberation theology" stakes its hopes on a total renovation of the social order that should include spiritual renewal. Such endeavors share many features with utopias that were pursued in the past. But a utopia being, by definition, a "nowhere land," it should not be read as a program for action. It is a symbol of the desire to know and to love that is at the heart of humanity. As is illustrated by the fall of Marxism as a political system, utopias are not good instruments of economic and social development.

Like the expectation of the kingdom of God in history, the prophecy of a new Pentecost is a utopia. It evokes an intrinsic though often concealed dimension of the Church of Christ: a deep desire for the gifts of the Spirit lives in the heart of the community as it lies at the heart of the faith. Indeed, the Church always looks forward to the Holy Spirit's generous outpouring. But it never presumes to know "the times and the moments" (Acts 1:7) that are still hidden in the Wisdom of God.

For Further Reading

Jacques Maritain. *On the Church of Christ: The Person of the Church and Her Personnel.* Notre Dame: University of Notre Dame Press, 1973.

Cardinal Léon Suenens. *A New Pentecost?* New York: Seabury Press, 1975.

Kilian McDonnel. *Charismatic Renewal and the Churches.* New York: Seabury Press, 1976.

George Williams. *The Mind of John Paul II: Origins of his Thought and Action.* New York: Seabury Press, 1981.

Yves Congar. *I Believe in The Holy Spirit,* 3 vols. New York: Seabury Press, 1983.

Anthony Kelly. *The Trinity of Love: A Theology of the Christian God.* Wilmington: Michael Glazier, 1989.

14

Tomorrow's Church

The purpose of this concluding chapter is to give an overview of what has been seen so far regarding the Church, community of salvation, and to suggest some lines of thought and action for the future.

The community of salvation originated in the saving acts of God in Jesus Christ, the Word incarnate. The shape and scope of this community were, at the beginning, held together in a *vision* that was shared by the apostles and the other believers who became the first generation of the disciples of Jesus. This vision was inspired by the belief that Jesus Christ, who died on the Cross and rose from the dead by the power of God, is, by God's loving will, the only mediator between the Creator and the creatures. It was focused in hope on the unique relationship that linked Jesus with the One whom he called *Abba*, "Father" (Mark 13:36), and whom he revealed to his disciples as also their Father, "the one in heaven" (Matt 6:9). The Father of the Lord Jesus was no other than the Creator of the universe, the Source of Christ's own being and mission, the "Father of the lights" from whom "every good gift and every perfect gift descend" (Jas 1:17). This central vision was nurtured by and in the divine grace that is bestowed on the faithful in the Holy Spirit. In all subsequent periods of history, the experience of being the Church has therefore been inseparable from the two poles of the Christian faith—belief in the oneness of the Three divine Persons and belief in the incarnation of the Second Person, the Word of God, who "was made flesh" (John 1:14) for the salvation of the world.

As the years passed, this fundamental ground of the Church gave rise to a *tradition* that has continued into our own times. This is the continuous faithful transmission of the faith, through the Scriptures of the Old Covenant, where the great acts of God before the coming of the Christ are recorded, and through the writings of the New Covenant, in which eye-witnesses narrated their experience of the Word made flesh and of the preaching of the gospel under the guidance of the Holy Spirit. This double tradition has acted in a complementary way. As the second leg of it completed and interpreted the first, it also gained the status of sacred Scripture. Together, they have inspired images and symbols in thought, speech, and art that have been received and interpreted by successive generations of Christians whose lives have been nourished by them. This interpretation has peaked from time to time in the councils of the Church. It has found confirmation and its most influential models in the monastic experience.

In turn, the main *structures* of the Church and its life were born of the tradition. The task of serving the gospel took shape in a twofold ministry, the general ministry of all the baptized faithful, and the specific ministry of those who were ordained for leading Eucharistic worship (priests). The chief responsibility for teaching the gospel and promoting the people's fidelity was entrusted to a magisterium of ordained persons (bishops). Under their leadership, the whole people of God has symbolically offered the universe to God in doxological homage.

Finally, the actual horizon of the Church in the modern world highlights the heart of its life, throbbing in the ebb and flow of a multifold *dialogue*. The Christian community is a communion of human persons whom the Spirit brings into dialogue with God through Christ, who are involved among themselves in a constant dialogue of love, and who feel the tensions of a twofold ongoing dialogue with the secular dimensions of human society and with the spiritual dimensions of the other great religions of humankind.

Grace and Sin

Now this overview points to a contrast that is inherent in the experience of being the Church. This experience is lived at two levels. At the level of faith, the Church is all that has been said in the previous chapters. It is even more, since, as the repository of God's love for the creatures, the Christian Church has the promise of innumerable graces to come. But each one of the faithful lives and prays in a local community that is imperfect. Its members remain self-centered and commonly place their own interests before those of their neighbor. They are, and they often enjoy being, more knowledgeable about their own race and culture than about other clans, tribes, or nations. They are more concerned about their kith and kin than about strangers. Yet they also are aware of their shortcomings and their sinfulness. This local community daily confesses its sins and begs for divine forgiveness and grace.

At the level of the grace of God, the community is the recipient of God's gifts. It lives by the faith it has received; it looks forward in hope; and in the present, it bears the fruits of faith in love. Yet in its daily living, the community suffers from the sinfulness of its members. It is an imperfect embodiment of true Christian communion, service, and worship (*koinonia, diaconia, liturgeia*). Its life and witness ought to be a convincing argument for the Gospel of Jesus Christ. Indeed, the objective or positive apologetic that was in favor in the eighteenth and nineteenth centuries gave pride of place to the self-evidence of the marks of the Church, to the "moral miracle" of its survival through persecutions, and to what was taken to be the demonstrable superiority of its moral and spiritual teaching over those of all other prophets and teachers. However, this sort of apologetics failed in its purpose. For when it listed the very existence of the Church among the "miracles" that prove the truth of the gospel, it was banking on a certain idea of the Church, not on what was visible of the Church as it is. It argued from the Church in hope rather than from the Church in reality. But in a scientific and technological civilization like ours, theory needs to be confronted with reality, the Church in hope with the Church in fact.

Such a comparison, however, brings out an unexpected contrast between claims and achievements. In spite of the heroism of its missionaries through the centuries, the Christian community has failed to persuade most of the Jews that Jesus is indeed the Messiah who was foreseen under the Mosaic Covenant. It has also failed to persuade the majority of humankind that Jesus and his revelation of the Father are indeed the God-given fulfillment of the religious aspirations of humanity. In addition, agnosticism, unbelief, and indifference to the Church's witness and teaching have spread far and wide in areas and countries that were formerly identified with Christendom. The social and political traditions of old Christian lands have given way to humanistic liberal conventions that owe more to the philosophy of the Enlightenment than to the gospel. Scientific research, the political organization of nations, the production, distribution, and consummation of wealth, and even the practice of medicine and of the health professions are premised on the principle that humanity has "come of age." Having reached adulthood, it now considers that the "hypothesis of God" is superfluous in the organization of the public domain.

Being then pushed aside to the periphery of public attention, the Christian faith takes refuge in the purely interior realm of individual consciences where it is legally protected by freedom of thought and the right to privacy. As to the Church, it is protected, or merely tolerated, under the freedom of association and the freedom of speech that are identified as basic human liberties and are therefore, in most places, constitutionally guaranteed. Nonetheless, there remains a dwindling number of small regions where the mentality of past Christendom may still be experienced and where spontaneous social pressure functions in favor of the Church. But these are only enclaves of religiosity in a non-believing world. They cannot bear the burden that used to be borne by the whole Church. Rather than the spearhead of a new Christendom, they are commonly seen as relics or museums of a past that cannot be revived. This is all the more striking as the demographic balance of the world shows that Christians are multiplying naturally, through the birth process and the education of children in the faith of their ancestors, at a lower rate than other great religions of humankind such as Islam, Hinduism, and Buddhism. In spite of the spread of Christianity in Latin America and in many parts of Africa and Asia, the population explosion is making the Christian Church into a proportionally dwindling minority, even as it expands numerically.

The reasons for this triple failure cannot be examined at this point. The factors that favored Christian expansion in the Roman empire, among the Celtic and the Germanic tribes of Europe, and later among the Slavs, were themselves quite complex. So were the mixed causes and motivations at work in the pre-colonial and colonial periods of the Christian missions. But one should note that the preaching of the gospel has had little impact in areas of advanced civilization and developed religions such as the Islamic world, India, or China, in contrast with its greater success among the Animist religions and in the highly structured but fragmented tribes of Africa, Asia, and the Americas. The Church's problem is not how to remedy the shortcomings of the past; it is how to remain or to become the community of salvation for the people of today and of tomorrow. Now, when one tries to assess the chances of the Church and its members in the present world horizon and the promise of the future, one is faced with two fundamentally different interpretations of the contrast between the Church in hope and the Church in fact.

An End or a Beginning

In what was written in the aftermath of Vatican Council II, the idea was frequently expressed that the Church had reached the end of an era: the end of Christendom or of the Counter-Reformation or of sociological Catholicism. But another idea was also broached: the council marked a beginning, a new start, a new Pentecost. The two notions, of course, need not be contradictory. Only when something is ending can something else take its place. But there is a striking contrast between the Church's yesterday and its present day: what is beginning does not belong to the same category as what has ended.

What has ended is the practical identification of the Christian Church with recognizable temporal structures and a recognizable public way of life, those of Europe or of Christian countries or of Christian society. What has begun, however, is not a new identification with temporal structures and ways of life. It is a return to the situation of the Church in its first centuries when it lived in a diaspora situation, small clusters of believers in a sea of paganism. Yet this cannot now be a true diaspora. A diaspora presupposes a basic relation to a stable homeland or center. But unlike the Judaism of old and unlike the early Church as long as it could relate to Jerusalem as to its source and Mother-Church, the modern Christian community cannot appeal to a geographic or spiritual home base. Rome itself is not such a base since according to the Catholic tradition the Church in Rome is *mater et magistra* only of the Churches of Western Europe and of those that have been established by their missionaries. Even when they acknowledge the primacy of "the first Rome" and of its bishop, Oriental Christians do not confuse the Latin with the universal Church. They owe their knowledge and preservation of the gospel not to Rome and its guidance but to the Greek Fathers and to fidelity to the Holy Spirit in their midst. By the same token, the confessional primacies that may be identified with Constantinople and Canterbury cannot anchor a Christian diaspora. And in any case, the continued existence of all primatial sees is itself contingent on certain temporal conditions that a mere earthquake or a nuclear accident could end forever.

The choice, then, lies between assuming that the Church is shrinking because the world is nearing its end, and the opposite assumption: the diaspora situation of the Church signals the edge of a new expansion. The first option has little need of illustration. It is rampant in the fundamentalist sections of Protestantism where the end of the world is expected for the near future. In the Catholic Church, it takes a different form. It is not infrequent in devotional writing. Priests bemoan the lack of vocations to the priesthood and try to assure one another of the genuineness of their own calling. Many spiritual authors look back with nostalgia on the ages of faith, and they try to renovate the Christian life by advocating modes and methods of mental prayer that are often borrowed from other religions. As they do so, however, they flirt with apocalyptic, unearthly spiritualities that have little in common with the traditional Christian focus on the Word and the sacraments. We now live, as Paul Tillich wrote of himself, in a "boundary situation,"[1] in an uncertainty between two worlds, between sin and justice, between destruction and renewal, between apostasy and fidelity. The only ways open are the inner ways of the Spirit who can, as a familiar prayer goes, "renew the face of the earth." This of course entails an invitation to Christian hope. But hope is unable by itself to read the mind of God and to foresee the shape of things to come.

In terms of theology and anthropology, the thought of Pierre Teilhard de Chardin may illustrate the second option. Only recently have the sciences begun to understand the interior structure of matter, the shape of the cosmos, and the history of time. In the vision of the universe that is emerging from modern research, it is likely that humanity is much nearer to its starting point

---

[1]Paul Tillich, *The Religious Situation* (New York: Henry Holt and Company, 1932); *On the Boundary* (New York: Scribners, 1966); *My Search for Absolutes* (New York: Simon and Schuster, 1969); George H. Tavard, *Paul Tillich and the Christian Message* (New York: Scribners, 1962).

in the past than to its end in the future. Teilhard saw this in terms of a pro-gressive, open-ended humanization and spiritualization which he projected into the eschatological future of Christian hope. This would be ultimately crowned by a cosmic encounter with the Christ of faith who is not only the means and the goal of the spiritual ascent of each human but also the "Point Omega" of the evolution of the universe according to God's ultimate design.[2] Were Teilhard alive today, he would refine his model. For it is now more obvious that humanity is reaching a point of no return beyond which it needs to function differently from what it took for granted in the past. There are astonishing changes in nature due in part to the unregulated exploitation of natural resources. Moreover, humanity holds in its hands the capability of destroying the human habitat and that of all other species through poison-ing of the natural environment; and it has the possibility of destroying life altogether through nuclear explosions. These are signs that fresh principles of human organization and behavior are absolutely required for survival. Humanity has to choose to live or not to live, to ensure the conditions of continuing life or to stifle them. The refusal to choose would itself be a choice for death, for it would doom our descendants to extinction within the span of a few generations.

In these conditions, the Christian hope is inseparably tied to the expecta-tion of a new lease on life for humankind. If the human world is nearing its end, so is the Church. If the universe remains inhabitable for humankind, the Church has an indefinite future ahead of itself, possibly for many mil-lennia.

If the World be doomed . . .

In the first case, the Christian Church can hardly continue to live on as though history had an indefinite course in front of itself. The end of the world, at least of the human world, is near. But what should be the duties of the Church as signs of the end of the world multiply?

We are of course not used to thinking in such terms. The very idea is strange. Yet the answer is easy to give, if harder to apply. As the Church nears the end of the world, Christian preaching and catechesis should aim at pre-paring the people for the end. It should give priority to the doctrines of eschatology, to the notion that life on this earth is not the supreme good, that it is radically evanescent, that it should be lived and organized, not for its own sake or for the glorification of temporality, but as a preparation for death in readiness for resurrection and eternal life in God. Since neither resur-

[2]Pierre Teilhard de Chardin, *The Phenomenon of Man,* New York: Harper and Row, 1959; *The Future of Man,* New York: Harper and Row, 1959; *Science and Christ,* New York: Harper and Row, 1968. See Francisco Bravo, *Christ in the Thought of Teilhard de Chardin,* Notre Dame: University of Notre Dame Press, 1967.

rection nor eternal life can be described, the preparation must be for the radically unknown, for looking forward to a total change in our mode of being and knowing. As the saved humanity enters the heavenly kingdom of God, it shall pass from vesperal knowledge to matutinal knowledge. These Scholastic expressions designate two ways of knowing reality. In the present world we are like Adam and Eve on the evening of each day of creation, as in the biblical myth (Gen 1). We know the creatures first and God second, from what the creatures reflect of the Creator. In the heavenly kingdom, one knows God first and the creatures second, as they stand in God's design and power and chiefly as they are subsumed in the attributes of God.

In the last decades before the end of the world, the Church will have to act and speak against the human and natural despair that is then likely to invade the secular mind. It will have to be persuasive in insisting that death is better than birth, that the beyond is more wonderful than the here and now. And since greater spiritual detachment from temporal and spatial conditions can only be gradually obtained and is best urged by those who practice it, the Church will have to set the example. It will have to give lesser importance to its temporal and spatial structures, to stress the indwelling of the Holy Spirit and the sovereignty of the Word, to teach meditation and the mystical way, to abandon all the trappings of human honor and glory that have accompanied the exercise of the ordained ministry.

At the same time, the Church will have to recover or reemphasize the theology of the Second Advent, the return of Christ. This theology was common in the early years of the Church when the world was already believed to be old and overcrowded and Christ was expected to come back soon. In a different form, it was familiar to several periods of the Middle Ages when sculptors represented the Last Judgment at the central porch of gothic churches and when, in keeping with the theology of history of St. Augustine, it was believed that the sixth and seventh ages of the world, running concurrently, were nearing their end to be followed by the eighth day of eternity in a new heaven and a new earth.

Such speculations on the end-time, however, cannot be convincingly taken over from the past unless they are also reshaped and reinterpreted. One cannot be content with the stand of some of the Protestant fundamentalists who speak of the return of Christ as though Jesus could suddenly appear anywhere on earth in his earthly body or maybe on the clouds of heaven with the spiritual body of his resurrection. Were this the case, there is a great likelihood, as was foreseen by Dostoevsky in the legend of the Great Inquisitor,[3] that Christ would not be acknowledged, even in the Church. After all, nothing in the Scriptures or the traditions explains how to recognize him. When Christ returns, it can only be not in the flesh but in the Holy Spirit. This has been implicitly affirmed in the traditional rejection of all forms of

[3]In his novel, *The Brothers Karamazov.*

millennialism: Christ will not reign on this earth in a temporal kingdom. By the same token, he will not return in order to substitute his Kingdom for the nations of this world. Christian eschatology must be given a more refined shape and orientation than that. What this shape should be, however, may be difficult to imagine before the need arises. But searching for possibilities should provide the main item on the theological agenda as soon as it becomes clear that humankind is unwilling or unable to stem the deterioration of our planet.

How many decades has the Christian Church before it can reasonably decide whether to prepare for an imminent end or for an ongoing future of many centuries? If the environment continues to decay at the speed it has decayed in the first hundred and fifty years of its modern exploitation, there will not be much time. By the year 2050 or before, our successors should know what to expect.

If the Spiral goes up

The spiral is one of the overall images that Teilhard de Chardin employed to suggest the ongoing march of creation. A spiral shows at the same time advance and convergence, the advance of the universe toward the new, and the convergence of all its energies in pursuance of the new. The plan that Teilhard proposed was simple. After slowly giving birth to life (formation of the biosphere) and then to humanity (formation of the noosphere), the universe is itself being transformed by the evolution of humanity under the impact of Christ (formation of the Christosphere). Each age follows a curve: a long process of warming up leads to a saturation or boiling point. At this point, a mutation takes place in the structure of the universe.

This model, borrowed from the past, is then projected into the future. A slow perfecting of the Christosphere must take place through the action of the Holy Spirit in what can well be many millennia. It must eventually reach a saturation point. Then, the balance of matter and of spirit in the structure of the universe will be reversed: spirit will take the lead. This moment will be marked by the emergence of "ultra-humanity." Until this point, spirit (the *nous* or spiritual element in humanity) has been supported by matter. From this point on, matter is subsumed under spirit. The point itself is not a point in the strict sense. It is likely to be a long period without definite edges as were the passages from matter to life and from life to spirit, recognizable only after the fact. Like the universe itself, yet long before, the human world must eventually come to an end. The material conditions of this end have been inscribed in its physical make up even since it began. But if one holds to the Christian hope that is intrinsic to Teilhard's projections, the conclusion follows that when the end comes, it will be at the point where "ultra-humanity" will in turn reach spiritual maturity. Then the prospect of the end will not be one of inescapable doom and gloom as it presumably would be today for most of humankind. It will be a time of free and joyful self-abandonment, of gratitude for all divine gifts, and of love for God, knotted together in a "paroxysmal state" of "super-consciousness."[4]

In this perspective, the future of the Christian community is viewed as humanly bright. One may of course criticize the details of Teilhard's outline. Science has evolved since it was conceived. Paleontology, Teilhard's own field of expertise, and astronomy have made remarkable progress. The knowledge of both the infinitely small and the infinitely great, of the structure of matter and of the shape of the universe has evolved considerably. But it is not the details of Teilhard's argumentation that matter; it is the overall orientation.

If humanity has many millennia before it, then so has the Church. But a mutation of humanity should be matched by a mutation of the Church. Whatever its make up, an ultra-humanity can be at home in nothing less than an Ultra-Church. In the meanwhile, a Church that is confident of such a long life can surely not be satisfied with its present form and shape at the end of the second millennium.

The In-Between Time

As it prepares for the future, the Church of Christ will be called to resituate itself in relation to humanity and to the universe. A global reshaping may be required and a reformulation of its identity, not in relation to God and to Jesus Christ, but in relation to creation. For the prospect of the end belongs in the first place to the doctrine of creation. An eschatology is implied in the way one understands the relation of this world to its Maker. Until our present age, the Church has been worried by the immediate pastoral problems and difficulties that have arisen from the conditions of each passing period of humanity. It has commonly put its energies at the service of momentary needs that were soon displaced by others. It has exalted the value of magisterial decisions that were made obsolete, sooner or later, by the evolving conditions of civilization.

This recurring focus on the immediate has been the occasion for wonderful deeds and for lives consecrated to God and neighbor. The saints have often been women and men who discerned the "signs of the times," perceived in them a call from God, and responded generously, devoting their being and life to assuaging the needs of the people and the community, far or near. The Church has believed divine Providence to be at work in the circumstances of human history. But this belief does not erase the radical ambiguity of the human condition. The focus on the immediate that has deter-

[4]Teilhard, *The Future of Man*, p. 298-308.

mined pastoral goals and regulated pastoral prudence has always tended to cause nearsightedness among the Church's members and leaders. And this in turn has been the cause or the occasion for a process of decadence. The Church has lived through cycles of growth, decay, and reformation, all three of which have affected its spiritual as well as its material dimensions.

This is well illustrated by the curve of Counter-Reformation ecclesiology. Beginning toward the middle of the sixteenth century, the Catholic Church and its members adopted a defensive position before the spread of the Reformation. This was embodied in the doctrinal and reformatory decrees of the council of Trent (meeting intermittently from December 1545 to December 1563). The council, acting as a starting point, inspired a new departure. But this new departure, often called the Catholic Reformation, was affected by the negative reaction to Protestantism called the Counter-Reformation. The defensive stance became aggressive. Often in the course of the next four centuries, the Catholic Church behaved as though it lived in combat conditions.

With the French Revolution and its active persecution of the Church, the aggressive disposition retrenched into a siege mentality, for the popes of the nineteenth century could not be reconciled with the principles and the consequences of the Revolution. Pius VI (1775-1799) had been a prisoner of Bonaparte who led the revolutionary armies into the Papal States. Pius VII (1800-1823) had been forced by Napoleon into a compromise. But Pius IX condemned most features of the modern world, and he called Vatican I largely as a means to condemn modern philosophy and the politics of nationalism. Leo XIII declared invalid the ordinations made in the Church of England, thus condemning the inroads of political power into the spiritual domain of the Church. Pius X, in rejecting Modernism, delayed the impact of modern philosophy on theology and of methods of historical and literary criticism on the study of Scripture. Benedict XV and Pius XI judged that the ecumenical movement, active and growing in other Christian Churches since 1910, could not be trusted and encouraged. In *Humani generis* (1950), Pius XII condemned several scientific hypotheses and their impact on theology. The fortress mentality that had grown from the Counter-Reformation kept on hardening its features. The Catholic Church behaved as though the horizon of conflict were bound to be universal and permanent.

The history of the Church since the sixteenth century clearly points to the basic reform that is needed to face the future. The Church has to overcome the temptation to eternalize the conditions of the present moment. It needs to search for new solutions, not to return to old solutions. The final promise of Christ to the small band of his disciples, "I will be with you all the days until the consummation of the world" (Matt 28:20), must be read in a heuristic perspective and even with a sense of serendipity. This will mean not that Christ and the Spirit will always preserve the Church in its present form and structures but that, as new ages open for humanity, the Church will be able to find the appropriate forms and structures for these ages. Yet this requires that the Church's members be open to such new forms and openly search for them with faith and trust.

One should not exaggerate the problem. As the siege mentality developed in the Church, there were also signs of openness to the future. The same popes who suffered from the French Revolution and its impact accepted some aspects of modernity. In their social encyclicals, Leo XIII and Pius XI foresaw the problems that would arise from both capitalism and communism. And not all Catholics were displeased that the popes lost their temporal sovereignty over the Papal States and that Churches and clergy were progressively deprived of their ancient privileged status in society.

Forward to Tradition

In the hypothesis of an indefinite future ahead of humankind, the Church's fundamental outlook on itself stands in need of reform. It is, to be sure, neither the Gospel and its doctrinal explanation nor the essential ecclesial structure that I have in mind in this statement. It is the basic perspective from which the gospel is lived and preached, doctrines formulated and taught, the ecclesial structure organized and made effective. Until the end of the twentieth century, the tradition has acted and has been heard mainly as a voice from the past. The year 2000—if we may choose that year for its symbolic value as the start of the third millennium in the Christian calendar— should elicit the other role of tradition: it is not only a voice from the past, a record of events, and a memory of things acted out; it also is a call from the future, an anticipation of the fulfillment of the promises of God, a participation in the times that lie ahead and, ultimately, in the eschaton.

I am not proposing that the Church discard its past—an impossible task anyway—but that it develop a dimension that has always been inherent, but partially dormant, in the tradition. As was pointed out earlier in this volume, the tradition is the Church's memory.[5] But in normal circumstances, memory exists and functions not for the sake of the past that is remembered but for the sake of the present and the future. Neither tradition nor memory, despite popular notions about them, are intended to inspire nostalgic looks at touching moments of youth once the youth is gone. They are meant to equip for the future out of the strength that was experienced in the past, to thrust ahead out of the trust that has accumulated from the gifts already received, to look forward to the new because it should be, in anticipation, cherished at least as much as the best of the remembered moments of the past.

[5]See above, chapter 9.

When it is approached from this point of view, the tradition of the Church does not look primarily like a deposit that has been transmitted from the beginning and has grown in the process of its transmission or, in a more dynamic understanding, like the mode and method of its transmission. It is a current experience of symbolic or imaginative reconstruction. The deposit of faith is present as we reconstruct the Christian origins and the Christian past. Such a reconstruction belongs to the awareness of being the Church. Yet the heart of the tradition is neither the past nor its reconstruction in the present. Seen as past, the tradition is dead and gone. Felt as present, it is ambiguous and hesitant, caught as it is between the old and the new, compared as it must be with the signs of the times and the exigencies of the situation. Only as anticipated future does tradition display its full scope. For then it takes shape not only as a reconstruction of the past but also as a preconstruction and precomprehension of what is to come.[6]

Tradition as Reception

One of the theological questions of the moment, closely tied to an ecclesiology of communion, regards the nature and function of reception in the ongoing tradition of the community. This question is often approached narrowly, as though it concerned only the way in which the laity of the Church receives, accepts, and applies the decisions made by the hierarchy. But this is only one aspect of the question. Reception is actually the key to many things in the Christian life. Just as there would be no creation unless there were creatures, so there would be no grace unless it was received from God, no covenant unless a promise was received from the initiator of the covenant, no gospel unless the hearers of the word of God received it, no baptism unless an actual person welcomed it in faith, no sacrament unless the "element" and the "word" proclaimed over it were enlivened and activated for the believers by the Holy Spirit.

In the traditioning process, it is possible to place the accent on the giver or on the receiver. Since the ultimate Giver is God whose gift is transmitted through Christ and is received in the Holy Spirit, there is an essential primacy of the gift. But apart from inward gifts of grace and call that come directly from God, the Giver always proceeds through created and chiefly human instruments and channels. There ensues a spiritual relationship between the instrumental or sacramental agent and the receiver. The agent stands in a special relation to God who acts through the divine Word that is channeled through human agents. The receiver stands in a special relation to the Holy Spirit who enables and ensures the proper reception of God's gifts.

---

[6] I have explored this point of view in the conclusion of *La Tradition au XVIIe siècle en France et en Angleterre,* Paris: Le Cerf, 1969, p. 493–512.

This work of the Spirit flows from what the Spirit is in God, the One who eternally receives the divine Word in reciprocated love.[7]

It follows that the process of reception is not purely passive. The receiver is not a mere patient. On the one hand, one cannot be actuated by the Holy Spirit without participating in the freedom of the Spirit: free gifts are freely received. The Church, in which the giving takes place and the tradition is implemented, should therefore be reorganized as the realm of spiritual freedom where law has given way to gospel, compulsion to suggestion, domination to respect, where authority does not proceed by power but by persuasion, where it is not formulation and definition by those in authority that occupy the center of the stage, but reception, welcome, and thanksgiving by the whole believing people.

On the other hand, the process of tradition is never done once for all. It continues. What has been received must eventually be passed on. But there can be neither a proper handing on of memory unless its contents have been experienced as memorable nor a proper education of hope unless the promises have been experienced as trustworthy and received as worthy of hope. Here again, reception is the key to handing on what has been received. Such a reception is turned not to the past but to the future. Memory remembers the past and transmits it because it also remembers the future and the expected transformation and recapitulation of all things in Christ. The Church is the horizon in which the believers focus their lives on this expectation.

Tradition as Consensus

There naturally is an intrinsic purpose at work in the reception of divine grace, of the gospel as the good news of salvation, of the Church's teaching concerning the great acts of God in Jesus Christ and concerning the doctrines of the Trinity and of the incarnation. This purpose is the upbuilding of the community of believers in unanimity of heart and mind. As the community of salvation lives on through the many centuries that will precede the end-times, its main need as a community will be to reach and preserve consensus. In the first two millennia, this consensus was generally obtained by way of authority and obedience. It was accepted that the clergy or the bishops or the pope speak with authority and are to be obeyed and followed. This authoritative structure of the Church emerged in its main lines during the first centuries of Christianity. From time to time, it was modified or added to in view of a new cultural and political context, as happened in the Middle Ages regarding the relative authority of the emperor and the pope or in the nineteenth century in the matter of papal primacy and infallibility. Even the

[7]See the last chapter of my book, *The Vision of the Trinity*, Washington: University Press of America, 1981, p. 119-140.

Protestant Churches did not alter the pattern radically. They only introduced various checks and balances by which the exercise of authority by
ordained ministers has to find its way through committees and parliamentary
processes borrowed from democratic systems of government.

Yet it is difficult to imagine that this structure has now reached its permanent shape. One may presume, on the contrary, that it will be radically modified in the future in keeping with a sharper conviction in the baptized laity
that they share with the ordained clergy the awareness of being the Church,
in keeping also with the access of women to full equality with men in society,
and with the greater sense of spiritual freedom that will be brought about by
a growing emphasis on the Holy Spirit. Consensus will be obtained, but not
through a quasi-political system of authority.

It is not possible or advisable to try and delineate in advance what these
structural changes will be. Yet the Christians of tomorrow will need to open
their hearts in this direction. The Church as a whole received from Christ
the promise of durability (Matt 16:18). If something in the Church's structure shares this durability, it is more likely to be the sacramental structure
of grace than specific elements in the structure of authority.

The Church of the Spirit

This investigation of tradition and reception has not taken us out of ecclesiology. On the contrary, it helps us to see the Church of the future. For
if there is an area where the Church of today has an unfinished task, it is in
the realm of Trinitarian doctrine specifically regarding the Holy Spirit. Returning for a moment to Vatican II, I have been puzzled by one point: while
the opposition to the conciliar majority dwindled to a handful of votes on
most questions, why did it remain considerable on the apparently peripheral
query whether a chapter on "the Virgin Mary in the Mystery of Christ and
the Church" should be located at the end of the constitution on the Church,
or should constitute a separate document?

This, I believe, was not due to major differences in piety. It obviously reflected different orientations in mariology. Yet all mariologies could easily
accommodate the ecclesial perspective that sees the Virgin not only in the
horizon of the incarnation as the *Theotokos* and the beloved bride of the
Spirit but also in the horizon of the reception of faith as the Church's most
loved daughter and most perfect model.

The reason for the lack of unanimity in the mariological episode of Vatican
II lies, I suspect, in latent ties between mariology and pneumatology. The
place of the Virgin in Christian faith and doctrine is bound to depend on the
perceived action of the Spirit at the annunciation. This story of the infancy
gospels has indeed been thoroughly examined exegetically, thoroughly investigated theologically. Furthermore, mariology is one of the major lin-

gering points of contention between Catholics and Protestants, and pneumatology still remains as a point of contention between Western and Eastern Christians. In addition, the Virgin *Theotokos* does not stand by herself. Even under the Cross of Jesus, she is, according to the Johannine Gospel, with the Apostle John from whose presence she receives comfort and eventually a home. In the person of John, the whole community of believers is involved.

All this points to a crossroads of doctrines that may well provide a theological agenda for the next millennium: the eschaton, the Holy Spirit, the unanimity of believers, the life in God exemplified in the Virgin Mary and the saints. Reflection at this crossroads should bring further light to bear on the nature of the Church as the God-given, Christ-centered, Spirit-empowered community of salvation.

For Further Reading

Avery Dulles, *A History of Apologetics,* New York: Corpus Instrumentorum, 1971.

Hans Schwarz, *On the Way to the Future,* Minneapolis: Augsburg Publishing House, 1972.

Hans Küng, *Eternal Life? Life after Death as a Medical, Philosophical and Theological Problem,* New York: Doubleday, 1985.

T. P. Weber, *Living in the Shadow of the Second Coming,* Chicago: University of Chicago Press, 1987.

Zachary Hayes, *Vision of the Future: A Study of Christian Eschatology,* Wilmington: Michael Glazier, 1989.

Peter C. Phan, *Eternity in Time.* Selinsgrove, PA: Susquehanna University Press, 1988.

Index

Animals I See at the Zoo

GORILLAS

Reading consultant: Susan Nations, M.Ed., author/literacy coach/
consultant in literacy development

WEEKLY READER®
PUBLISHING

Please visit our web site at: **www.garethstevens.com**
For a free color catalog describing our list of high-quality
books, call 1-800-542-2595 (USA) or 1-800-387-3178 (Canada).

Library of Congress Cataloging-in-Publication Data

Pohl, Kathleen.
    Gorillas / Kathleen Pohl.
      p. cm. — (Animals I see at the zoo)
    Includes bibliographical references and index.
    ISBN 978-0-8368-8219-3 (lib. bdg.)
    ISBN 978-0-8368-8226-1 (softcover)
    1. Gorilla—Juvenile literature. I. Title.
  QL737.P96P65   2008
  599.884—dc22   2007006038

This edition first published in 2008 by
Weekly Reader® Books
An imprint of Gareth Stevens Publishing
1 Reader's Digest Road
Pleasantville, NY 10570-7000 USA

Copyright © 2008 by Gareth Stevens, Inc.

Editor: Dorothy L. Gibbs
Art direction: Tammy West
Graphic designer: Charlie Dahl
Photo research: Diane Laska-Swanke

Photo credits: Cover, pp. 5, 9, 13 © T. J. Rich/naturepl.com; title © Photos.com; p. 7 © Kevin
Schafer/CORBIS; p. 11 © Bruce Davidson/naturepl.com; p. 15 © Suzi Eszterhas/naturepl.com;
pp. 17, 19 © Anup Shah/naturepl.com; p. 21 © Gerald & Buff Corsi/Visuals Unlimited

Printed in the United States of America

1 2 3 4 5 6 7 8 9 11 10 09 08 07

Note to Educators and Parents

Reading is such an exciting adventure for young children! They are beginning to integrate their oral language skills with written language. To encourage children along the path to early literacy, books must be colorful, engaging, and interesting; they should invite the young reader to explore both the print and the pictures.

The *Animals I See at the Zoo* series is designed to help children read about the fascinating animals they might see at a zoo. In each book, young readers will learn interesting facts about the featured animal.

Each book is specially designed to support the young reader in the reading process. The familiar topics are appealing to young children and invite them to read — and re-read — again and again. The full-color photographs and enhanced text further support the student during the reading process.

In addition to serving as wonderful picture books in schools, libraries, homes, and other places where children learn to love reading, these books are specifically intended to be read within an instructional guided reading group. This small group setting allows beginning readers to work with a fluent adult model as they make meaning from the text. After children develop fluency with the text and content, the books can be read independently. Children and adults alike will find these books supportive, engaging, and fun!

— Susan Nations, M.Ed., author, literacy coach, and consultant in literacy development

I like to go to the zoo. I see **gorillas** at the zoo.

Gorillas are big **apes**. They are the biggest apes.

They look like big
monkeys, but they
do not have tails.

Gorillas walk on their long arms and legs.

They use their
hands the same
way people do.
They can pick
up things and
hold food.

They use their fingers to pick dirt and bugs out of each other's fur.

In the **wild**, gorillas make nests out of leaves and grass. They sleep and nap in their nests.

Gorillas eat plant stems, leaves, and fruits. In the zoo, they eat **monkey chow**, too.

I like to see gorillas at the zoo. Do you?

Glossary

apes — furry animals that look like big monkeys without tails

gorillas — the biggest kinds of apes

monkey chow — a special kind of food for zoo animals such as apes and monkeys

wild — an animal's natural home

For More Information

Books

Bender, Lionel. *Wild Animals: Gorilla*. London: Cherrytree Books, 2005.

Milton, Joyce. *Gorillas: Gentle Giants of the Forest*. New York: Random House, 2003.

Stone, Tanya. *Wild, Wild World: Gorillas*. San Diego: Blackbirch Press, 2003.

Thomson, Sarah L. *Amazing Gorillas!* New York: HarperCollins Children's Books, 2005.

Web Site

Zoobooks Virtual Zoo – Pet the Gorilla

www.zoobooks.com/newFrontPage/animals/virtualZoo/petgorilla.htm

Learn about gorillas, take a gorilla quiz, pet a gorilla, and listen to the sounds a gorilla makes.

Publisher's note to educators and parents: Our editors have carefully reviewed this Web site to ensure that it is suitable for children. Many Web sites change frequently, however, and we cannot guarantee that a site's future contents will continue to meet our high standards of quality and educational value. Be advised that children should be closely supervised whenever they access the Internet.

Index

About the Author

Kathleen Pohl has written and edited many children's books, including animal tales, rhyming books, retold classics, and the forty-book series *Nature Close-Ups*. Most recently, she authored the Weekly Reader® leveled reader series *Let's Read About Animals* and *Where People Work*. She also served for many years as top editor of *Taste of Home* and *Country Woman* magazines. She and her husband, Bruce, share their home in the beautiful Wisconsin woods with six goats, a llama, and all kinds of wonderful woodland creatures.